D0615581

"When I hear the word 'evangelist,' the first face I imagine is always that of Billy Graham. And when I think of careful analysis of Graham's monumental reshaping of the world religious landscape, the only name I can imagine is that of renowned historian Grant Wacker. In this illuminating book, Wacker demonstrates why Graham was a distinctive voice at a determinative time. This book steers away from both sentimentality and cynicism in ways that can equip generations to come to learn from one who was, arguably, the most significant Christian evangelist since the Apostle Paul."

— RUSSELL MOORE, author of *The Storm-Tossed Family:*
How the Cross Reshapes the Home

"This fast-paced biography cuts through Billy Graham mythology to reveal who the great evangelist really was as a human individual. Wacker guides us behind the banner headlines, blockbuster revivals, and White House visits to explore the psychological depth, historical contingency, and internal contradictions that made Billy Graham one of the twentieth century's most effective preachers—with a complex legacy that his fans and his critics still debate today."

— MOLLY WORTHEN, author of *Apostles of Reason:*
The Crisis of Authority in American Evangelicalism

"Wacker's portrait of Graham is as warm and engaging as his subject, but it holds Graham to account for his mistakes and misjudgments. Easily the best short biography of Billy we are likely to get."

— KENNETH L. WOODWARD, author of *Getting Religion:*
Faith, Culture, and Politics from the Age
of Eisenhower to the Ascent of Trump

"This is a beautifully crafted, eloquent, and deeply illuminating account of Billy Graham's unparalleled evangelistic career, penned by one of the most eminent American religious historians of our time. Structured as historical 'scenes' interspersed with lively and insightful 'interludes' about the man himself, this is the best single overview of Graham's ministry to date. Highly recommended for general readers and scholars alike."

— R. MARIE GRIFFITH, John C. Danforth Center
on Religion and Politics

"Grant Wacker is the finest Billy Graham scholar in the world today. The writing is vintage Wacker: clear, concise, and brilliantly articulated. Wacker makes Graham and his remarkable career in the pulpit come alive for readers at all levels. It is a must read for anyone interested in the amazing story of evangelical revivals in the late twentieth and early twenty-first centuries."

— HARRY S. STOUT, Yale University

LIBRARY OF RELIGIOUS BIOGRAPHY

Mark A. Noll and Heath W. Carter, series editors

Religion shapes every story. Regardless of our beliefs, the cultural influences and religious commitments that surround us help forge our deepest convictions. And in religious biographies, we see these dynamics at work in the lives of influential people throughout history.

The Library of Religious Biography is a series of original biographies that bring to life important figures in American history and beyond, showing the sometimes surprising influence of religion on these subjects and the world they inhabited. Grounded in solid research, these volumes link the lives of their subjects to the broader cultural contexts and religious issues that surrounded them. The authors are respected historians, each a recognized authority in the period of religious history in which his or her subject lived and worked.

Marked by careful scholarship yet free of academic jargon, the books in this series are well-written narratives meant to be read and enjoyed as well as studied.

Titles include:

A Short Life of **Jonathan Edwards**
by George M. Marsden

Sworn on the Altar of God: A Religious Biography of **Thomas Jefferson**
by Edwin S. Gaustad

The Miracle Lady: **Katherine Kuhlman**
and the Transformation of Charismatic Christianity
by Amy Collier Artman

Abraham Lincoln: *Redeemer President*
by Allen C. Guelzo

Aimee Semple McPherson: *Everybody's Sister*
by Edith L. Blumhofer

George Whitefield: *Evangelist for God and Empire*
by Peter Y. Choi

For a complete list of published volumes, see the back of this volume.

ONE SOUL AT A TIME

The Story of Billy Graham

Grant Wacker

WILLIAM B. EERDMANS PUBLISHING COMPANY
GRAND RAPIDS, MICHIGAN

Wm. B. Eerdmans Publishing Co.
4035 Park East Court SE, Grand Rapids, Michigan 49546
www.eerdmans.com

Published 2019
Printed in the United States of America

25 24 23 22 21 20 19   1 2 3 4 5 6 7

ISBN 978-0-8028-7472-6

Library of Congress Cataloging-in-Publication Data

A catalog record for this book is available from the Library of Congress.

For Nathan Hatch, Laurie Maffly-Kipp,
George Marsden, Mark Noll, and Skip Stout.
God is everywhere, soulmates aren't.

When wealth is lost, nothing is lost; when health is lost, something is lost; when character is lost, all is lost.

BILLY GRAHAM

Contents

CONTENTS

Contents

Preface

When I entered my small Methodist church one Sunday morning last winter, Bob Maddry, a retired truck driver and old chum, walked over. "I lost a dear friend this week," he said. "Billy Graham brought me to Jesus. He saved my life." Bob paused, then added, "I never shook his hand."

A couple of weeks later I asked Bob if he remembered where and when his conversion had taken place. He answered immediately and precisely. "Raleigh. Wednesday night, September 26, 1973." At that moment I knew that Bob spoke for countless others, salt-of-the-earth folk, everywhere. They never personally met Graham, but his ministry had remade their lives.

Graham had died quietly in his sleep in his home in Montreat, North Carolina, on Wednesday, February 21, 2018, four days before I talked with Bob. The preacher was ninety-nine. On Saturday the hearse bearing his body motored the 130 miles from Montreat to Charlotte. Along the way the highway patrol blocked the on-ramps with wooden barricades and yellow tape. Fire trucks parked on overpasses, and cars in the oncoming lane pulled over. Officers saluted, grievers dabbed their eyes, and simple well-wishers quietly waved handkerchiefs.

The following week Graham's body would rest in three places. First up was Graham's childhood home, rebuilt on the grounds of the Billy Graham Library in Charlotte. On Monday former president and first lady George W. and Laura Bush visited. On Tuesday former president Bill Clinton paid his respects. On Wednesday the body was moved to the Rotunda of the United States Capitol, where it would lie "in honor" for two days. Graham was the fourth civilian and first religious leader in American history to be honored this way. On Thursday the body was moved back to the Billy Graham Library in Charlotte for the funeral and interment the next day.

The service was an evangelical version of a state funeral. It unfolded under a 28,000-square-foot tent reminiscent of the one that had sheltered Graham's breakout revival in Los Angeles in 1949. The event attracted President and First Lady Donald and Melania Trump; Vice President and Second Lady Mike and Karen Pence; North Carolina governor Roy Cooper; former North Carolina governor Pat McCrory; both North Carolina senators, Richard Burr and Thom Tillis; the Gaithers; Christian singer Michael W. Smith; five hundred members of the media; representatives from fifty countries; and 1,800 ticketed friends from the political, business, government, entertainment, and religious worlds. Former president Barack Obama did not attend but said that Graham "gave hope and guidance to generations of Americans." Former presidents George H. W. Bush and Jimmy Carter sent regrets, unable to come because of age.

By 2018 attention of this magnitude was an old story. At the dedication of the Billy Graham Library eleven years earlier, former president George H. W. Bush had called Graham "America's pastor." The label stuck. When Graham died, it showed up everywhere. For sure, some journalists had their doubts. In light of the nation's pluralism, one said "America's pastor" was meaningless. A small but vocal minority felt that Graham not only did not deserve the honor but also had inflicted grave harm upon the nation. But clearly the great majority accepted the label, either as a statement of simple sociological fact, or as an expression of their own feelings, or both.

Graham's death revealed the breadth of the shadow he cast across the religious landscape. "His message," said Saphir Athyal, an Indian Syriac Christian theologian, was "his life as well as his words." The Roman Catholic archbishop of New York, Timothy Cardinal Dolan, spoke for many journalists, possibly a majority of Americans, and countless Christians around the world. "As anyone growing up in the 1950s and 1960s can tell you, it was hard not to notice and be impressed by the Reverend Billy Graham," the cardinal intoned. "Graham . . . always [preached] the same message: Jesus is your Savior and wants you to be happy with Him forever."

Writing for the *Religion News Service*, journalist Yonat Shimron framed Graham's achievement in more historical terms. The preacher worked, she said, "with a combination of zeal, integrity and graciousness that won him admirers the world over." For millions, he seemed somehow to stand above the partisan controversies of the era. An ordinary man, filling an extraordinary role.

*　　　*　　　*

Billy Graham lived an enormous life. It would be hard to find a religious leader—or leader of any sort, for that matter—who traveled more widely, or met more people, or addressed more pressing issues of the day than he did. It would take multiple fat volumes to tell his whole story. So in the interest of coherence, not to mention economy, I hope to simplify the task by focusing on one thread. I try to tell the story the way I think he would do it.

More or less, anyway. The "more" part is that from time to time I add details he might not think to include, or events he was too modest to dwell on, or episodes that he clearly preferred to forget. The "less" part is that I mainly stick to Graham's public life, the things he did and said in public for everyone to see and hear. Two wrinkles slightly qualify that promise. Graham's wife, Ruth Bell Graham, weaves in and out of the narrative because she was very much part of his public presentation. And their son Franklin emerges in the later chapters, for the same reason.

Otherwise I omit many interesting details about Graham's daily life that he might want to slip in, such as his chronic insomnia, or attraction to sunny beaches, or fondness for lemon cake and Big Macs. But interesting is not the same as important. What is important about Graham—what people will want to know about a century from now—is his public life.

As much as possible, *One Soul at a Time* follows the main events in Graham's life chronologically, in the order in which they actually took place. Of course, Graham, like most people, didn't actually live his life that way, in simple chronological order. Experiences overlapped. But the biographer cannot unfold multiple narratives at the same time. So in each of the chapters—or scenes, as I prefer to call them—I try to highlight the main thread, the one that I think Graham himself probably would isolate as the key feature. When necessary, I sketch in the background or peek ahead to the outcome, but only when I need to in order to make sense of the moment.

It is important to stress that *One Soul at a Time* is not an abbreviated version of *America's Pastor: Billy Graham and the Shaping of a Nation*, a detailed thematic study of Graham that I published in 2014. In *America's Pastor* I focused on Graham's relation to American culture. Here I focus on the man himself. The two volumes recount some of the same basic facts, of course, and some of the same basic ideas too. In this volume, however, I frame similar facts and ideas in different ways for different purposes.[1]

Today biographers of Graham have to figure out how to find him behind the huge cumulus cloud that his son Franklin Graham has created.

The son looms in the daily news as an extraordinarily influential evangelist, humanitarian, and culture warrior in his own right. Sometimes Billy and Franklin really did resemble each other, but at other times they differed dramatically.

Discerning the optics of that complex relationship would be a worthy project in itself, but it falls outside the scope of this book. One of the purposes of this study is to help readers see Billy himself, as he really was, in his own times, and leave Franklin for another day.

A few words about my point of view may be useful. Though I try to tell Graham's story as objectively as I can, I am the first to admit that the lens I use inevitably colors how I see him. So I suppose I should say a bit about that lens.

I place myself in the broadly evangelical tradition of American religion that Graham did so much to create and shape. Usually I find myself rumbling around somewhere on the left side of that tradition, both theologically and politically. But it is big enough and diverse enough that I feel comfortable thinking that we are all part of the same family.

Viewing Graham from this perspective, then, I see him as one of the most influential Christians, and certainly the most influential evangelical Protestant Christian, of the twentieth century. He was a great man, who helped bring spiritual meaning to the lives of millions around the globe. At the same time, Graham, like all great men and women, also had serious character flaws and made serious mistakes. I certainly believe that the strengths far outweighed the weaknesses. Yet that complexity means that his story has much to teach us about the complexities of faith in the modern world.

All that being said, I seek to avoid evaluating Graham for good or for ill. When he lived up to his own highest ideals, that should be evident. And when he failed to do so, that should be evident too. I try to let the reader judge.

*   *   *

The book's title—*One Soul at a Time*—deserves a word. It comes from Ken Garfield, a journalist who covered Graham's crusades for the *Charlotte Observer* for many years. In 2013 Garfield said that the evangelist "made people feel that he cared for them, one soul at a time." Garfield was Jewish and never considered converting to evangelical Christianity. But he appreciated the gentle, inclusive spirit of the man who invited others to find a new faith or to renew an old faith grown cold. When Graham died five years later, Garfield wrote, "We mark Graham's passing with gratitude and grief. He offered the promise and comfort of Jesus to the last person in the last row in the most distant venue on Earth."

But there is more. In one sense Graham seems to be the last person on earth whose approach should be described with the words "one soul at a time." After all, he perfected the art of mass evangelism. He preached to 215 million people in 185 countries in crusades, rallies, and live satellite feeds. Of those, some 77 million saw him face-to-face in more than seventy countries.[2] More than 3 million souls responded to his invitation to profess faith in Christ.[3] He broke numerous attendance records, sometimes speaking to more than 100,000 people face-to-face in a single service. Indeed, twice he spoke to more than 1 million in one event.

If we add the folks who encountered Graham through his books, magazines, motion pictures, daily newspaper columns, and syndicated radio and television programs, the number swells beyond any easy reckoning. Hundreds of millions more, possibly billions, seem likely. "With the possible exception of Pope John Paul II," said religion journalist David van Biema in *Time* magazine, "Graham . . . touched more lives for Jesus than anyone else in the modern era and . . . extolled him directly to a greater swath of humanity than anyone else in history."

Even so, Graham said that he always saw himself speaking not to audiences, let alone to nameless multitudes, but to individual hearts. That is where enduring change ultimately had to begin, with each person making their own decision to follow Christ. Or not. "This is not mass evangelism," he liked to say, "but personal evangelism on a mass scale."

Billy Graham very much wanted to invite every person on the planet to embrace the gospel. And he hoped to inspire them to try to reform society as a whole, from top to bottom. But his method—the way he sought to do it—was always the same. One soul at a time.

Acknowledgments

I have found that the acknowledgments section of a book is usually the hardest to write. After studying American religious history for four decades, and working on Billy Graham for one of them, the list of people who have given me ideas and encouragement stretches out into the horizon. So where should I draw the line?

In order to keep this section to a tidy length yet not dilute the appreciation I owe to the people who have contributed to this book specifically, I have kept the list fairly brief. But I want to stress that my debts range far beyond the people I can reasonably name in the following few paragraphs.

As usual, priority goes to the librarians and archivists who helped more than their jobs required. Like pretty much everyone who writes seriously about Graham, I must begin with Bob Shuster, the polymath archivist at the Billy Graham Center Archives (BGCA) at Wheaton College. Bob not only directed me to obscure resources but also offered new ideas for the narrative all along the way. Paul Ericksen, Director of the BGCA, provided wise counsel throughout. Katherine Graber, Public Services Archivist, came flying to the rescue whenever I called (or e-mailed).

It would be difficult to exaggerate my debt to David Bruce, Executive Assistant to Mr. Graham in Montreat, North Carolina. Though it is a cliché, sometimes a cliché is the only word that fits. His assistance was priceless.

Readers of the manuscript included John Akers, David Bruce, Jean Graham Ford, Leighton Ford, Aaron Griffith, George Marsden, Mark Noll, and Anne Blue Wills. All read every word. They helped save me from factual mistakes, wobbly concepts, and missteps into too much praise—or criticism. These folks proved that the best friends are the ones who present the bracing medicine of honest critique before—not after—the book sees light. They also proved that a dollop of encouragement, offered at just the right time, can restore the patient to robust health.

Others contributed in important ways too. More than once Scott Kelley, Diana Langston, and Ray Woody—friends since high school days—sent me back to the drawing board with penetrating questions. Edith Blumhofer, Allison Brown, Ken Garfield, Jim Lutzweiler, Daved Anthony Schmidt, and my research assistant, Max Feiler, provided a steady stream of data bytes I never would have found on my own. Jean Graham Ford, Leighton Ford, Bob Mayer, Garth Rosell, and Bob Shuster carved time from their busy schedules to find and provide a majority of the (mostly unpublished) photos of Graham that grace this volume.

The list goes on. Vincent Bacote, Uta Balbier, Catherine Brekus, Anthea Butler, Elesha Coffman, Heather Curtis, Darren Dochuk, Betsy Flowers, Spencer Fluhman, Marie Griffith, David Heim, Brooks Holifield, John Huffman, Helen Jin Kim, Katie Lofton, Mandy McMichael, Kristopher Norris, Dana Robert, Jon Roberts, Garth Rosell, Nathan Walton, and Todd von Helms prompted me to think about Graham's legacy in fresh ways. Nannelle Griffith shared her memories of the 1953 Chattanooga crusade. Heath Carter and Mark Noll, the editors of Library of Religious Biography, acting solely on faith, invited me to submit the manuscript before they had seen a word of it.

Perennial conversation partners and dear friends Randall Balmer, Martin Marty, Matt Sutton, and Ken Woodward, speaking with Episcopal, Lutheran, secular, and Catholic voices, respectively, helped me remember that if this book doesn't make sense to readers beyond Graham's evangelical tradition, it doesn't make sense at all.

My regular coffee-swilling mates at Duke—Kate Bowler, Stanley Hauerwas, Richard Hays, Dick Heitzenrater, Greg Jones, Xi Lian, Rick Lischer, and Will Willimon—kept me from slacking off by recurrently asking, "How's it going?" My nine-year-old grandson, Henry Beck, put teeth in the question: "Have you finished your Billy Graham book *yet*, Grandpa?"

Andrew Finstuen and Anne Blue Wills, two of the three editors of *Billy Graham: American Pilgrim*, let me pretend to be the third and equal partner, even though they did more than two-thirds of the work. Their generosity proved that the study of American religious history is often a labor born of deep affection among colleagues.

The five people named in the book's dedication know that words can go only so far. But sometimes you have to try.

My copy editor, Tom Raabe, well earned his keep—and more. He caught embarrassing factual howlers and applied his scalpel to excess prose without mercy. Some of my best writing ended up on the cutting room floor. For which readers should be as grateful as I am.

My debt to David Bratt, the executive editor at Eerdmans, is hard to measure. David recognized that the detailed thematic study of Graham that I published several years ago left a need for a concise narrative biography. He selected this book's title, smoothed out lumpy prose, posed the two governing questions that *One Soul at a Time* tries to answer, bolstered my courage to take stands on controversial questions, spotted paragraphs the world could do without, batted ideas back and forth in person and over the phone, and did not bark at me when the manuscript grew larger and took longer than he expected. Through it all he turned out to be a wonderful friend as well as editor.

And then there was Billy himself. Four visits with him in his mountaintop home near Montreat, North Carolina, when he was in his late eighties and early nineties, permanently etched themselves in my memory. Given his age, I made no attempt to "interview" him, at least as journalists and historians ordinarily do. But he interviewed me. He did it partly by asking a lot of questions about my own life—dogs, kids, grandkids, Blue Devils—but also and more memorably by letting me experience firsthand the extraordinary humility, graciousness, and spiritual depth of a truly great man.

My wife, Katherine Wacker, did not type a single word or, after the preface, read a single page of the manuscript. Something about "been there, done that" was, I think, what she said. But a half century of putting up with me, as I drifted off wondering how to phrase the next sentence, gives the biblical image of the "pearl of great price" new dimensions of meaning.

Cary, North Carolina
March 2019

Landscape of a Life

By the time Billy Graham was thirty years old, probably most adult Americans had heard of him. By the time he was thirty-five, his name had spread around the globe, and by forty, he had become an iconic figure in Christian circles everywhere. Graham retained that status until he effectively retired from public ministry in 2005.

Hard, quantitative signs of Graham's importance on the religious landscape crop up almost everywhere we look. Probably more people saw or heard Graham preach than any other person in history.[1]

Graham's endeavors set records in other ways too. Between 1955 and 2017, he won a berth in Gallup's list of the "Ten Most Admired Men" sixty-one times. President Ronald Reagan, his closest rival, appeared "only" thirty-one times, while former president Jimmy Carter and Pope John Paul II appeared twenty-seven times apiece.

Exact figures about the size of Graham's media empire—the numbers of listeners, viewers, and readers—are extremely hard to pin down. Even so, allowing for significant variations in data-gathering methods, the overall picture is clear enough.

First up were the network broadcasts. *Hour of Decision*, a weekly syndicated radio program, was released in November 1950. One hundred fifty ABC-affiliated stations carried the first broadcast. Within weeks twenty million potential listeners were tuning in. In 2010 nearly one thousand stations around the world still carried the program, by then airing in five languages.[2] Graham's syndicated national television program, also called *Hour of Decision*, which started in June 1957, soon ranked as one of the most widely viewed religious television broadcasts in the nation.[3]

Believing that words lasted longer in print than over the airwaves, Graham moved toward the publishing market with even greater vigor. His daily newspaper column, "My Answer," which he launched in 1952, ran in seventy-three newspapers. In time it reportedly hit two hundred venues with a circulation of fifteen to twenty million potential readers.

The fortnightly *Christianity Today*, which followed four years later, almost immediately established itself as the normative voice of mainstream evangelicalism.[4] At the time of Graham's death in 2018, it claimed a print circulation of 120,500 (36,000 free), a readership of 240,000, and five million discrete visits each month for its online version.

The popular monthly magazine *Decision*, issued in three—later six—languages and a Braille edition, started landing in readers' mailboxes in 1960. By 1975 this monthly—written with a mass audience in mind, and lavishly illustrated with black-and-white and soon full-color pictures—was reaching five million readers. Except for two Jehovah's Witness publications, it likely ranked as the most widely circulated Christian-related magazine in the world.[5]

Graham's books appeared on average every other year, from his first in 1947, *Calling Youth to Christ*, to his last in 2015, *Where I Am: Heaven, Eternity, and the Life Beyond*, when he was in his late nineties. All together, he authored or authorized thirty-four volumes, which were translated into at least fifty languages and sold millions of copies.[6] Three of them sold more than one million apiece. Graham's third book, *Peace with God*, published in 1953, served as his signature work. This compact volume of two hundred or so pages sold more than two million copies and saw translation into thirty-eight languages.[7]

Graham personally knew all thirteen presidents from Harry Truman to Donald Trump.[8] Most of them became his friends—some his close friends. When Graham died, his home state of North Carolina initiated the complex process of replacing the statue of one of its two favorite sons in the US Capitol (Charles Aycock) with one of Graham.

Factoids and anecdotes might actually tell us more about Graham's influence than any number of raw statistics or listing of awards and honors. First the factoids. For two years in the mid-1950s Graham won more magazine and newspaper space than any other person in the nation, including the president. Also, the BGEA's photograph archive contains more than 1,100,000 negatives. Photographers knew a good, not to mention marketable, image when they saw one.

Second, the anecdotes—or what we might call cultural snapshots—reveal worlds within worlds about Graham's place on the American religious landscape. Two, coming from surprising corners of American life, are especially worth quoting. Harold Bloom, a leading literary scholar at Yale, and not especially sympathetic to Graham, brilliantly captured his impact in a cover article published in *Time* magazine in 1999 entitled "100 Most Important People of the Century": "You don't run for office among us by proclaiming your skepticism or deprecating Billy Graham."

In 2014, in *AARP The Magazine*, Bob Dylan reflected on his own legendary career with a remarkable extended reference to Graham.

[He was] the greatest preacher and evangelist of my time—that guy could save souls and did. I went to two or three of his rallies in the '50s or '60s. This guy was like rock 'n' roll personified—volatile, explosive. He had the hair, the tone, the elocution—when he spoke, he brought the storm down. Clouds parted. Souls got saved, sometimes 30- or 40,000 of them. If you ever went to a Billy Graham rally back then, you were changed forever. There's never been a preacher like him. He could fill football stadiums before anybody. He could fill Giants Stadium more than even the Giants football team. Seems like a long time ago. Long before Mick Jagger sang his first note or Bruce strapped on his first guitar—that's some of the part of rock 'n' roll that I retained. I had to. I saw Billy Graham in the flesh and heard him loud and clear.

Granted, Graham never came close to winning universal approval. Secular pundits found his theology absurd in the clear light of modern thinking. Mainline preachers, both Protestant and Catholic, recoiled from his unflinching presentation of his interpretation of the gospel. Fundamentalists scored him for cooperating with Catholics and liberal Protestants in order to win popularity.

Graham's perennial hobnobbing with the rich and the famous, his unsteady (initially hawkish, later ambivalent) support for the Vietnam War, his dogged defense of Nixon during Watergate, and his noxious private comments about Jews and the media in Nixon's office in 1972 tarred his reputation. Repeated apologies never erased the damage.

Death offered no protection, either. After Graham's demise, historian Matthew A. Sutton, writing in the *Guardian*, judged that Graham had positioned himself on the "wrong side of history." His backward-looking posture "may be his most significant, and saddest, legacy," said Sutton. Writing in the *New York Times*, historian David A. Hollinger, in turn, dismissed Graham's career as "largely a story of missed opportunities," one that promoted "childlike religious emotions and obscurantist ideas."

Historians were not alone in their dismissal. In an obituary essay headlined "Billy Graham Was No Prophet," the conservative columnist George F. Will found the subtitle of my book *America's Pastor: Billy Graham and the Shaping of a Nation* "inapposite." Far from being a shaper of the culture, Will argued, Graham was shaped by the culture, and not by its best parts, either. Though Graham "gave comfort to many people and probably improved some," Will allowed, the preacher was neither a prophet nor a theologian. In Graham's dealings with presidents, for example, he "mixed vanity and naivete."

Other journalists used Graham's death as an opportunity to denounce him. In an essay revealingly titled "The Soul-Crushing Legacy of Billy Graham," posted at *RollingStone.com*, journalist Bob Moser found him "a Machiavellian backroom operator . . . a conniving hypocrite with a layman's grasp of the Bible and a supernatural lust for earthly power." Actress Nia Vardalos showed that a scalpel could cut deeper than a cleaver. "Billy Graham, Rest In Peace sir," she intoned. "I hope God bunks you with Liberace."

*   *   *

These jabs notwithstanding, this book will show, I think, that historian Martin Marty got it right when he told a 2013 gathering at Wheaton College, Graham's alma mater, that Graham belonged on the Mount Rushmore of American religious history. Millions of evangelicals worldwide used his views to settle debates, exegeted his words as if they were biblical proof texts, and wrangled about what "Billy really meant."

When reporters said, as they often did, that Graham was the closest thing to a pope that Protestants had—columnist Murray Kempton dubbed him "the Pope of lower Protestantism"—they were using Graham not simply as a handy symbol but were also stating a fairly indisputable historical fact. At the time of his death, Ashish Ittyerah Joseph, an Indian eulogist, dryly observed that for Protestants "he is what Mother Teresa is for Catholics." A Protestant saint.

Perhaps the most historically important point about Graham is not whether he was a villain or a saint but that millions of people, both inside and outside the United States, positioned themselves on the religious and cultural landscape by virtue of their view of Graham. Historian George Marsden said that an evangelical could be defined as "anyone who liked Billy Graham." The line was a quip, but funny precisely because it cut so close to the quick. "For more than 50 years," said another historian, Daniel Silliman, "Graham was so famous people felt like they had to have an opinion about him. Whether they liked him or didn't like him, he became a lodestar of religious identity." The story that this book tells helps us know why.

Two questions run throughout the following pages. The first one is simple. What made Graham different from other evangelists of his era and, with the possible exception of George Whitefield in the eighteenth century, from all other evangelists in American history?[9] Granted, Graham emerged from a long, rich tradition of schools, newspapers, magazines, radio programs, missionary organizations, sturdy denominations, country pastors, pulpit princes, media stars, and itinerant preachers like himself. Still, in the late 1940s, before he was thirty, he rapidly moved to the front of the pack, and for the next six decades no one else came close.

Why?

In this book I will try to show that Graham became singularly successful because he displayed an extraordinary ability to embrace the trends of the age and then turn them to his own evangelistic and moral-reform purposes.

All successful evangelists did the same, of course, but Graham did it more skillfully than anyone else, and with remarkably few missteps along the way. He spoke to multiple audiences at once: politicians, journalists, denominational leaders, local pastors, and ordinary folk ranging from earnest seekers to ardent skeptics. And he made it all look so easy.

At a certain point a difference of degree became a difference of kind. His singular ability to appropriate the trends of the times enabled him to stay relevant, year after year, decade after decade. Like everyone else, he aged, and changed with age, and yet, unlike most people, he somehow remained strangely ageless.

The answer to the second question is simple too. How did Graham connect so strongly with so many people for so many years? I will try to show that multiple versions of Billy Graham strode across the stage. His ability constantly to change enabled him to reach many different kinds of people — usually positively, occasionally negatively — at many different places in their lives. Few actually knew him in person, yet millions felt that they did.

How did this happen? First of all, Graham changed over time. In the decades stretching from 1945 to 2005, at least four Graham figures marched across the public stage: "Young Barnstormer," "Leading Evangelist," "Priestly Prophet," and, finally, "Senior Statesman." This volume is divided into four parts to reflect those stages.

Moreover, Graham not only developed over time but there was also a change in how his managers projected him, how the media portrayed him, and how the public saw him. The stages involved considerable overlap, of course, but viewed from afar, they are unmistakable.

Graham also changed according to the situation. Virtually all leaders did, of course, but Graham seemed to vary more dramatically than most. More precisely, he presented different faces to different people at pretty much the same time. So which was he? An old-time evangelist or the CEO of a sprawling business organization? A down-home farm boy or an up-town trendsetter? A humble carrier of the gospel or a name-dropping ally of the White House? Historian Steven Miller got it just right. Graham was, said Miller, "America's most complicated innocent." Duplicitous, rarely; evasive, often; sincere, always.

In short, then, the two recurring questions that mark Graham's long career boil down to a few words. First, how do we account for his unique-ness (or, if we count Whitefield, virtual uniqueness) in American reli-gious history? And second, how do we account for his power to connect? Persuasive answers to these two questions also boil down to a few words. His uniqueness grew from his singular ability to appropriate the trends of the age and then put them to work for his purposes. And his power to connect grew from his ability constantly to change, over time and from situation to situation. This propensity meant that people of his generation experienced him as a pastor for all the seasons of their lives.

*   *   *

One more matter needs brief attention. Humpty Dumpty once told Alice: "When I make a word work a lot, I always pay it extra." Since the word "evangelical" turns up often in the following pages, I probably should say a bit at the outset about what it means in this book.

I use "evangelical" to describe people who believed that the Bible is the final authority for all the truly important questions about God, peo-ple, and the world. In their minds the Bible called for repentance for sin, faith in Christ, holiness of practice, mission to others, and the promise of eternal life. Taken together, these tenets constitute the gospel—or good news—of salvation.

This is basically a theological definition of "evangelical." Other defini-tions, more attuned to society or culture or history, are useful too. In due course we will encounter all of them and see how sooner or later most of them felt the imprint of Graham's hand.

PART 1

Young Barnstormer

SCENE 1

Southern Farm Boy

One of the most important things to remember about Billy Graham is that he was a Southerner. Born November 7, 1918, Billy Frank—as his family liked to call him—always took pride in his Southern roots. Indeed, he rarely missed a chance to remind audiences where he came from.

In his late-life memoir, *Just as I Am*, published in 1997, Graham showcased his two grandfathers. Both had fought for the Confederacy, and both had suffered grave wounds that impaired them for the rest of their lives. One took a bullet in the leg, and the other lost a leg and an eye. Graham did not say anything about his grandfathers' view of slavery, but he did make clear that they believed the region of their birth was worth defending. He did too, often arguing that the South was doing a better job of coming to terms with its grim racial history than the rest of the nation.

Graham's natal family was, as the Southern novelist Flannery O'Connor might have put it, "good country people." More precisely, good prosperous Southern country people. Graham's father, William Franklin Graham, had received only a third-grade education, but he proved a hard worker, strict disciplinarian, shrewd businessman, and generous neighbor. His mother, Morrow Coffey Graham, completed a year (perhaps more) at Queens College in Charlotte. She helped out by giving private piano lessons. Billy Frank was the first of four children, followed by Melvin, Catherine, and Jean.

Graham kept the Southern lilt in his accent to the end. Indeed, visitors found that in casual conversations he revealed it more strikingly than when he was preaching to national and international audiences outside the South. One New York journalist called his accent "Carolina stage English." I am not exactly sure what that meant, but presumably it suggested something like a Southern lilt with a slightly uptown touch.

Graham's accent rode the crest of another powerful Southern tradition: public speaking. Graham never got caught up in the antievolution crusade, as William Jennings Bryan did, but he would have felt right at home with Bryan in that sweltering Tennessee courtroom in 1925, proclaiming the Word of Truth, with dramatic flourish, to the press and commoners alike. That kind of barnstorming oratory permeated the air he breathed.

Graham's personal style, at once neighborly and unbuttoned, expressed an informal way of life also characteristic of his region.

In these respects, he resembled his almost exact contemporary and fellow North Carolinian, Andy Griffith. To the end of his ministry, people talked about how approachable Graham seemed. Once stung by a famous preacher who brushed him off when he asked for an autograph, Graham vowed never to fall into that pattern. And by all accounts, he kept his word.

* * *

The senior Graham supported his family as a dairy farmer. The farm thrived. Graham grew up in the comfort of a solidly upper-middle-class home. Undergirded by a three-hundred-acre dairy farm, with four hundred regular customers and seventy-five cows, the family was the first in the area to own a car and put in a telephone. The farm did go through a rough patch when the elder Graham lost his savings at the height of the Depression. But hard times did not last long. The adult Billy usually—not always, but usually—acknowledged the favorable circumstances of his upbringing.

The Graham family worshiped nearby at the Chalmers Memorial Associate Reformed Presbyterian Meeting House. The congregation was affiliated with the Associate Reformed Presbyterian Church, a small but sturdy denomination that traced its roots back to Scotland. It favored rigorous Calvinist theology, strict observance of the Sunday Sabbath, daily family devotions, and chanting psalms rather than singing hymns in its meetings. It represented a minor yet thoroughly respectable segment of the Southern Protestant mainline.

Unlike the Protestant mainline in the North, which was theologically liberal, the Southern mainline in general, and the Associate Reformed Presbyterian Church in particular, remained theologically conservative. It also positioned itself in the center or even center-right of Southern society and culture. Its partisans were mannered and well connected. If Graham's crusade meetings, especially in the middle and final thirds of his career, were marked more by decorum than by emotion, we should not be surprised.

Biographers hunting for signs of exceptional promise in Graham's youth will hunt in vain. Billy was not a great student, but not a terrible one either. With mostly average grades in his pocket, he graduated from Sharon High School in three years, which was customary in those days.

The adult Billy Graham often talked about the work disciplines of his rural childhood and adolescence. Routinely getting up in the wee hours of the morning, he milked the cows, and milked them again when he got home from school in the afternoon. The regimen of hard labor stayed with him to the end, but not farm life. He vowed that the two occupations he never would go into were undertaking—and farming.

Later on, Graham took care to portray himself in his teenage years as a typical red-blooded male. Baseball figured large. After watching Babe Ruth play, he fancied a career in the sport. He boasted that he was good enough to play a couple of innings with a minor league team in Charlotte, but confessed that he was not good enough to go pro. Fast cars also played a big role. Careening along country roads, with an occasional pileup in the ditch, was part of the narrative. The youthful Graham was no pacifist. He remembered bloody fist fights and tough-guy confrontations. He also remembered that one night soon after he got married he used his .22 rifle to graze a burglar who had broken into their house. (The burglar escaped.)

Not surprisingly, the biggest part of Graham's memory of his adolescence involved young women. Many years later he admitted that he had been more smitten with one girlfriend than most people knew. Yet he always insisted—and there is no reason to doubt—that his relations with young women never went beyond hugs and kisses—though plenty of those.

The family business introduced Graham to men and women hailing from a wide range of racial, ethnic, and economic locations. These included an African American foreman and his wife, at least one Hispanic laborer, and other farm hands. In his memoir he admitted that as a young man growing up in the South in the 1920s and 1930s he had enjoyed the company of black friends but never saw them as social peers.

*   *   *

One thing that did not figure large in Graham's memories of his youth was religion. But this easygoing approach to faith changed in the fall of 1934. The senior Graham and a band of local businessmen had invited Mordecai

Ham, a dapper, fire-breathing evangelist from Kentucky and Oklahoma, to come to town for a revival. It ran twelve thunderous weeks from August 30 to November 25. Ham's followers met in a wood-frame tabernacle, with a tin roof and sawdust aisles, seating five thousand souls, about six miles from Graham's farm.

Night after night Ham railed against liquor and sins of the flesh. The revival was the old-fashioned kind, with passionate preaching (often aimed at local clergy), nightly meetings, soul-stirring music, and, at the end of the sermon, a call for sinners to step forward and give their lives to Christ.

At first Graham resisted even going to the meetings. The drive was too far and there was too much emotion. But somewhere near the end of the revival—the exact dates are not clear—he yielded to the insistent invitations of a friend and headed to town.

After several services, in which he ended up even singing in the choir, Graham gained a sense that Ham was preaching directly to him. The tension was too much. On November 1, 1934, six days before his sixteenth birthday, during the last verse of the gospel hymn "Almost Persuaded, Now to Believe," the young man got up and walked to the front. He never looked back.

Graham later pointed to that evening and that experience as the moment of his conversion. Though he had professed Christian faith and tried to live a Christian life as far back as he could remember, he had never clearly repented of his sins and given his heart to Christ in a direct, personal way. Even so, it was a tearless conversion. The next day, he remembered, he felt no different inside. But the world looked different outside.

This event is probably best understood not as a classic conversion experience, a sudden transition from darkness to light, but as the culmination of a long process of serious self-examination. It symbolized a threshold when Graham decided to stop, take stock, and become the kind of young man he knew he wanted to be.

Viewed from afar, there really was not much for Graham to be saved from. By all indications his home and church had already inculcated strong moral principles and the basics of Calvinist theology in his life and heart. But the kind of independent revivalism that Ham brought to town clearly felt different.

The summer after graduating from high school, Graham found himself in South Carolina selling Fuller Brushes door to door. He also found that he was good at it. By the end of the summer, he had posted the best record of any salesman in the state. And he learned a key lesson. If the product was good, sell it with all the energy and skill you've got. This lesson served as a portent of things to come.

And then, off to college. Another Southern evangelist, this one named Bob Jones, had preached at Graham's high school during his senior year. Jones's commanding style impressed the young man. Though Graham had considered enrolling at the University of North Carolina at Chapel Hill, three hours northeast of Charlotte, Jones's example, and his mother's preference, led him to Bob Jones Bible College in Cleveland, Tennessee, in the fall of 1936.[1] He was seventeen.

College Years

Graham's four months at Bob Jones Bible College were not happy ones. He found that Jones ran the school with an iron fist. The rigid rules, especially those governing relationships between male and female students, seemed unreasonable. And so did the emphasis on rote education. He flunked math. Beyond that, the climate was damp and chilly, and Graham could not shake a stubborn cold. For a young man who cherished blue skies and balmy weather, these were not small matters.

About then, Florida Bible Institute (FBI), in Temple Terrace, Florida, near Tampa, entered Graham's zone of possibilities.[1] A high school friend at FBI had told him about the sunshine and orange trees. Equally important, his mother saw an ad for the school in *Moody Monthly* and liked what she saw. She valued its close relationship with the Christian and Missionary Alliance, commonly known simply as the Alliance. Another small but sturdy denomination, it emphasized private devotions, foreign missions, divine healing, the premillennial return of Christ, and practical training for Christian service.

Graham told Jones that he was thinking about transferring. Jones shot back that if he did, he would end up "a poor country Baptist preacher somewhere out in the sticks." Unfazed, Graham enrolled at FBI at the beginning of the spring semester. He soon found himself enjoying the adjacent golf course and swimming in the Hillsborough River—albeit full of deadly water moccasins—running near the campus.

In the Sunshine State, Graham experienced his first major romantic disappointment, or at least the first one he wrote about. Though only nineteen, he asked a fellow student named Emily Cavanaugh to marry him. She agreed, but soon decided for another swain. Heartbroken, Graham later took his sorrows to the golf course. Surrounded by moonlit trees draped in moss, he remembered, he fell on his knees and committed his life to full-time Christian service. Years later a reporter asked him if he thought Emily had made a mistake when she dumped him. He answered—we can almost see the grin— "I *always* thought she was wrong."

*   *   *

If Graham saw emotional growth at FBI, he also saw the priority of evangelism. That is not to say that FBI was unconcerned with correct doctrine, including the facticity of the Bible, the necessity of a personal relationship with Christ, the soon coming of the Lord, and a mandate to "go into all the world and preach this gospel." At this phase of his life, Graham was still, in George Marsden's words, a "purebred fundamentalist." That being said, the key point here is that Graham *presupposed* this theological outlook but harbored no taste for fighting about the details or forcing it on others. And he never would.

At FBI Graham learned something else: the craft of preaching. It is easy to forget that Billy Graham was not always Billy Graham. He had to master the tools of the trade just as any other craftsman would. Over the years, he said that when he walked behind the pulpit, he often had no idea what he was going to say and had to rely on the Holy Spirit to fill his mouth. That might have been his self-perception, but the plain truth is that most of the time he had a pretty good idea about what he was going to say and, just as important, how he would say it.

Graham's professional career started out slowly. He began in the Tampa area by preaching on a local radio station, on street corners, in "trailer parks," and even in jails. Alligators on the riverbank heard the word too. Determined to perfect his timing and gestures, he watched himself in a mirror. He memorized passages from the sermons of fundamentalist warhorses. He even copied the mannerisms of famous ones vacationing at FBI in the winter.

Graham's first big evangelistic outing took place at Bostwick Baptist Church in Palatka, Florida, a few miles north of Tampa, on Easter Sunday, March 28, 1937. The young flamethrower had four sermons in his back pocket, planned for forty-five minutes apiece. He preached all four in eight minutes flat.

The opportunities for preaching in the area when Graham was a student at FBI gave him his first taste of serious opposition. He was heckled and once even knocked to the ground. He never retaliated, but he never retreated, either.

Here we might pause to note one of the many paradoxes about Graham's life. There is no evidence that he ever backed away from a public talk—including ones in potentially unfriendly settings—because he feared hostility. At the same time, he was irenic to his toenails. He took strong positions on numerous issues, doctrinal and otherwise, but rarely if ever entered into formal debates about them, and certainly not personal quarrels.

Before long Graham graduated from street corners to wooden pulpits, showing up most often in Southern Baptist and in Alliance churches in Tampa and central Florida. In 1938, his senior year, he was baptized by adult immersion in Silver Lake at a Baptist camp meeting, and the following year ordained by Baptist deacons. He freely admitted that he switched from the Presbyterian to the Baptist fold for practical reasons. If he was going to preach in Baptist churches, he figured, he ought to join them.

With one fleeting exception (noted below), Graham remained loyal to the Southern Baptist Convention the rest of his life, yet he rarely emphasized Baptist distinctives and never let his Baptist identity constrain him. Years later he even told one journalist that he found himself most comfortable in the evangelical wing of the Anglican Church. In his own mind, at least, his primary identity was always that of a broadly evangelical Christian.

*   *   *

Graham was no academic, and never pretended to be, but as his FBI days were drawing to a close, he knew he needed more training. His mother wanted him to go on to Wheaton College, located in Wheaton, Illinois, a small Norman Rockwell–looking town twenty miles west of downtown Chicago. The school was fundamentalist, academically rigorous, and fully accredited. As it happened, in his senior year at FBI, he had caddied for snowbird visitors who also had connections with Wheaton. One of them offered to help pay for his first year.

Graham graduated from FBI with a B.Th. (bachelor of theology) degree in May 1940 and matriculated at Wheaton in the fall as a second-semester freshman. Though he had three years of Bible school under his belt (one semester at Bob Jones College and five at FBI), Wheaton gave him only one semester of academic credit. With good reason, Wheaton—which may have been the only evangelical school strong enough to exercise a selective admissions policy—was often dubbed the Harvard of the fundamentalist world. He majored in cultural anthropology, not Bible or theology, as one might expect. Later he said he had wanted to prepare for a missionary career by learning about the diversity of human cultures.

We do not know his grades, but we do know that Graham's main professor, a charismatic Russian émigré named Alexander Grigolia, had recently received his PhD in anthropology from the University of Pennsylvania. Graham took his anthropology studies seriously. One textbook, which has survived, is well underlined and annotated.

Given Wheaton's fundamentalist academic environment, he probably learned very little about cultural relativism, even from Grigolia. Yet the sparse evidence available suggests that he learned a good deal about the differences among cultures. And he also learned that despite those differences, people's need for salvation from sin, which Christ alone provided, was universal.

During his junior and senior years at Wheaton, Graham also served as the interim pastor of an Alliance church that gathered in a rented Masonic hall just off the Wheaton town square.[2] With two hundred to three hundred attenders, the church—widely known as "the Tab" (for United Gospel Tabernacle)—boasted a reputation for vigorous evangelistic services. Graham preached every Wednesday night, Sunday morning, and Sunday night. He later admitted that the regimen both honed his preaching skills and harmed his grades.

When Graham entered Wheaton College, he identified himself on a matriculation card as "CMA"—for Christian and Missionary Alliance. And the Tab identified itself as Alliance, too. Graham never explained how that self-ascription fit into his public identification as a Southern Baptist. Perhaps for a few years he just flew both flags at once.

The larger significance of Graham's fleeting dual denominational identity is that in those days the boundary lines between those two traditions, as well as among many other evangelical traditions, were not firmly fixed. They all preached the same gospel and sang the same soul-saving gospel hymns, and that was all that really mattered to him.

*   *   *

College life drew Graham into wrestling, acting in a production of *Macbeth*, and part-time work moving furniture. Yet he was still a rural Southerner at heart. Feeling desperately lonely and embarrassed about his clothes, unstylish by Wheaton's prim standards, he seriously thought of withdrawing and heading back home. But he soon found a reason to stay. The reason had a name. It was Ruth Bell.[3]

Ruth's roots ran deep in the Southern Presbyterian tradition. Her parents, Dr. L. Nelson and Virginia McCue Bell, were conservative Southern Presbyterian missionaries in China. Nelson was a surgeon. Born in 1920, Ruth Bell grew up in Tsingkiangpu, China. Her parents ran the Love and Mercy Hospital, which Pearl Buck's father, Absalom Sydenstricker, had founded in the 1880s.

Ruth grew up in a family accustomed to reading—often out loud to each other—classics of British and American fiction. And incessant letter writing to folks back home. When she was ready for high school, her parents sent her, against her wishes, to a prestigious missionary boarding school in (North) Korea, Pyongyang Foreign School.

Ruth entered Wheaton—the college of choice for upper-class missionary kids—two years before Billy. But she dropped out in her sophomore year in order to help care for her sister, Rosa, who had fallen gravely ill with tuberculosis. When Ruth returned to Wheaton, she found herself in the same cohort—and frequent contact—with Billy.

Ruth Bell was smart, witty, pious, strong-willed, and, by all accounts—most emphatically including Graham's—a head turner. He styled her as a "hazel-eyed movie starlet." Smitten at first sight, he fervently pursued her. Ruth soon returned his attention, but the courtship was rocky. He later admitted that he treated her paternalistically, and she didn't appreciate it. Besides, she had planned to become a missionary in Tibet, and spending her life as the wife of an evangelist in America was not what she had in mind. But Billy persisted. They married in August 1943, three months after they both graduated from Wheaton.

The ceremony took place in Montreat, North Carolina, where Ruth's parents had located after being forced to leave China by the onset of World War II. The community was a Southern Presbyterian retreat center tucked in the Blue Ridge Mountains near Asheville. After two years in Western Springs, Illinois (noted below), the young couple moved to Montreat. That was the fall of 1945. In time, they would parent five children: Virginia—nicknamed Gigi—in 1945; Anne, in 1948; Ruth—nicknamed Bunny—in 1950; Franklin, in 1952; and Ned, in 1958.

Billy and Ruth first lived with the Bells but soon bought a house across the street. Free babysitting for a rapidly growing family probably was part of the reason staying close. Their second house was set on 125 acres atop a peak looming over the village below. They borrowed money to pay the $13 per acre price. Ruth oversaw the work, buying discarded timbers and big fireplace stones from residents of mountain cabins in the area.[4] Construction started in 1954, and the family moved in two years later. Dubbed Little Piney Cove, the house would be Billy and Ruth's home for the rest of their lives.

These family connections help explain Graham's willingness to live in the quaint remoteness of Montreat and, more to the point, portended Nelson Bell's powerful impact on his son-in-law. Graham dedicated his most recognized book, *Peace with God*, to his father-in-law. Graham later said that Bell was the most influential man in his life. To the end of Bell's days in 1973, Graham called him "Dr. Bell."

Youth for Christ

Soon after their marriage, Billy and Ruth hit the revival circuit in Ohio. Shortly into the trip, Ruth became ill. The situation quickly became serious enough that the young bridegroom placed his bride in a local hospital—and then headed back out to the sawdust trail.

This pattern of placing work before family marked Graham for most of his career. For many decades he averaged something like eight months a year away from home. He missed the birth of the first of their five children. In his old age, Graham regretted his numerous and extended absences. Yet here, as elsewhere, he exemplified the evangelical faith tradition, which lionized men and women who willingly—even eagerly—sacrificed family for mission.

In June 1943, just before their marriage, Graham accepted an invitation to become the pastor of a Baptist church with thirty members in Western Springs, Illinois, a small town halfway between Wheaton and downtown Chicago. Ruth was dismayed that Billy had said yes without consulting her. Not that she disagreed with the decision, but she was upset about being left out of the loop. Graham vowed never to do it again.

Western Springs Baptist Church was the only church Graham ever served as a regular pastor. His short tenure with this fledgling congregation revealed a cluster of aptitudes that marked his ministry for the next sixty years: an engaging personality, shrewd entrepreneurial skills, a knack for exploiting the media—and restless feet.

Graham took a variety of steps to make the church both visible and appealing. He changed the name to a more nondenominational-sounding one, Village Church. Soon the young pastor would establish a monthly dinner for civic leaders, which he tellingly called the Western Suburban Professional Men's Club. He featured celebrities such as *Lutheran Hour* speaker Walter Maier and the *Chicago Daily News* Pulitzer Prize–winning cartoonist Vaughn Shoemaker. Though Graham did not explicitly say so, it is easy to believe that he wanted to attract men of prominence not only for the financial contributions they might make but also for the status they might bring.

Bursting with ambition, Graham reached out in additional ways. He constantly traveled the Upper Midwest, holding revival services in fundamentalist churches and at Youth for Christ rallies (more below). He itinerated so much in fact that a regular substitute started filling in when he was out of town. Graham published a slim monthly magazine, *Songs in the Night*, which summed up—and touted—the swirl of activities going on in the church.

In January 1944 Graham took over a financially struggling weekly radio broadcast, also called *Songs in the Night*, that had started eighteen months earlier in a church in downtown Chicago. He aired it from the sanctuary basement every Sunday from 10:15 to 11:00 p.m. The program was well named, for it featured forty minutes of live music by an organist, a "girls" quartet, the King's Karrollers, and Canadian soloist George Beverly Shea, along with a four-minute sermonette by Graham. No appeals for money interrupted the broadcast.

Graham's most important move in Western Springs—by far—was enlisting the remarkable singing skills of Shea (commonly known as Bev) for *Songs in the Night*. Ten years older than Graham, Shea had already won a wide following in the area for his vocalizing on *Hymns from the Chapel*, a daily program released over WMBI, Moody Bible Institute's powerful clear-channel station. Shea was in high demand, and Graham knew it. Later in 1944 Shea left WMBI and moved to *Club Time*, a nationwide hymn broadcast sponsored by the Club Aluminum Corporation and aired over the ABC network and Armed Forces Radio.

At the time, Shea's name was more widely recognized than Graham's, so it made sense to place it first in local advertising. Graham astutely saw that Shea could strengthen his radio ministry and expand the church. Shea was gifted with a "deep molasses-barrel baritone" voice, just made, it seemed, for crooning old-time gospel hymns on the radio. His live renditions on the program proved a stroke of genius for both men.

The Village Church gave Graham useful experience. He learned the daily ups and downs of a local pastor. He also learned how to market his message through the deft use of media. But this ceaseless whirl of activity proved more useful for Graham than for his flock. Tensions rose. He later admitted that he had not been a very good pastor. And so the young preacher and the church eventually came to an amicable decision that his gifts lay elsewhere.

Graham's active time at the Village Church lasted about sixteen months. He effectively left sometime in the fall of 1944. The official termination date is not clear—likely October 1945—but that probably is a distinction without much of a difference. By then everyone knew that his heart lay elsewhere.

*   *   *

Graham's blossoming public career did not unfold in a political vacuum, of course. The horrors of World War II greeted him every day when he opened his morning newspaper. Like many other Americans who felt called to serve, he applied for chaplain's training in the army. The military turned him down for being underweight. After a second try, he won a commission as a second lieutenant.

But the young pastor never started actual training because in October 1944 he came down with a severe case of the mumps. So severe, in fact, that he and his physicians feared for his life. After a two-month convalescence, Graham concluded—and the army agreed—that with the war ending he should resign his commission and go into full-time ministry with a recently organized independent evangelistic organization.

Youth for Christ (YFC) was founded in 1941 as a nondenominational ministry for soldiers who were cast adrift in cities on weekend leave or returning from active duty without spouses and families waiting for them. YFC aimed to provide lively but uplifting entertainment, with a dash of patriotic fervor thrown in. Eventually YFC saw itself as an antidote to the real or perceived spurt of juvenile delinquency, too.

YFC was muscular Christianity on steroids. Its meetings headlined "all the gimmicks that reason would allow: famous athletes, stunts, music." Athletes such as Gil Dodds, the "Flying Parson," who held the American and world records for the mile run, enjoyed high billing. And so did the flamboyant wardrobe—pastel suits and hand-painted ties for starters—of YFC's featured speakers. Catching the eye was part of the game. Graham enthusiastically embraced all of it.

Graham's first major outing took place under YFC auspices. Always keen for maximum effect, YFC organizers scheduled the meeting for the Saturday night preceding Memorial Day 1944,[1] in Chicago's prestigious Orchestra Hall. Looking out on the three thousand partisans gathered to hear him, the young preacher swallowed his fears and marched himself out on to the stage. At the end, forty souls walked forward and gave their lives to Christ. Before long everyone knew that "closing the deal" would prove to be Graham's greatest gift in evangelism.

YFC perfectly fit Graham's bursting aptitudes for travel, schmoozing, and fiery preaching. In the fall of 1944—while he was still technically pastor of the Village Church—he started itinerating and preaching for YFC. The following year he became its first full-time evangelist, logging at least 135,000 miles—more than any other civilian passenger—on United Airlines. In time he would speak for YFC in forty-seven states and throughout Great Britain.

One of the most important developments that emerged from Graham's association with YFC was his chance encounter with Cliff Barrows. In 1945, at a YFC meeting in Asheville, Graham's scheduled song leader failed to show. Barrows and his bride, Billie Barrows, who were honeymooning in the mountains, happened to be at the meeting. When Barrows heard the news, he volunteered, but he warned Graham that he was not a trained musician. Barrows recalled: "He grabbed both of my hands and said, 'No time to be choosy!'"[2]

Born in 1923 in central California, Barrows was, like Graham at the time, a fundamentalist Baptist. Though Barrows was not quite as tall as Shea and Graham, he was, like them, handsome and safely married. Also like them, he was preternaturally talented. Historian Edith Blumhofer notes that Barrows's gifts—which would soon manifest themselves—included the ability to organize and run Graham's meetings, direct the crusade choirs, lead the congregations in familiar songs, serve as the announcer on Graham's radio and television broadcasts, choose all the guest artists, and, above all, keep the increasingly complex machine running smoothly.

*   *   *

YFC marched under a flagrantly mixed-metaphor motto that folk in the evangelical world soon internalized like a Social Security number: "Geared to the Times, Anchored to the Rock." Graham did not invent the motto, but he might as well have, for it captured the heart and soul—or perhaps we should say, hands and feet—of Graham's ambition for bringing the nation and soon the rest of the world to faith in Christ.

But Graham was too visionary—or at least too restless—to stick with any one plan for long. He held his first revival meeting on his own—that is, independent of YFC backing—in his hometown of Charlotte in November 1947.[3] Simultaneously flying under two flags—his own and YFC's—he conducted several more YFC meetings in 1948, the last one in Des Moines, Iowa, in September of that year. There is no evidence of conflict with YFC. Rather, he seemed simply to outgrow it. Undoubtedly there was an element of muscle flexing too. Though Graham was too politic to say so, he knew he was airborne and just did not need YFC any longer.

YFC helped move Graham to the top of his game in multiple ways. In those years he built a fat folder of sermons, learned how to preach to large audiences as if he were preaching to small ones, saw the wisdom of turning over the organization of his meetings to local committees, polished strategies for dealing with the press, developed a tough hide against criticism, and, most important, perfected the art of networking with other rising evangelical leaders.

Whether Graham made YFC or YFC made Graham is a good question. Either way, the knot was tied in the midst of the cultural exuberance of America and Europe in the half-dozen years following World War II.

SCENE 4

England Calls

Fresh off the successes of the YFC revivals in the mid-1940s, Graham felt that he was destined for a wider mission field. And so it was that in March 1946 he and four friends made a brisk tour of England and the Continent under YFC auspices.[1]

The ambitious band consisted of Torrey Johnson, an influential YFC-related pastor in Chicago; Charles Templeton, a popular YFC evangelist; J. Stratton Shufelt, a YFC soloist; and Wesley Hartzell, a Hearst newspaper reporter. The presence of an influential pastor, a popular preacher, an acclaimed vocalist, and a professional journalist showed how the YFC band expected to deploy the savvy marketing tactics that worked so well back home.

Graham and his group received more—or, depending on one's perspective, less—than they bargained for. The response was mixed. The British wondered why these young Americans would be coming all the way to the British Isles—where Christianity had prospered for fifteen centuries—to explain to them why and how they needed to scrub up their spiritual lives.

They also found Graham's approach odd. His flamboyant attire raised eyebrows among folks accustomed to seeing clergy in black robes and tab collars. The Graham team surely looked like Americans selling religion the way Americans sold everything else: as a commodity for the taking. Still, these Graham/YFC meetings attracted a respectable turnout in some places, and hundreds—possibly thousands—made new commitments to Christ. The aggregate crowds reached one hundred thousand over forty-six days.

The lure of globalizing the gospel message soon beckoned again. In the fall of 1946, Graham headed back to Great Britain, this time with Barrows; Barrows's wife, Billie; Shea; and a travel arranger. Ruth later joined them. The results were better than the first time around. Graham toned down his approach, used more conventional language, and donned business attire when he preached. In the meantime, his British audiences had gained a better appreciation for Graham's personal integrity and the sincerity of his mission. Some Church of England clergy even invited him back. This journey, which posted 360 meetings over six months, intimated the extraordinary stamina that marked Graham's career for the next five decades.

Hearing of his successes across the Channel, evangelical pastors in Germany and in France invited him to try his revival hand in their countries too. Data on the results of this initial excursion to the Continent are scarce, but Graham gave every indication that he was pleased. A December 1946 vacation with Ruth, relaxing on a sunny beach on the Riviera, brightened his assessment of things too. The point here is not trivial: one of the less appreciated features of Graham's story is that throughout his life he worked extremely hard, but he also knew the importance of taking short sabbaticals.

The trip to Britain bore an outcome that Graham surely did not anticipate but held powerful consequences for the rest of his ministry. Simply put, it cemented his commitment to itinerant evangelism. It also toughened him against the loneliness of extended absences from home and the kind of fierce criticism that he received from the British press and from other religious leaders in the country.

Beyond that, he encountered a degree of deprivation in the UK in the months immediately following World War II that eclipsed anything he had imagined, let alone actually experienced, at home. Food shortages and lack of heat in homes and churches left this comfortable American speechless.

Like young Mormon missionaries knocking on doors and getting hostile responses, Graham learned anew that evangelism in general, and evangelism in Europe in particular, was hard going. But there was no turning back—and no sign that he ever considered it. Graham arrived back home in March 1947, surely knowing that he was in for keeps.

Becoming Billy Graham

In hindsight—and probably even at the time—the next turn in Billy Graham's life would seem like the strangest one of all. William Bell Riley, a patriarch of fundamentalism, begged Graham to take over Riley's Northwestern Schools in Minneapolis, which he had founded over four decades before. The schools included a Bible-training institute, a liberal arts college, and a seminary. Graham reluctantly agreed. Just twenty-nine, he became the youngest college president in the nation.

It wasn't just his youth that made Graham an unusual choice for the position. His most prestigious degree was a BA from Wheaton College—nothing to sneeze at in the evangelical world but thin preparation for running a college or seminary, let alone both. Yet somehow he found a measure of success at Northwestern. Under his leadership, the institution increased enrollment, built new buildings, and even started a radio station. The challenge of keeping the station going prompted Graham to create a mailing list of supporters. "We have to capture those names!" he told his business manager.

Yet, whatever success Graham had at Northwestern, the experience made clear to him that he was cut out to be a preacher, not a college president. A little over four years into the experiment, he resigned as president of Northwestern Schools. In the future he would receive more offers, including two that would make him head of a Billy Graham University, but he always said no.

*   *   *

Graham's primary vocation as an evangelist continued apace even during the Northwestern years. In the fall of 1948, he made one of the most important moves of his career. He, along with Barrows, Shea, and associate evangelist Grady Wilson, was in Modesto, California, holding a campaign.

One evening, in their motel, they started talking about the traps that had snared other evangelists.

After praying about it, the band concluded that four seemed most common: misuse of money, sexual immorality, not cooperating with other clergy, and dishonesty about numbers. They promised each other that they would avoid these pitfalls. That promise came to be known as the "Modesto Manifesto." Graham never called it that, and no one typed it up in a document of any sort. But it functioned as if they had.

First up was their determination to erase the Elmer Gantry image of the evangelist as a money-grubbing charlatan. In popular culture Elmer Gantry—the protagonist in Sinclair Lewis's 1926 novel of that name—symbolized the roving preacher who squandered followers' hard-earned dollars on booze and women.

Graham knew the risks that money posed. In YFC meetings he had turned over all offerings to the sponsoring committee and then drew a salary from YFC. But now that he had launched into independent meetings on his own, he was paid the same way most evangelists were paid.

At the end of a service, or string of services, they passed the hat for a "love offering." This venerable practice begged for abuse. It encouraged preachers to wring as much money as possible from audiences with emotional appeals. And since the money came in cash, there was no public accounting for the amount received or whether the amount was reasonable for the services rendered.

At the time, Graham evidently did not know exactly how to deal with this problem, but he promised to downplay the offering and rely as much as possible on whatever money the local organizing committee had raised and provided.

Next up was sexual morality. They knew that all evangelists toiled in the shadow of Gantry not only as a charlatan but also as a skirt-chaser. They also knew that they, like most young men, were vulnerable to temptation, especially being away from home for long stretches. And they knew the destructive power of rumors of impropriety, regardless of what the actual actions or intent may have been. So they determined to avoid even the appearance of immorality—let alone the sin of it—by never dining or traveling alone with a woman outside their families.

This commitment immediately caught the eye of journalists, who incorrectly elevated it to the first and most important of the four. Journalists also failed to see that Graham aimed for the rule to work in commonsense ways. The point (confirmed to me by one associate) was to prevent candlelit dinners in faraway places, not routine business interacticns in fully public places.

Next, the four men specified willingness to cooperate with—not fight—other clergymen (in those days, almost always men). The fundamentalist army that Graham had grown up in fought nonfundamentalist Christians as much as they fought the unsaved world. After criticizing another preacher when he was just starting out in ministry, Graham concluded that his job—his sole job—was to proclaim the gospel, not to bad-mouth people in other Christian traditions or, for that matter, in non-Christian traditions.

And finally, there was the challenge of honesty about the arithmetic. Everyone knew that evangelists—especially faith healers—exaggerated the number of people who came to their meetings as well as the number who claimed to be saved or healed. Journalists rightly grew wary.

Graham responded by insisting that the team must scrupulously avoid inflating successes in their advertising and reporting. Soon he started to rely on turnstile counts, or aerial checks, or police or journalists' estimates, not the guesses of his own workers, who had a vested interest in making the numbers as high as possible.

Even more important, in 1950 he started to insist on calling the people who came forward and signed decision cards "inquirers," not "converts." Only God knew who the converts really were. All that he could affirm was the number of people he could actually count. Journalists were slow on the uptake, as they peppered him year after year with questions about how many people had been converted in his meetings. To which he almost always gave the same answer: effectively, I have no idea, only God knows.[1]

As things turned out, the Modesto Manifesto proved to be a working blueprint for how the members of the team ran their personal and professional lives for the next six decades. Graham would be assailed for many things, some of them valid, but critics rarely targeted him for failing to abide by the manifesto's principles. Partisans often referred to the content of the manifesto simply as "The Graham Rules." Eventually it ranked as one of the keystone "texts"—or more precisely, oral traditions—of American evangelicalism.

*   *   *

In 1948 and the first half of 1949, Graham had other things on his mind, too. The plain truth is that his career was sputtering. The testing took two forms. First, the revivals that he led in those months, mostly in the South and Midwest, not rarely went unheralded in both the religious and secular press. One, in Altoona, Pennsylvania, in July 1949, is best described as a flop, and he knew it. Few people attended, and few professed a new birth experience. It was "the sorriest crusade we ever had," Grady Wilson later admitted. Contrary to the myth that Billy Graham always was the biggest news in town, he was not invincible.

Second, and more to the point, Graham's faith went through a time of trial. He never went into great detail about it—he was not an introspective or self-revealing man—but he said enough for us to know that he was grappling with the Bible's authority. The trial reached a turning point in the most unlikely of places: on a mountaintop in a remote stretch of land in Southern California.

Mears and Templeton

Like virtually all male evangelicals in those years, Graham held patriarchal views about women's place in the home and in the pulpit. He urged married women to understand their appropriate roles as housewives. Viewing the man as the main breadwinner, he advised women to keep the house neat, dress attractively, and cook good meals. A widely touted photograph by the famed *Life* magazine photographer Cornell Capa, taken during Graham's 1957 New York crusade, showed Ruth dutifully ironing her husband's shirt in their hotel room before he went on stage. In this case, a picture really did speak a thousand words.

Yet Graham was never simple in his views, as his connection with Henrietta Mears shows. Years later he would say that she exercised "a remarkable influence both directly and indirectly on my life." Indeed, he added, "no other woman outside my wife and mother has had such a marked influence." Mears played a dramatic role in the postwar evangelical story, and certainly in Graham's own story too.

In the 1930s and 1940s Mears taught a Sunday school class boasting an attendance of more than four thousand at First Presbyterian Church of Hollywood. The class attracted celebrities such as UCLA football great Donn Moomaw, and members of the faculty of Fuller Theological Seminary in Pasadena. Though evangelicals never doubted women's equality before God, they doubted that women should teach men, and certainly not males and females together.

Yet through sheer force of personality, Mears simply did it, and no one asked questions.

Setting aside venerable principles about the inappropriateness of women instructing men, she taught her students how to accept the authority of Scripture, not as an inerrant textbook to be read with wooden literalism, but as a living, trustworthy guide to salvation. Mears had the clout to speak without much fear of contradiction. In time her signature volume, *What the Bible Is All About* (1953), would sell three million copies, and it continues to sell to this day.

Besides teaching, Mears made a practice of taking young people on camping trips to arboreal spots in California for times of spiritual renewal and commitment. In 1947, seeking a permanent site, Mears and four colleagues formed a nonprofit corporation and purchased Forest Home, a retreat center in the San Bernardino Mountains east of Los Angeles. Meetings at Forest Home attracted evangelical heavyweights such as Bill and Vonette Bright, founders of Campus Crusade for Christ, and Dr. J. Edwin Orr, an internationally respected Irish historian and evangelical conference speaker.

Forest Home emphasized many features of ministry that prefigured and perhaps directly influenced Graham. These included a stress on making a clear-cut decision for Christ and for Christian service. Mears and Forest Home also stressed the integrity of distinct denominational traditions within the larger evangelical family, tolerance for moderately differing theological views, the multiracial and international character of the evangelical movement, the menace of global Communism, a willingness to exploit the communication potential of television and motion pictures, and an eagerness to feature the testimonies of Christian converts of distinction in the secular world, including the entertainment industry.

*   *   *

In August 1949 Mears invited Graham to speak at a College Briefing Conference at Forest Home. As it happened, about the same time he found himself grappling with the challenge to biblical authority that his old friend Charles (Chuck) B. Templeton was insistently raising and challenging Graham squarely to face.

Templeton was a looming presence in the early years of Graham's ministry, though not as large as many accounts have suggested. His tumultuous spiritual life provided enough contrast to Graham's to make him an ideal foil for journalists and, later, historians writing about Billy.

Templeton was multitalented. Born into a working-class family in Toronto in 1915, he landed a job as a sports cartoonist for the *Globe and Mail* when he was just seventeen. Four years later he experienced a powerful religious conversion in a local fundamentalist church. Though Templeton never finished high school, he became an itinerant evangelist for YFC, where he and Graham met.

Soon fast friends, the two men started traveling and preaching together in Canada, the United States, and Great Britain. Many thought that Templeton's skills surpassed Graham's, and Graham readily agreed. Predictably the Canadian's rugged good looks earned notice too.

In the late 1940s, however, Templeton began to doubt the message that he and Graham were proclaiming. In an effort to shore up his faith, Templeton won admission to Princeton Theological Seminary as a special student. But his old convictions continued to erode.

Graham took Templeton's doubts seriously. Though he later said that he himself had considered going on to seminary—Oxford more than Princeton—he never actually applied. Regardless, Graham acknowledged the gravity of Templeton's challenge about the Bible's truthfulness. Did Scripture contain errors? If so, could it still be a trustworthy guide to salvation?

What happened next has been told so many times it has acquired the patina of Holy Writ. Though the precise chronology is not clear, apparently later in the week when Graham visited Forest Home, he hiked up a nearby mountain trail in the moonlight. (It may be relevant that this event, or at least the narration of it, resembled Graham's calling experience on a moonlit golf course in Florida a decade before.) Finding a glade, he laid his Bible on a tree stump. After soul-searching prayer, he determined that he would not try to defend the Bible but simply accept it on faith as God's authoritative Word.

Graham knew he was not equipped to take on Templeton's higher-critical arguments. But he also knew that the Bible fulfilled its stated purpose. When he quoted its passages in his sermons and then called people to come to Christ, they did. Later Graham would say that the Bible served as the foundation of his life, the center point that enabled him to orient everything else. Elsewhere he likened the Bible to the pen, phone, and dictating machine on his desk. He kept them handy because they worked.

Graham was not an intellectual gladiator. As we have seen, he avoided point-by-point debates over theology, and he never argued for the Bible's inerrancy either. Indeed, amidst the millions of words he uttered in print and in person, the word "inerrancy"—which soon became the touchstone of orthodoxy among fundamentalists and many evangelicals—rarely if ever cropped up.

But Graham did talk about the Bible's *infallibility*. While he did not think that the Bible contained factual errors, at least if it was translated correctly and interpreted fairly, he insisted that factual accuracy was not the point. Rather, the point—the one worth defending—was the Bible's power to shine a light on the path to salvation.

Templeton and Graham never again saw eye to eye on these matters. The Canadian told Graham he was committing "intellectual suicide." Yet Graham parted from Templeton energized. Looking at the results his preaching usually produced—lives claimed or reclaimed almost everywhere he went—it is easy to imagine that Graham found those results all the proof he needed.

Templeton stayed at Princeton only one year. He soon joined the staff of the National Council of Churches, and then the Board of National Missions of the Presbyterian Church USA. He held evangelistic meetings under its auspices, and represented the Protestant view on CBS's Sunday morning program *Look Up and Live*. In 1955 he issued *Life Looks Up*, a winsome and elegantly crafted defense of Christian commitment in the face of modern pressures.

Yet Templeton kept traveling left theologically. Eventually he declared himself agnostic, gave up ministry altogether, and moved back to Toronto. In his home city he displayed an impressive range of skills, including toy designer and news commentator. In 1996 he published a poignant memoir, *Farewell to God: My Reasons for Rejecting the Christian Faith*.

The friendship between Graham and Templeton grew wobbly but somehow survived until Templeton's death in 2001. At one point Templeton said, "Much of what he says in the pulpit is puerile nonsense," but then added, perhaps wistfully, "there is no feigning in him. . . . he believes what he believes with an invincible innocence. He is the only mass evangelist I would trust. And I miss him."

City of Angels

In one sense the most momentous public event in Graham's life unfolded the month after the famed "mountaintop experience" in August 1949. Back in April, the Christ for Greater Los Angeles Committee, an arm of the local Christian Businessmen's Committee, had invited Graham to come to the City of Angels for an extended revival.

At first Graham turned them down, not sure if it was the right thing to do. One might imagine too that the young preacher, just thirty years old, felt intimidated by the setting. Los Angeles was, after all, the third-largest metropolitan area in the nation, home of the movie industry with its reputation for suspect morals, and a vortex of ethnic diversity. Did he have the chops for it? Would he be dismissed as just another Southern barnstormer? Above all, was it really the Lord's will, or just his own ambition motivating him?

But then the Lord spoke—or so it seemed to Graham. He agreed to launch a three-week revival on September 25. Given the magnitude of the task, it would take preparation, and lots of it. His experience with YFC had taught him that revivals had to be worked up as well as prayed down. He required the committee to pay more attention to logistical details, raise more money, and triple the advertising budget.

By far the most important step, Graham later insisted, was the neighborhood prayer chains that started up months ahead of the campaign. Whether prayer chains had any effect on God is not a question that historians can answer. But this much is clear: Graham's conviction that he enjoyed God's blessing not only energized his efforts but also steeled him against criticism—and adversity from Mother Nature. The same surely could be said of the countless people who prayed for the meetings. Believing that they were doing the Lord's work empowered them.

As September 25 approached, both Graham and the committee proved to be masters of public relations. They won support from eight hundred local churches and endorsements from prominent business and civic leaders, including the mayor. They also proved to be masters of advertising. Unlike many of his peers on the revival circuit, who sometimes pretended that the Holy Spirit was doing all the work, Graham never apologized for advertising. His Fuller Brush experience taught him a lesson he never forgot.

And so it was that a blizzard of handbills, newspaper ads, and strategically placed road signs trumpeted every superlative in the book. People read about a "mammoth tent," "6000 free seats," "inspiring music," "unprecedented demands," "dynamic preaching," and "America's foremost evangelist." Adjectives such as "huge," "vital," "young," "golden," "thrilling," "dramatic," "magnetic," "eloquent," "compelling," "persuasive," "tremendous," "outstanding," "enthusiastic," "international," "interdenominational," and, perhaps best of all, "free" proliferated. Whether these booster terms came from Graham's hand or from his publicists' matters little; they merged to form the leading edge of his public presentation.

Graham opened the meetings right on schedule, under a 480-foot tent pitched at the corner of Washington and Hill Streets. The organizing committee touted the tent as one of the largest in the world, direct from a Ringling Brothers circus. And it stood in the heart of the city where it would be easy to find. The committee also erected a powerful searchlight on the site, every night beaming a tower of radiance into the Southern California sky.

Even so, at first the crowds disappointed. The weather was unusually cool for that time of the year, and in a tent the lack of heat was no small problem. Actually, throughout Graham's career, bad weather—heat, cold, rain, sleet—would often be a problem for his outdoor meetings. But he invariably interpreted adversity as opportunity, and the crusades rolled on. Then too the revival failed to catch fire in the local press. Though the committee had placed many ads in the local papers, few stories resulted. Three weeks in, Graham and friends were just about ready to pack up and go home.

But then things changed. Crowds started to surge. Latecomers were forced to gather on the street outside the tent and listen via loudspeakers. The six thousand chairs in the tent, originally placed as far apart as possible to make the tent look full, were now jammed together to make room for three thousand more. Graham and the committee decided to extend the meeting another three weeks.

The reasons for the turnaround are easy to see. For one thing, the weather had shifted. The breezes were so balmy that the ushers had to raise the flaps on the tent. Moreover, a large minority of the city's population were migrants from the lower South and old Southwest. As word of mouth began to spread among them, Graham's accent must have seemed like a comforting note from back home.

But good weather and good memories were not the only factors. The campaign started to attract celebrities. Stars professed conversion to Christ, and they talked about it. The first famous convert—or inquirer— was Stuart "Stew" Hamblen, a rough-hewn radio host and horse gambler. Hamblen had grown up a Methodist preacher's kid in Texas but strayed far from the church. After persistent coaxing from his wife, Hamblen attended a meeting on Sunday night, October 16. The next morning he "gave his heart to Christ." Hamblen proclaimed his life change on the radio. He also stopped hawking his sponsor's cigarettes, which cost him his job.

In the coming weeks, other celebrities, including the Olympic track star and war hero Louis Zamperini, followed.[1] Hamblen and Zamperini prefigured one of the most conspicuous features of Graham's crusades for the next six decades: testimonies. Graham instinctively understood that the theology textbook was no match for the word of the satisfied customer.

By far the biggest boost came from a source no one expected. A day or two after making the decision to keep going, Graham walked into the tent and found reporters milling around, flashbulbs popping, notepads flipped open. When he asked an unnamed journalist what was going on, the journalist said, "You've just been kissed by William Randolph Hearst."

Legend holds that Hearst, one of the most powerful newspaper moguls in the nation, had told his staff to "puff Graham." Like most creation stories, that one almost certainly was not literally true, but it carried enough truth to gain legs.

A couple of years before, Hearst had told his reporters to "puff Youth for Christ." In Los Angeles he evidently issued a more general directive to his reporters to pay special attention to Graham's meetings. The two men never met, and there is no evidence that Hearst shared Graham's evangelical convictions. But he probably approved Graham's fierce anti-Communism and stress on public morality. He also knew that a winsome face on the front page sold papers.

*   *   *

Hearst was not the only one who appreciated the marketing value of a handsome star player. Nearly every newspaper account of the revival in Los Angeles mentioned Graham's looks, often in the first paragraph. But there was more to it than a commanding visage and warrior heart.

In Los Angeles Graham's explosive speaking style captured attention. One journalist later dubbed him a "preaching windmill." He paced the platform relentlessly, sometimes racking up more than a mile per sermon. Song leader Cliff Barrows reeled the cord for Graham's lapel microphone in and out like a fishing line.

Graham talked fast. He said that he had listened to successful newscasters like Gabriel Heatter, H. V. Kaltenborn, Drew Pearson, and Walter Winchell, and that was how they read the news: fast. "God's machine gun," one journalist called him. Back in England in 1946, a stenographer clocked him at 240 words a minute. Despite the speed, he seemed never to garble a word, or pause to find one, or fall into grammatical errors.

And loud. Just about everyone, including Graham himself when he looked back on his career years later, said that he blazed away with deafening volume. That was his sister Jean's verdict too: "He preached *so loud*." *Time* magazine's take was even more memorable: "trumpet-lunged."

With two deft sentences, one local journalist seemed to capture everything. "Tall, slender, handsome, with a curly shock of blond hair, Graham looks like a collar ad, acts like a motion picture star, thinks like a psychology professor, talks like a North Carolinian and preaches like a combination of Billy Sunday and Dwight L. Moody. . . . He uses few illustrations, no sob stories, absolutely no deathbed stuff."

The content of Graham's sermons won as much attention as the style. Graham saw peril everywhere he looked, and he looked everywhere. Nations warred against nations, factions against factions, churches against churches. Individuals even warred against themselves. The solution was as clear as it was simple: confess your sins and find a new life in Christ.

If one peril stood at the top, it was Communism. Graham targeted it repeatedly and forcefully. No wonder. On September 23, 1949, two days before the revival started, President Truman announced that the Soviet Union had recently detonated an atomic bomb. Americans knew that day would be coming sooner or later but few expected it sooner. And then on October 1 Mao's "Reds" won control of mainland China. Graham's preaching about Communism, which persisted into the mid-1970s, gained power because millions of Americans saw the threat exactly as he did: lethal, imminent, and unavoidable—unless the nation changed its ways.

Initially the committee had planned for the Los Angeles campaign to run three weeks, but swelling crowds prompted two extensions, stretching it to eight weeks altogether. This flexibility proved typical of Graham. He prudently left time between campaigns to allow for the possibility that the meeting should be longer. He knew the Holy Spirit would decide, but he wanted to make the Holy Spirit's work as easy as possible.

*   *   *

Graham's schedule in the City of Angels was brutal. Determined to accept every invitation that came his way, he gave countless talks to local churches, civic groups, and neighborhood klatches. He met celebrities in their homes. One photo shows him—all of thirty years old—casually schmoozing with Jimmy Stewart, Jimmy Durante, and Katharine Hepburn in someone's well-appointed kitchen.

Graham spoke every night (except Monday, when everyone took a breather) and twice on Sunday, and sometimes twice on Saturday too. When the revival started, he had a repertoire of twenty-five sermons, but he soon ran out and had to write new ones from scratch. Or not. Once he simply recycled Jonathan Edwards's classic "Sinners in the Hands of an Angry God," giving Edwards credit. In the eight weeks of the revival, he preached sixty-five sermons. Observers judged the number of visitors to be 350,000—possibly 400,000—souls. Something like 6,000 persons either committed or recommitted their lives to Christ.

A week before Thanksgiving 1949, Billy and Ruth finally boarded the train home to Minneapolis, where Graham was still more or less overseeing Northwestern Schools. During the crusade Graham, who was lean to begin with, dropped twenty pounds and fought crushing exhaustion. When he got home, he looked back on the Los Angeles marathon with wonderment about what the Lord had done. He would have been more than human if he had not taken at least a smidgen of pride in his own role too.

Graham could not have known that those eight weeks would soon make him a national celebrity and then an international icon. The Associated Press proclaimed that the rising evangelist "tops Billy Sunday." *Time*, too, declared that "no one since Billy Sunday" has plied "the revival sickle" as successfully as this "blond . . . North Carolinian." *Life* magazine, with 13.5 million readers in the 1940s, trumpeted his achievement. *Quick*, *Newsweek*, *Los Angeles Times*, and *London Illustrated* joined the parade.

The time was ripe. American cultural historian Anne Blue Wills points out that Peter Marshall—pastor of New York Avenue Presbyterian Church in Washington, DC, and twice the chaplain of the United States Senate—had died at age forty-six in January 1949. Though Marshall was a minister, not an evangelist, he had filled a niche in popular Protestant culture. Graham was an evangelist, not a minister, but in many ways he filled—and soon exceeded—Marshall's celebrated role.

SCENE 8

Beantown

Just six weeks after Graham left Los Angeles, he headed out again, this time to Boston. On New Year's Eve 1949, he launched another extended revival. The whole story had a surreal quality. For one thing, the city was a citadel of East Coast respectability, with its academic elites, finance mavens, and social aristocracy. It also served as the historic home of Unitarians, Christian Scientists, and a rapidly swelling number of Catholics of mostly Irish extraction.

The Boston invitation came from a coalition of evangelical ministers who were worried about the forbidding forces surrounding them and eager for broad spiritual awakening. The Reverend Dr. Harold John Ockenga, the senior pastor of Boston's historic Park Street Church, led the coalition.

A Congregationalist, Ockenga was, by any measure, a formidable presence. The main founder of the National Association of Evangelicals back in 1942, he also labored as president of Fuller Theological Seminary in Pasadena, California, at the same time he served as pastor of Park Street. And he was one of a tiny few evangelicals who held an earned PhD in a secular discipline, philosophy, from a secular school, the University of Pittsburgh.

And then there was Park Street Church, where Graham held the first, fourth, and fifth meetings of the revival. If evangelical Protestants in New England had a sacred site, this Federal-style church, built in 1809, was it. On July 4, 1831, people first sang "My Country, 'Tis of Thee" on its steps. Esteemed for tradition and respectability, the church had served as a launching site for evangelical abolitionists before the Civil War and for myriad famous evangelists afterward. Charles Finney, Dwight L. Moody, Billy Sunday, and other luminaries had preached from its pulpit. The edifice overlooked the famed Boston Common on one side and the site of the Boston Massacre and the Old Burying Ground on the other.

In short, Boston, Ockenga, and Park Street Church posed a daunting challenge—and radiant opportunity—for a young preacher from the rural South with few connections outside his tightly enclosed evangelical world. Under the circumstances, it is surprising that Graham accepted the invitation at all, especially since there was not much time to set the stage, either for himself or for the city. After all, extensive preparation already served as a hallmark of his meetings. But he went anyway, undoubtedly feeling the Holy Spirit's prompting and a sense of personal challenge too.

Graham started off on Friday night, December 30, at Park Street Church, one night before the meeting officially opened at Mechanics Hall on New Year's Eve. Two thousand jammed into the church on December 30, and six thousand into the hall on December 31. Seeing the unexpected size of the response, the organizers scheduled another service in the hall for the next afternoon, New Year's Day. Seeing another filled room, they moved the evening service to Park Street Church, which also filled, with two thousand turned away.

After two nights at Park Street, they moved the meetings back to Mechanics Hall, then to the Opera House, then to Symphony Hall, and finally to Boston Garden, the city's largest indoor facility, for the concluding service on January 16. The Garden meeting drew twenty-five thousand, with ten thousand turned away.

*   *   *

All this moving around attested to three of Graham's most enduring traits. The first was his pragmatism. His willingness to mount the hallowed pulpit of Park Street, even though he lacked a seminary degree, along with his willingness to move to four of the largest and most prestigious venues in the city, should occasion no surprise given his practical proclivities. He simply needed the room.

The second trait was his eye for situating his meetings in cities and sites with high cultural visibility. It was no accident that in Los Angeles he had pitched his tent in the heart of the city. In years to come he would choose venues with political significance, such as the steps of the United States Capitol, or sports significance, such as the Rose Bowl, or architectural significance, such as Central Park.

The third trait, closely related to the first two, was an astute sense of timing. He knew *when* to launch—or conclude—meetings. In Boston he officially opened the meeting on New Year's Eve, a calendar landmark that evangelicals traditionally had set aside for a "Watch Night Service." In later years he would take advantage of Christian celebrations, such as Easter afternoon, or national holidays, such as July 4, or countless political events, such as presidents' and governors' prayer breakfasts and inaugurations.

*　　*　　*　　*

Graham's preaching in Boston may have set a record, at least for him, for shameless showmanship. He interpreted the Bible in preposterously literal terms, hurled slang words, and tried to reenact biblical stories on the stage. Heaven, he thundered, will be "sixteen hundred miles long, sixteen hundred miles wide, and sixteen hundred miles high." And how would saints pass the time? "We will sit around the fireplace and have parties and the angels will wait on us and we'll drive down the golden streets in a yellow Cadillac convertible." He called an Old Testament feast a "shindig" and acted out the parable of the prodigal son by pretending to slop hogs. Ruth, watching from the sidelines, worried.

Shameless showmanship aside, several unanticipated outcomes crowned the Boston campaign. One was Graham's efforts to work with, not against, the city's Catholics in a common enterprise of fighting personal sin and social injustice. Archbishop (later Cardinal) Richard James Cushing reciprocated, directing the archdiocesan newspaper to showcase Graham's work. When Graham's evangelical friends advised him not even to meet with Cushing, Graham said, "When I accepted the call to ministry, I told God I'd go anywhere he wanted me to go. I'd go to hell if he'd give me a safe conduct out."

These gestures by Graham and by Cushing took courage on both sides. In 1950 most evangelicals regarded the pope as the antichrist, sometimes not only metaphorically but also literally. Ockenga led the pack in voicing strident opposition to Catholicism. And Catholics largely relegated Protestants to the dominion of the lost, too, for there was no salvation outside the Catholic Church. Yet the manifest friendship and mutual support between Graham and Cushing signaled a beachhead, and it would grow.

Another major outcome was the surprising rapport that Graham established with the elite academic community. He accepted invitations to speak at MIT, Wellesley, and Harvard in the Boston area, as well as other prestige schools in New England such as Yale, Vassar, Amherst, and the University of Massachusetts.

Data on these early visits are scarce. We do not know how many invitations came from student groups, or affiliated churches, or faculty

43

members, or administrators. Historian Andrew Finstuen estimates that probably more than half came from student groups.[1] Whatever the origins of the invitations, few contemporaries discerned the significance of a country boy with modest educational credentials walking into academic lions' dens and emerging with mutual respect.

The press coverage of the Boston meeting formed one more major outcome. It was extraordinary, both in the sheer number of articles published and in the range of details about his life and ministry journalists covered. Headlines emphasized the size of the crowds and Graham's stamina, his dynamic presentation, his smashing looks, and his hearthside life with Ruth and their young children. Journalists even rummaged around for stories about his fitness regimen and eating habits. One big photo of Graham in a T-shirt spoke volumes. The press could not get enough of him.

Graham kept moving. From Boston he itinerated on to standing engagements in the South and elsewhere in New England. Later he came close to admitting that he had made a mistake abandoning the white-hot revival in Boston. Was it possible, he mused, that it might have replicated the revivals of the Great Awakening? One of the great paradoxes of Graham's story is that he rarely lacked confidence about what he should do next, but sometimes, years later, he looked back and wondered if he had made the right decision.

Wins and Losses

First the wins. In February 1950 Graham was heading south again, this time to Atlanta, where he addressed the Georgia state legislature, and then on to a three-week campaign in Columbia, South Carolina. Given Graham's unerring eye for influence, it is not accidental that he settled on the state capital—also the home of the University of South Carolina—for a major revival in the South. The final meeting of the Columbia crusade, held in the university's stadium, saw attendance records smashed. Yet two additional events in the city influenced his career more clearly.

South Carolina governor Strom Thurmond threw his support behind the campaign by inviting Graham to address the South Carolina legislature. Though he had won the endorsement of the mayor of Los Angeles before the Los Angeles revival, the backing of the governor of a state signaled government support at a dramatically higher level.

Evidently it did not occur to the governor—or to Graham, or to anyone else, for that matter—that this arrangement might cross a boundary between church and state. There is no reason to think that Graham found Thurmond's segregationist views troubling, either. But there is plenty of reason to think that Graham was pleased to win the support of a sitting governor.

A second outcome portended far greater consequences for the long run. When Graham was preaching in Columbia, the magazine mogul Henry R. Luce—who was vacationing on the Carolina coast—heard about the young evangelist. Luce rivaled Hearst in the publishing world; they were two of the most powerful publishers in the nation. Some said he was the most influential private citizen in the country, for he owned *Time*, *Life*, and *Fortune* magazines and later created *Sports Illustrated*. Luce liked what he heard about Graham and invited him for dinner. They hit it off.

Luce and Graham had a lot in common. Unlike Hearst, Luce was an active churchman. A lifelong Presbyterian, he had grown up in China, where his parents had served as educational missionaries. Both Luce and Graham held traditional values about hard work, public service, and old-fashioned patriotism. Both believed that Communism posed a lethal threat to America's survival. And both determined to throw their energies behind their nation's defense.

The constant attention that Luce showered on Graham in his magazines decade after decade gave the preacher priceless publicity, not to mention uptown legitimation. *Life*'s lavish pictorial spreads capitalized on Graham's visual appeal. Graham readily admitted that he owed a big part of his success to Hearst and, especially, to Luce. More broadly, Luce's approval marked the beginning of a long and fruitful relationship with journalists.

The South Carolina meeting saw the American debut of a major name change that Graham actually had introduced four years earlier in England. Campaigns became "crusades." Graham might have picked up the idea from Billy Sunday, who called his engagements crusades, too.[1]

The point of the name change was to make clear that the meetings actually started long before the evangelist arrived in a city and continued long after he left. The advance planning men, with their families in tow, typically relocated to the site three months ahead of a meeting and sometimes one or even two years ahead. They stayed for three or so months afterward to oversee follow-up efforts with folks who had signed decision cards.

In the spring of 1950 Graham returned to Boston. He held a massive service on the Boston Common on Sunday afternoon, April 23. Despite driving rain, he drew the largest crowd in the history of the Common. He also drew unprecedented press coverage. Predictably Graham preached on sin and Christ as the answer for it. Just as predictably, he preached on Communism and Christ as the answer for it too. He was establishing a pattern. Audiences came expecting certain topics and left satisfied.

*   *   *

But there was also a big loss. In July 1950 Graham—just thirty-one years old—wangled a meeting with President Harry S. Truman in the Oval Office. "Wangled" is the right word, too, for Graham had made several efforts in the previous year to secure the meeting. He sent letters. He tried without success to get Truman publicly to congratulate Northwestern Schools when they launched a radio station. He telegrammed Truman his firm support for Truman's muscular prosecution of the Korean War. Truman ignored the preacher. Graham finally succeeded only by calling in favors from politician friends.

This meeting proved to be one of the most memorable incidents in Graham's long life, but for all the wrong reasons. A half century later he would rehearse the story on the very first page of his memoir. Perhaps he was trying to quarantine it by giving it a front-row seat.

In any event, colleagues Grady Wilson, Cliff Barrows, and Jerry Beaven accompanied Graham to the White House that day. The little knot of preachers got off to a rough start by dressing in pistachio-green suits with white buck shoes. Graham had somehow gotten the idea that the president liked garish attire. That was his first mistake.

Graham and friends talked with the president in the Oval Office for an hour. Toward the end, he asked Truman where he stood with God. Truman, a mainline Baptist, and reticent about religious matters anyway, answered that he tried to follow the Sermon on the Mount and the Golden Rule. Graham, in classic evangelical fashion, told Truman that was not good enough. He had to accept Christ's offer of salvation, personally, in his heart.

Graham then asked Truman if it would be okay if he prayed with the president. Truman reportedly said, "It can't do any harm." Whereupon Graham invoked God's blessing on the president, buttressed by Barrows on the sidelines, urging, "Amen!" "Do it, Lord!"

When the group left the Oval Office and walked to the front lawn of the White House, they were besieged by reporters who wanted to know every word the president had said. Graham naively obliged, kneeling on the grass, as if the group had knelt in the Oval Office too. There is no evidence that they had. Graham then dutifully rehearsed every word he had said to Truman and that Truman had said to him. Photographers captured the scene, and reporters spread the words they heard.

Truman was furious. He made clear to his staff that Graham was never to be invited back to the White House. He declined to attend or endorse Graham's prayer meeting on the Capitol steps in 1952 or Graham's crusade in Washington that year, despite multiple requests from him for a morsel of support.

Truman never forgave the preacher. Years later, when Graham visited the aging former president and tried to make amends, Truman was polite but unmoved. After the visit, Truman said that he just didn't "go" for preachers like Graham. All they wanted, he snapped, was to get their names in the papers. Of the thirteen presidents Graham would personally meet, Truman was the only one he visibly alienated.

Yet Graham learned a valuable lesson: never talk about private conversations with the president of the United States, or any other top leader, for that matter. Presidents simply presupposed confidentiality. A single violation meant that he would never be invited back.

Later we will see that Graham's determination to follow the rule of confidentiality got him into hot water with the press in the 1960s when he refused to tell journalists the content of his conversations with Presidents Johnson and Nixon about the Vietnam War. Graham learned that navigating the tiny patch of land at the pinnacle of power was never easy.

SCENE 10

Launching the Ship

At the end of the summer of 1950, Graham accepted an invitation to hold a two-week campaign in Portland, Oregon. In one sense Portland did not rank with the earlier campaigns in Los Angeles, Boston, and Columbia as a landmark in his career. Though the attendance was good, it did not win close attention from the press, as the others had done. But in another sense, Portland ranked even higher, for those weeks saw Graham turning his hand to organizational details.

First of all, during the Portland meeting Graham incorporated the Billy Graham Evangelistic Association (BGEA),[1] initially for tax-accounting purposes. The campaign had brought in $25,000 cash in order to launch a national radio program, *Hour of Decision*. Graham's associate Grady Wilson stuffed the money in a shoe box and stashed it under his hotel bed. In the morning Graham took it to a local bank for safe keeping. Though Graham intended to use the money for his ministry, he quickly saw that as soon as he took possession, he was liable for income tax on it.

And so it was that Billy and his always-levelheaded wife, Ruth, realized that they needed to form a nonprofit organization. Graham brought in George W. Wilson, business manager of Northwestern Schools back in Minneapolis, to set up and run the BGEA.

In 1950 Graham's vision also focused on the opportunities offered by electronic and print media. In November of that year he launched *Hour of Decision*, a nationally syndicated radio program aired over 150 stations on the ABC network.[2] This initial move into radio was just a baby step compared with the massive strides of later decades into television, satellite, and digital technology. Yet it betokened the boldness that marked Graham's career from beginning to end.

Hour of Decision drew on a venerable tradition of religious broadcasting, including Aimee Semple McPherson's *Sunshine Hour*, Walter Maier's *Lutheran Hour*, Charles E. Fuller's *Old Fashioned Revival Hour*, and Monsignor Fulton J. Sheen's *Catholic Hour*, which later morphed into his enormously popular *Life Is Worth Living* television program.[3]

Together, these broadcasts attracted millions of listeners every week for their uplifting, seemingly nonsectarian approach to Christian faith. By 1950 Graham was an old hand with the medium. As noted earlier, he had preached on radio during his student days in Florida, orchestrated *Songs in the Night* at his pastorate in Western Springs, and built a station at Northwestern Schools. He knew how it worked.

Hour of Decision's format was reassuringly predictable. Every broadcast began with Barrows's crisp baritone pronouncement: "Each week at this time . . . for *you* . . . for the *nation* . . . *this* is the *Hour of Decision!*" Barrows's explosive vocative "*this*" underscored the importance of the moment. Decide for Christ or against Christ, but—he clearly was saying—whatever you do, *decide*, up or down. Rousing hymns, sung by multihundred-voice (later, sometimes multithousand-voice) choirs, followed.

Graham's *Hour of Decision* sermons, timed to run exactly eighteen minutes to fit network specifications, followed. A few were extracted from actual sermons he had preached in the crusades, but most were prerecorded in studios or in his hotel rooms. Audiences were primed for the sermon with Barrows's invariable lead-in: "And now, as always, a man with God's message for these crisis days, Billy Graham."

Unlike its venerable predecessor, Charles E. Fuller's *Old Fashioned Revival Hour*, there was no folksy chitchat. Graham plunged to the point. World, national, and personal crises rampaged everywhere. Christ alone offered the answer. Barrows followed with a short appeal for "your prayers and support." He rarely mentioned money explicitly, just "prayers and support." As we have seen, within weeks *Hour of Decision* ranked as one of the most widely heard religious broadcasts in the country, reportedly with twenty million potential listeners.

In September 1951 a television spin-off of *Hour of Decision*, also called the *Hour of Decision*, started broadcasting over the ABC network, first in fifteen- and later in thirty-minute segments. Taped in a studio, sometimes with interviews of guests and edited clips from live audiences, the program consisted of music and a short sermon from Graham. The BGEA quietly discontinued it in 1954. If Graham was good at starting new media ventures, he was just as good at knowing when they had served their purpose and should be gracefully laid to rest.

In 1952 the BGEA established World Wide Pictures. This ministry eventually produced more than 130 films—including 35 feature-length ones—that were shown around the globe in seventeen languages with an aggregate of 175 million viewers (as of 1988).

The BGEA's first movie, *Mr. Texas*, actually appeared in 1951, the year before World Wide Pictures was organized. The organization's second feature-length production, *Oiltown, U.S.A.*, appeared in 1954. Both movies showcased heartwarming stories about hardened sinners turned around by Graham's simple gospel message.

In the beginning the production quality was not so great and the acting amateurish at best, but World Wide Pictures' productions rapidly improved on both counts.[4]

Graham's next major venture into media took the form of a mass market daily newspaper column, "My Answer," which he launched in December 1952 in the *Pittsburgh Sun-Telegram*. The column featured commonsense responses to a wide array of questions grassroots followers posted to Graham. Assistants did the actual writing, but Billy and Ruth spot-checked the columns to make sure the writers all spoke with the same voice. Year after year the underlying theological assumptions remained the same, but the specific questions evolved with the times, and so did the specific answers.

SCENE 11

Korean War

The Korean War raged from June 1950 through April 1953. Unlike the Vietnam War in the late 1960s and early 1970s, Graham did not say much about it. But he said enough that we can follow his line of thinking and see how he changed, or at least partly changed, between the start and the end of the conflict.

In the beginning, Graham was the fiercest of hawks. In his mind the Korean War was not a war against the sovereign nation of North Korea but a war against worldwide Communism. One Chicago newspaper, quoting *Pravda*, famously dubbed him "Communism's Public Enemy Number One."

Though Graham may have been exceptionally strident, his voice constituted but one in a massive choir. He spoke in concert with the highest officials of government, including Senator Karl Mundt, Congressman Walter Judd, Secretary of State Dean Acheson, President Harry Truman, and Democratic presidential candidate Adlai Stevenson, as well as countless leaders in the business, entertainment, and religious worlds. The atrocities of World War II felt fresh enough to keep fears of a global replay alive.

From the perspective of the early 1950s, Communism posed a lethal threat. Relentlessly expansionist, Communist forces were, Graham preached, "knifing" their way across southeast Asia. Soon they would be slicing up many other parts of the world too.

Communists were hard and disciplined, while Americans were soft and flabby. Communists were masters of treachery. "The pinks, the lavenders, and the reds . . . have sought refuge beneath the wings of the American eagle," Graham thundered. They had already infiltrated America's schools and media and even some mainline churches.

Worse, "Commies" had slithered into the highest chambers of the American government. Indeed, they were so good at it that most citizens did not even see them. Graham's rhetoric blended Communism with the military might of the Soviet Union. Graham did not claim that the United Nations itself, which oversaw the war, was Communist. But he thought the UN certainly leaned left, and it hardly had America's interests at heart.

Communism was more than a military menace, however. It was also a spiritual menace. It functioned like an alternative religion, albeit atheistic, "competing with Christianity for American souls." Like Christianity, it provided a total worldview, an explanation for social conflict, and a promise for where history was heading.

The movement's soldiers marched not only on their feet but also quietly in disguise in the nation's classrooms, in the halls of Congress, and in the court system. It inspired not only loyalty but also a willingness to sacrifice, even die, for its cause. It persecuted Christians in other lands. And it was unspeakably cruel, willing to subject its victims to physical torture or death if they disobeyed or resisted.[1]

This is the context in which Graham's grim view of the hostilities in Korea made sense. In April 1950, two months before armed fighting actually started, he telegrammed Truman and urged him to fight the North Korean Communists without quarter.

One year later the preacher was still in a belligerent mood. The Allied commander, General Douglas MacArthur, had invaded North Korea against Truman's orders. As a result, Truman relieved MacArthur of his command in April 1951. Graham rushed to the general's defense. Though claiming to be politically neutral—a ruse hardy anyone really fell for—Graham repeatedly scored Truman for dithering in Korea, which MacArthur did not.

Graham spent most of December 1952—including Christmas Day—touring the war zones in Korea as a special guest of the Pentagon. He visited small Christian congregations, where he found himself impressed by the strength of their commitment. He marveled as they endured subfreezing temperatures in early morning hours to hear him speak in makeshift chapels on mountain sides. Graham also visited soldiers in combat zones and wounded ones in field hospitals. He said the trip gave him heightened appreciation for the bravery of the soldiers who risked—and often gave—their lives to heed their country's call.

On returning, Graham reported that he went to Korea a boy but came back a man. The trip marked the beginning of lifelong admiration for soldiers and the profession of soldiering. Graham never esteemed combat itself, as some leaders like Teddy Roosevelt had done, but he displayed an enduring respect for military valor as a mark of character. Later Graham would compare Korean War soldiers favorably with Vietnam War soldiers because of the former's greater discipline.

As the conflict wore on, and as UN forces suffered humiliating reversals, Graham seemed to change his tune. He never had doubts about the war, which he supported from the outset, but about Truman's seemingly halfhearted way of fighting it. Graham denounced him for dragging the United States into a major and bloody foreign conflict, with no clear plan for victory, and without popular support. Just before the 1952 election, he argued that just as Adam's sin in the garden had implicated the entire human race, Truman's decision to enter the Asian conflict had implicated the entire nation, like it or not. "How many of you voted to go into the Korean War?" he demanded. "I never did."

Indecisiveness in combat, which Truman's fecklessness exemplified, was just as bad as indecisiveness in religion. Either fight all-out or go home. In some ways Graham remained a strong man at heart, for into the 1970s, and sometimes later, policemen, generals, and admirals were frequent and honored guests on his platforms.

Even so, Graham was never simple. Photos of him bending over wounded soldiers on their cots revealed a compassionate, even tender, side that stood in sharp contrast with the two-fisted bravado of his rhetoric.

The experience in Korea did not turn him into a pacifist. He would not entertain deep doubts about the utility, let alone morality, of total war between nations until many years later. But the Korea visit marked the beginning of those doubts, for it prompted him to begin to think twice about the staggering human cost of global conflicts.

SCENE 12

He Liked Ike

Graham's political—and especially partisan—identity was complicated.

On one hand, he was a lifelong registered Democrat. A July 1949 article in *Christian Life Magazine* referred to Graham, with evident disapproval, as a "known . . . Roosevelt-Truman Democrat."

Lyndon Johnson ranked as one of his closest friends. Indeed, Graham said that it was impossible to be around Johnson for very long and remain a Republican. The preacher resisted enormous popular pressure to support Senator Barry Goldwater over Johnson in their run for the White House in 1964. Graham almost certainly voted for Johnson.

Graham was a golfing-schmoozing friend of other prominent Democrats too, including Peace Corps director Sargent Shriver, Florida senator George A. Smathers, Vice President Hubert Humphrey, Texas governor John Connally,[1] Arkansas governor and later president Bill Clinton, and Arkansas first lady and later New York senator Hillary Clinton. Graham likely voted for Clinton in 1996 (though not in 1992). In time, he would support some of the Democrats' key legislative initiatives, such as the civil rights acts and, far more strongly, the SALT treaty.

On the other hand, the preacher's Democratic ties were loose ones. He said that he was a registered Democrat by virtue of being born in the South, not by partisan choice. Until he got to Wheaton, he admitted, he did not know that being a Southerner and being a Democrat were not the same.

Adding to the complexity was Graham's diffidence about his actual voting choices. He insisted that he told no one, including his wife, how he actually voted. He quipped that once he did not know how he had voted because one lever on the voting machine stuck and so he pulled the other one.

Yet the main claim—that he kept his choices to himself—simply was not true. In 1948 he publicly supported the stolid Republican candidate for president, New York governor Thomas Dewey. In most—though not all—

of the subsequent presidential elections, and in some gubernatorial ones too, he left multiple hints that he had voted for the Republican candidate. The historians Nancy Gibbs and Michael Duffy, who carefully studied Graham's relationship with the presidents, concluded that overall he is best described as a moderate Republican.

*　　　*　　　*

Partisan leanings—sometimes Democratic, usually Republican—aside, Graham's love for the political process ran deep. From time to time friends pressed him to make a run for the Senate or even the presidency. He admitted that once he had "briefly" considered the idea but quickly dismissed it. He also admitted that, lest there be any doubt in his own mind, Ruth had dismissed it for him. She assured him that the American people would not accept a divorced president.

Even so, in Graham's case there was a big difference between actually running for office and plunging deeply into the political discussions of the day. He remained an avid imbiber of current events. Journalist visitors to Graham's home routinely reported seeing most of the major newsmagazines and papers—*Time, Newsweek, US News & World Report*, the *New York Times*, and the *Times of London*—strewn around his office. For a time, Graham even had a UPI teletype machine installed in his kitchen.

Given these deep-seated proclivities, it is not surprising that a young Graham responded positively when in the fall of 1951 Sid Richardson approached him with an idea. Richardson—a Dallas oil tycoon and one of the richest men in America—offered to introduce Graham by letter to General Dwight D. Eisenhower. The general was living in Paris and serving as the supreme Allied commander in Europe. Graham took Richardson up on the offer and traveled to Paris, where he met Ike in person.

The preacher encouraged the general to run for president, telling him, "Upon this decision could well rest the destiny of the Western World." Eisenhower took Graham seriously, even though he was amused by the young man's melodrama, which an elderly Graham would remember with a grimace. There is no evidence Graham talked Ike into doing anything he would not have done anyway, but Graham's enthusiastic support surely helped.

The 1952 presidential campaign tempted Graham to step into the thicket of partisan politics, and he did not try very hard to resist. Graham left no doubt that he embraced the views of millions of other Americans who pinned "I Like Ike" buttons to their shirts and glued "I Like Ike" stickers on their bumpers. After the general accepted his party's nomination for president, he invited Graham to supply scriptural passages for his stump speeches, which he did.

Though Graham claimed to be nonpartisan, in supposedly offhand comments he not so subtly supported Ike in 1952 and again in 1956. He even disparaged the Democratic candidate, Senator Adlai Stevenson, for being divorced (a problem he would quietly overlook when the divorced Ronald Reagan ran for president thirty years later). Formally denying that he supported one candidate over another while informally doing exactly that prefigured a lifelong pattern.

Graham and Eisenhower were never close, yet they clearly enjoyed each other's company, especially on the golf course. And they shared a judicious temperament about public policy matters. Graham initially supported Senator Joseph McCarthy's crusade against domestic Communism, for example, but backed away from McCarthy at the same time that Eisenhower did. And for the same reason: McCarthy had gone too far.

Graham and Eisenhower worked together to establish consensus-building rituals, which the overwhelming majority of the American people supported. First was the Presidential (after 1970 National) Prayer Breakfast, which Ike founded in 1953. Though initially reluctant to cross the church/state boundary, Ike agreed to attend and speak.[2] The following year Graham played a role in persuading Eisenhower to add "under God" to the Pledge of Allegiance and in 1956 to make "In God We Trust" the nation's motto and add it to the nation's bills.

*   *   *

Graham and Eisenhower also shared a measured approach to the other looming issue of Ike's administration: race. The Supreme Court's 1954 *Brown v. Board of Education* decision decreed that "separate but equal" facilities in public schools were unconstitutional. The demand for racially integrated schools fueled one of the most sustained and sometimes violent reactions in American history. Both the preacher and the president were drawn into the middle of it, less by choice than by the rolling tides of history.

It was a time of fear. Blacks despaired that whites in general and the white church in particular would ever muster the moral courage to rectify dire injustices. Whites dreaded race mixing, a sure consequence, they thought, of integrated schools.

Moreover, many whites were convinced that Communists were fomenting the civil rights crusade. The alleged camaraderie between Soviet leader Nikita Khrushchev and Martin Luther King constituted exhibit A. The absence of any evidence for this linkage did little to diminish the fear, since the threats that stoked the strongest fears ran underground, out of view.

In this context Graham and Eisenhower both believed that a slow but sure approach to racial justice was the only one that might work. Both hoped that all Americans—black and white—would seek incremental changes so that people could get used to them. Unless white folks internalized these changes as the right thing to do, they would never stick. Ike asked Graham to help mobilize black church leaders to support a program of gradual though steady transformation of people's attitudes. Graham agreeably complied.

The turbid seas of racial conflict—blacks demanding justice as long overdue and whites resisting their demands as premature—swept over the nation. In September 1957 Arkansas governor Orval Faubus defied a federal court order to integrate Little Rock Central High School. Instead he directed the Arkansas National Guard to surround the school and prevent nine African American students from enrolling.

The confrontation in Arkansas challenged all of Ike's strategic skills. On one hand, it undergirded his instincts about the justice of the demand for integration. On the other hand, it violated his instincts for doing things with due deliberation. He also worried about interfering with the rights of a state. Eisenhower consulted Vice President Richard Nixon, who backed the president's proposal to intervene with military force. Eisenhower then phoned Graham, who told the president that he had no choice. Hours later Eisenhower ordered 1,200 members of the Army's 101st Airborne Division to carry out the court's order and ensure the students' safety.

*   *   *

Graham admired Ike's intelligence, character, and judgment. Ike's religious seriousness impressed Graham too. Though reared in Kansas in the Brethren in Christ (or River Brethren), a strict sect with Mennonite roots, Eisenhower had never been much of a churchman. So he asked Graham to help him find a church.

Graham nudged Eisenhower toward the prestigious and venerable National Presbyterian Church, where he was baptized in February 1953, ten days after he was inaugurated. Ike became a member and attended for the eight years of his presidency. The friendship persisted after Eisenhower left office in 1960. As Ike approached his own death nine years later, he sought reassurance from Graham about the certainty of the life to come.

Here Graham proved true to his vocation. Partisan politics was one thing, faith another. Ministry was the higher calling. At the end of the day, he remained a pastor to the presidents.

Pulling Down the Ropes

The 1953 Chattanooga, Tennessee, crusade stands out as one of the mountaintop events in Graham's career. The metaphor is apt, for the city was set on a scenic plateau in the southern Appalachians and proved rich with Civil War lore and antebellum architecture. The significance of the event in the evolution of Graham's views of racial justice was far from evident at the time, but over the years its importance steadily grew.

Graham launched a four-week crusade in the city on March 15, 1953, housing it in a ten-thousand-seat tabernacle hammered together just for the purpose. At first the Chattanooga meeting ran according to the strict racial segregation that characterized the Jim Crow South, both legally and in practice. Three days into the revival Cliff Barrows announced that "there are no reserved seats on Sunday afternoons except for colored persons." The crusade chairman then announced that "seats had been reserved for colored for all services."

Until then, Graham's meetings in the South, like those of other white evangelists such as Billy Sunday and Aimee Semple McPherson, had been ghettoized. Blacks sat in the back and whites in the front, just as they did on buses. Sometimes people self-segregated and sometimes a rope divided them. Either way, Graham had followed the same pattern. This practice neatly paralleled municipal ordinances that prohibited the "promiscuous" seating of the races. In the 1940s Graham occasionally preached to entirely black congregations too.

As the story goes, the Chattanooga meeting's white organizers assumed that the event would honor the strict racial segregation that characterized the Jim Crow South. But one night—perhaps before Graham arrived in town, or perhaps just before he preached for the first time, or perhaps before one of his sermons, or perhaps before he preached the final sermon—his conscience started to gnaw. Over the opposition of the committee—or perhaps the white ushers—he strode out into the audience and personally pulled down the ropes that separated blacks from whites. And the ropes stayed down.

At least that is the conventional narrative.

Figuring out what really did happen in Chattanooga is not easy. Several problems pop up. For one thing, it is not clear what Barrows and the crusade chairman meant by "reserved." Did the word mean that whites could sit anywhere they wanted but blacks were restricted to the reserved section? Or did it mean that a special section had been dedicated for blacks only? Given Jim Crow customs, the former seems much more likely. Yet the latter is possible since the Graham crusades normally set aside dedicated sections for specific church groups.

Still, to the best of my knowledge, Graham did not mention any "rope incident" until a press conference in South Africa in 1973, two decades later. Even then he did not specify where it took place. Historian Stephen Miller reports that Graham did not identify Chattanooga as the site until he gave an interview to a Georgia newspaper in 1976. But by then he had preached hundreds of crusades and, as he later acknowledged, the specifics of individual crusades blurred in his memory. And none of the earliest biographies, including the authorized one by John Pollock in 1966, mentioned it either.

Additional complications arise. One eyewitness, Nannelle Griffith, age seventeen, sang in the choir every night. She affirmed (to me) in 2019 that she did not see ropes at the crusade—let alone see Graham pull them down—since the meetings were fully integrated to begin with. Nor did whites and African Americans self-segregate. Of course, it is possible that Graham pulled down the ropes in Chattanooga before the first service started. Yet Griffith heard nothing about it.

And Cliff Barrows insisted to the end of his life in 2016 that the "rope incident," or something very much like it, actually took place the year before in a crusade in Jackson, Mississippi. Since Barrows oversaw the logistics of all of Graham's meetings, it seems reasonable to assume that he would have known what happened.[1]

The questions that we ask today about Graham and race differ from the ones that contemporaries asked in the early 1950s. Indeed, they almost certainly differ from the ones Graham himself asked at the time. So the materials required to answer our questions with certainty are sparse and not always consistent. Sometimes educated guesses are the best we can do.

*   *   *

Regardless of the exact details and precise chronology, the Chattanooga story must be placed in the longer narrative of Graham's engagement with African Americans and the civil rights movement. We have seen that it started when Graham was a kid back on the farm. In his 1997 memoir, he remembered that back then he had known black farmhands, one black housemaid, and at least one Latino worker.

From Graham's perspective, the relations were friendly all around. Indeed, one of the workers had entertained the adolescent Graham with salty jokes.

But genuine integration lay beyond his imagination. No one in Graham's family or circle of white friends or white churchmates ever conceived such a thing. Years later Graham's sister Jean remembered that in the 1930s the family's maid had accompanied the family to church for worship but sat in the balcony.

In 1959 Graham told a press conference in Wheaton that Wheaton College was the first institution he had attended "where Negroes were on an equal footing with whites." At the college, he later said, he met an African American student. That was the first time he encountered a black person as a social peer.[2] The experience at least started to open his eyes to the grim realities of race and racism in America.

Gaining a clear picture of the mature Graham and race is difficult. The earliest contemporaneous reference to his views may have appeared in the July 1949 issue of the popular monthly *Christian Life Magazine*— the same one that identified him unfavorably as a "known . . . Roosevelt-Truman Democrat." In this case Graham's ideas provoked disapproval for another reason: "he was known to hold radical views on race." Exactly what constituted "radical" was left unsaid, but we might reasonably guess that it included some degree of sympathy for integration.

On the other hand, according to one secondhand account, as late as 1950 Graham, in private conversation, blamed British slavers for creating the race problem in America in the first place. And he endorsed the Jim Crow system of segregation as the natural order of things.

Graham may have gotten this idea in part from his strong-minded physician/theologian father-in-law, L. Nelson Bell. In 1944 Bell had written in the *Southern Presbyterian Journal*—an organ he had founded and helped edit—that God had drawn a permanent line between the races that was both biological and geographical. Though Bell called whites to end legal discrimination, be respectful to blacks, and acknowledge their spiritual equality, he deplored mainline Protestant efforts to blur the line in pursuit of "unrestricted social equality."

But the early 1950s saw significant changes in Graham's thinking. At a plenary meeting of his own Southern Baptist Convention in 1951, Graham denounced the denomination for barring blacks from its seminaries. To be sure, the preacher's words were not as prophetic as they seemed. Since 1941 the Convention had been issuing resolutions calling for "the protection of all the civil rights of the [Negro] race." Still, Graham pinpointed a problem that required a solution.

In 1952 Graham defied the governor of Mississippi and held racially mixed meetings in the state. In Jackson—perhaps the site where the ropes actually came down—he followed the Southern revivalist custom of segregated seating during the service. But he insisted that black and white people who responded to the invitation at the end of his sermon must walk and pray together. He said that the sight of black and white inquirers worshiping as one "at the foot of the cross" touched his heart.

Graham's awareness of racial justice did not tumble from the sky as a sacred meteor. It developed over time. The Dallas crusade, which ran from May 31 to June 28, 1953, saw the ropes go back up.[3] The problem is that the crusade organizer stipulated that the ropes should remain up until 7:00 p.m., then taken down. The service started at 7:30 p.m. The reason for the thirty-minute gap is not clear. It may have grown from the general practice in Graham meetings—noted earlier—of reserving blocks of seats for specific church groups. After that time the reserved areas were opened, and anyone could sit anywhere they wanted.

Or not. The extant evidence is too scarce to know exactly what happened, and why. Gaps in the record similarly limit our vision of what took place in crusades in Texas, New York, and Michigan in the fall of 1953. But the final meeting of the year, in Asheville in November 1953, almost certainly was fully integrated.[4] Ropes never again went up in a Graham crusade in the United States.[5]

Graham biographer Marshall Frady—generally not very sympathetic to him—said that his efforts in the early 1950s to address racism constituted his "handsomest hour."[6] But the story of Graham and race did not end in Asheville. In the following decades, it would continue to take twists and turns. Without doubt Graham was the most influential evangelical Protestant leader of his era. When it came to race, he may have been the most complicated, too.

PART 2

Leading Evangelist

Core Message

Graham started his day with prayer. Not a prayerful attitude, but down on his knees, sometimes even prone on his stomach. Graham was no mystic—his mind did not run that way—but he knew that theology was the distillation of faith, and faith was the distillation of a life of disciplined prayer.

To that purpose Graham committed himself to an hour of prayer and Bible study each day after breakfast. He began with five chapters of Psalms, he claimed, to know how to get along with God, and one chapter of Proverbs to know how to get along with other people. That way he read each book through once a month. Graham said—and colleagues agreed—that he constantly sought God's will for the course ahead, for power to keep himself away from sin, and for continual reminders that his strength came from the Lord, not himself.

When Graham died, his publicist A. Larry Ross attested that Graham made a point to pray in snatches throughout the day, as opportunity offered. Graham's lifelong associate and close friend T. W. Wilson put it this way: "Let's just say Billy tries to keep himself prayed up all the time."

*   *   *

But piety of this sort was never the whole of it. Graham also committed himself to writing down the basic skeleton of the theological principles he believed and preached. By 1953 his convictions had settled into a definable format. The format did not exactly add up to a systematic let alone comprehensive account of evangelical Protestant belief and practice. We will see premises undefended and gaps ignored. But it was complete enough and ordered enough to provide a scaffolding for his thinking.

If Graham's theological convictions read like evangelical boilerplate, that's because they were. To a great extent he was the one who made it so.

Admittedly the movement traced its theological roots back to the Protestant Reformers of the sixteenth century, the Pietists and Puritans of the seventeenth century, the Wesleyans of the eighteenth century, and the revivalists of the nineteenth century. But in the minds of many American Christians, and countless more around the world, Graham's thinking on the subject was all they needed.

We might call the result Graham's core message. It was the *evangel*, the good news, delivered with little variation in countless venues, whether from behind a pulpit, in interviews with television personalities, or in engagements with college students.

That message took shape early on in his signature book, *Peace with God* (1953). As noted, this compact volume of two hundred or so pages eventually sold more than two million copies and saw translation into at least thirty-eight languages. A new edition, revised with considerable help from his wife, Ruth, appeared in 1984.

Peace with God came with two backstories. The first was the popular literary setting. Historian Andrew Finstuen notes that after World War II a steady stream of broadly similar books and magazines coupling Christian faith with self-help psychology permeated the market. Some of the most important ones included Rabbi Joshua Loth Liebman's *Peace of Mind* (1946), Claude Bristol's *Magic of Believing* (1948), James Keller's *You Can Change the World!* (1948), Harry Overstreet's *Mature Mind* (1949), Peter Marshall's *Meet the Master* (1949), and Charles L. Allen's *God's Psychiatry* (1953).

Without question, Norman Vincent Peale, pastor of New York City's prestigious four-thousand-member Marble Collegiate Church, led the Protestant self-help movement. With a half-million subscribers, *Guideposts* magazine, which Peale founded in 1945, focused on inspirational human-interest stories. *Guideposts* fostered *A Guide to Confident Living* (1948) and the record-setting *Power of Positive Thinking* (1952). "For him," said Finstuen, "sin was not an intractable condition, but a defect in personality that could be improved upon by positive patterns of thought."

The point here is not the real or perceived theological continuities between these works and Graham's *Peace with God*. Graham's focus, after all, fell on *God's* ways with humanity, not the reverse. But they all reflected a popular yearning to find accessible and workable answers to the anxieties of the age.

The second backstory illumines Graham's desire to define his theological voice in popular culture. He initially engaged Janet Blair, an accomplished ghostwriter, to come up with a draft using notes from his sermons. Reporter George Burnham said, "With the crowded schedule that Dr. Graham maintains, he doesn't have the time to do the actual writing of the book." But after reading Blair's draft, Graham said he discarded it because Blair had missed too many of his key points and emphases. With Ruth's help, he started all over again.

The fundamental message of *Peace with God* could be stated in abstract theological terms but Graham preferred the language of everyday experience. He aimed to show that however phrased, the New Testament's central message of human sin and divine forgiveness—the *gospel*—represented truly good news.[1]

Logically, if not always in practice, Graham's thinking about his basic principles started with the problem of authority. Who or what established the final rule of measurement for everything Christians should believe and practice? The answer, of course, was simple: the Bible. This sacred text talked about many things but, above all, it spoke of God's relationship with people.

The Bible's narrative arc was clear. It taught that the first human, Adam, had sinned by willfully rebelling against God's rules. So did every other person who came after Adam. Human pride was the toxic well that polluted everything else. Even nature, red in tooth and claw, suffered from God's wrath about man's defiance.

Yet God, in his infinite love, chose to save people by revealing himself in his Son, Jesus Christ, who was simultaneously fully God and fully man. Because Jesus lived a sinless life, his death paid the penalty for sin and his resurrection defeated the grave. If people repented of their sins, and embraced Christ as Lord and Savior, in a new birth of their entire heart, the Holy Spirit would enable them to live lives of inward peace and outward holiness.

In Graham's preaching, the *new birth* constituted the centerpiece of the gospel. It enabled converts to love their neighbors, even when their neighbors had wronged them (especially when their neighbors had wronged them). It also enabled converts to seek social justice for everyone, not just their own families and communities, and renounce personal habits that harmed their bodies and wasted God's money.

Graham knew perfectly well, of course, that Christian theology entailed many other claims. But since he saw himself as an evangelist called by God to invite people to faith, the new birth stood at the center. Many evangelicals used the term *born again*, and occasionally he did too, but he preferred *new birth*.

Christians could be confident that Christ would return at the end of human history. Other evangelical Protestants had fussed about the details surrounding Christ's return, but *Peace with God* downplayed them lest people lose sight of the main point: Christ would return and make things right.

After death, believers would enter into the everlasting joys of heaven and nonbelievers the everlasting sorrows of hell. Time counted. Believers were obliged to share this good news—or gospel—of salvation with others.

The whole story of God's redemption of individuals, society, and creation could be boiled down to fewer than a dozen terms: authority, God, Bible, sin, Christ, new birth, sanctification, justice, missions, second coming, and final destiny. *Peace with God* was not a work of systematic theology but rather a working manual for the Christian life.

Peace with God largely or entirely overlooked many of the key theological ideas that one or another evangelical Protestant sect held dear. The list was actually quite long: inerrancy, sanctification, glossolalia, sacraments, liturgy, miracles, polity, dispensationalism, confessions, creeds, and Eucharist, among many others. The import of this highly selective combination of doctrines is clear. Graham was shooting down the middle of the evangelical river, trying to make his message as streamlined as possible.

Later we will see that the message people actually heard in their cars or living rooms or stadium seats was even more streamlined than the one he articulated in *Peace with God*. In practice, Graham, like all good preachers, emphasized some parts more than others, especially later on as the years passed and situations changed. All of which is to say that the book served as a chartering document for millions of evangelicals. Yet, like most documents of that sort, it proved as pliable as time and place required.

"Harringay"

It ran twelve weeks, from March 1 to May 22, 1954. Graham and his associates came to remember the crusade at Harringay Arena in London with such vividness that they would call the entire event simply "Harringay."

A coalition of pastors from the British Evangelical Alliance had invited Graham to hold the meeting. Like the challenges of Los Angeles and Boston, the prospect was daunting. London was one of the largest, most diverse, and most cosmopolitan cities in the world. Moreover, leaders of the Church of England had conspicuously failed to support the invitation, fearing, as they put it, Graham's "high-pressure salesmanship."

But the Evangelical Alliance promised the same kind of deep financing, massive advertising, and meticulous preparation that Graham had come to expect elsewhere. After a year of negotiation about the details, he agreed, and they delivered.

When Graham docked in Southampton in late February 1954, he stepped off the boat on the wrong foot. A mock-up of a prayer calendar for Britain, drafted back in Minneapolis, preceded him. It said that Graham's revival would challenge "socialism with its accompanying evils." Advisers in Britain had urged Graham to change "socialism" to "secularism." Though he agreed, the change somehow got lost between the drawing board and the printing press.

Worse, when the calendar was finally printed and then distributed in the UK, the word "socialism" came out "Socialism." Though the change was an innocent one, made by a secretary, Britons saw it as a wildly inappropriate slam against the Socialist Labour government.

The British press and not a few ordinary folks took offense at Graham himself. They saw him as an American upstart who had the temerity, it seemed, to come to the UK with a political and economic as well as religious agenda. Even before he arrived, a headline in the *Daily Worker*, issued by the British Communist Party, ripped him as the "atom bomb gospeller."

But Graham readily apologized for the calendar mistake and sought to meet personally with journalists and clergymen skeptical of his visit. Most seemed at least placated, and many were fully supportive after meeting him in person and experiencing firsthand, they repeatedly said, his unpretentious ways and humble spirit.

Other problems thwarted Graham's effort. His style, both on stage and off, had grown more sedate, but it still rubbed many members of the British clergy the wrong way. Too unbuttoned, they thought. And the venue, Harringay Arena, did not help matters. Though it was the most affordable option the local organizing committee could come up with, it was comparatively small: a twelve-thousand-seat indoor arena best known for dog races and boxing matches. And it stood in a seedy, industrial part of the city.

Though Graham's anxiety ran high, the outcome defied expectations. The opening night was packed. After the second evening, which was riven with snow flurries and rain, people filled every seat for the remainder of the campaign, ultimately totaling two million visitors. The number of inquirers ran to thirty-eight thousand.

For the final night, the crusade moved "uptown" to Wembley Stadium, the largest venue in the British Isles. Anticipating that the stadium's 100,000 seats would be filled, the organizers also secured White City Stadium, seating 65,000. Graham preached first at White City and then motored to Wembley. Both stadiums filled, along with another 22,000 who were allowed to sit on the grass. Despite driving rain, the two crowds—totaling 187,000—constituted the largest audience ever assembled in British religious history, even greater than any crowd at the 1948 summer Olympics.

During the crusade, Graham worked relentlessly. Along the way he met with the Queen Mother and the queen's sister, Princess Margaret, by their personal invitation. He also spoke to 12,000 in Trafalgar Square, to 40,000 in Hyde Park, and to packed lecture halls at Oxford, Cambridge, and the University of London.

At the last one, the professor who introduced him pointed out that the school was founded on secularism, which won strong applause. The students then tried to mock antievolution views—which they somewhat inaccurately attributed to Graham—by bringing a fake ape into the hall. Graham instantly quipped that the ape reminded him of his ancestors, who, after all, came from Great Britain. The audience roared. It was classic Graham.

After Graham's several unsuccessful attempts to meet with Prime Minister Winston Churchill, the legendary leader issued an invitation of his own. Churchill bid Graham to meet him at 10 Downing Street, his private residence, the day after the historic Wembley gathering. After Churchill's death,[1] Graham reported that in the conversation Churchill wondered how Graham could have filled Wembley Stadium to the brim as he had done. Churchill joked that he (Churchill) and Marilyn Monroe together could not have done so.

The prime minister expressed his sense of hopelessness for the world as many as nine times in the course of a forty-minute conversation. Graham interpreted the prime minister's comments to refer to Churchill himself, too. With Churchill's agreeable consent, Graham spoke of the way of salvation, of Christ's return, and then prayed with him. On exiting, Graham, only thirty-six, remarked that he felt that he had just "shaken hands with Mr. History."

Why did the London crusade succeed in the face of such dour prospects at the beginning? Multiple factors were at work. One was a program that started earlier called Operation Andrew. Based on the biblical story of the apostle Andrew inviting his brother Peter to come to see Jesus (John 1:40–42), partisans were encouraged to bring a friend to the crusade, preferably an unchurched one.

Then too the meetings received growing legitimation. For example, high-ranking American statesmen in the UK such as Senators Stuart Symington of Missouri and Styles Bridges of New Hampshire publicly endorsed it, and in time dignitaries from the Church of England did too.

Graham's increasingly decorous style helped. The British press, academic establishment, and social elite were, as the saying goes, "pleasantly disappointed" to find Graham's sincerity and especially humility disarmingly genuine. And the services proved tamer than most people had expected. The choice of guest artists, choir music, celebrity testimonies, and dynamic preaching satisfied the faithful and evidently a good many doubters.

Then too the BGEA deployed the latest advances in communications technology. It pioneered the use of telephone landlines to carry the crusades to giant television screens (similar to those in sports bars today) in remote parts of the United Kingdom. This innovation—which is not sufficiently appreciated—prefigured Graham's lifelong determination to adopt the latest technology wherever he went.

Looking ahead for a moment, over the years the BGEA would distinguish itself for adopting, as soon as feasible, mass printing, radio and television coverage, satellite broadcasts, websites, digitized daily devotional materials, and social media. Using the latest technology predated the London crusade but gained a leading role there.

One more feature of the 1954 London crusade should be mentioned: advertising. This was hardly new, of course. Graham had arranged advertising for his work all the way back to his Florida Bible Institute days. Youth for Christ strategists, most assuredly including Graham, turned it into an art form. But the London venture signaled a qualitatively heightened level of application. Tracts, flyers, signs, and billboards blanketed the city.

Equally important was the approach of the advertising, which can be summarized with a single word: "minimalist." "Billy Graham, Harringay Arena, 7:30 Every Night." Or "Hear Billy Graham." Or just "Billy Graham," with his photo. Crusade organizers took a cue from advertisements for Cadillacs in the United States. They gave just enough information to arouse curiosity, implying that the product was so desirable it sold itself.

Graham kept moving. He followed Harringay with a hurried tour of the European continent, featuring short meetings that lasted from one to three days in Helsinki, Stockholm, Copenhagen, Amsterdam, Berlin, Frankfurt, Dusseldorf, and Paris. In each, the crowds ran in the tens of thousands, sometimes breaking stadium records.

Graham soon accepted an invitation from the Church of Scotland to hold a six-week crusade in Glasgow the following year, starting in March 1955. As in England, he encountered opposition, this time less from the established church than from high-church Calvinists who harbored doubts about his low-church methods and theology.

Though the 1955 Glasgow crusade received much less notice in the history books, Graham seemed more satisfied with it than with the London meetings. In his memoir he pointed out that Glasgow attracted 2.5 million attenders and generated 52,000 decisions in six weeks, while London posted 2 million attenders and 38,000 decisions in twelve weeks. Graham also pointed with manifest pride to the much wider range of social classes the Scottish crusade reached, including steelworkers, dock workers, and mill hands, as well as the very wealthy, theologians, and Scottish clergy.

On Good Friday he preached on the subject of the cross on the BBC to the largest single television audience since the coronation of the queen three years before. The final night, 100,000 souls jammed all spaces at Hampton Park, standing and sitting.

Four days after the Scotland crusade officially drew to a close, the inexhaustible Graham returned to London for a one-week meeting. Despite rain every night except the last—which turned out to be the coldest night of the year—the crusade attracted 450,000 attenders and generated 24,000 decision cards. The week was capped off with another packed meeting at Wembley Stadium on May 21, 1955.

The following day registered another landmark, as Graham delivered the Word for Queen Elizabeth II and Prince Philip (and one other couple) in St. George's Chapel on the grounds of Windsor Castle. This would be the first of a dozen occasions when Graham met with the Queen, whose faith he esteemed highly. In 2001 Sir Christopher Meyer, the British ambassador to the United States, bestowed on Graham an honorary knighthood on behalf of the Queen.

*   *   *

The results of the British campaigns of 1954-1955—or what Graham called "the harvest"—are not easy to assess. Short-term outcomes were elusive. Statistical tabulations varied greatly, depending on who asked the questions and how they were framed.

Anecdotal but substantial evidence suggests that Graham's meetings helped nudge a large number of Church of England clergy, especially seminarians, into a more evangelical understanding of Christian faith. Indeed, when Archbishop Michael Ramsey told Graham—whom he affectionately called Baptist Billy—that he feared that Graham's crusades might strengthen evangelicals too much, Graham deadpanned, "Yes . . . I'm sure that may be one of the side effects, and I rather hope it is."

Long-term results are even harder to measure. On one hand we know that in Graham's meetings, at home and abroad, some people were alienated by the perceived thinness of his theology and irrelevance of his message to the deeper needs of the times. On the other hand, others found the theology clear, direct, and relevant. One Anglican bishop, looking back, likened Graham's meetings to "divine adrenaline for a jaded church."

And so it was that thirty years later, Queen Elizabeth II invited Graham to join her for dinner on the royal yacht when it was anchored in San Francisco Bay. As he boarded the vessel, a British naval officer, part of a color guard, broke ranks and whispered two words in Graham's ear. "Wembley, '55."

SCENE 16

Christianity Today

Graham's London and Scotland crusades in 1954 and 1955, along with his work in South and East Asia in 1956, catapulted him into international visibility, especially within broadly evangelical circles. But in some important ways he never packed his suitcase, for the burgeoning evangelical movement at home required tending. For that task, he knew, there was no substitute for the power of the printed page.

In 1956 Graham founded the fortnightly *Christianity Today*. By then he had moved into every form of mass media except one: the magazine market. More precisely, the serious magazine market.

Graham later said that the idea of starting *Christianity Today* came to him about 2 a.m. one night in 1953. Trying not to disturb Ruth, he "slipped out of bed" and went to his study and scratched out a plan. Like most founding myths, this one was more creative than true. Graham and others of like mind had been talking about the project for several years.

Either way, Graham, with his typical golden touch, secured substantial financial backing from Philadelphia oilman J. Howard Pew. Graham's sympathy in those days for free-wheeling capitalism and his distrust of big labor undoubtedly helped endear him to the mogul, who not surprisingly held similar views.[1] Whatever the reason, Graham certainly found a sympathetic ear—and open wallet—in Philadelphia.

For some time, Graham and other evangelical leaders had been thinking about launching a fortnightly that would accomplish at least three goals: permanence, identity, and respectability.

Permanence was the simplest. Graham sensed that the message he proclaimed from the pulpit must be stabilized in a more enduring form. Words, he said, were evanescent, but print was not. Graham did not know much about church history—his sermons made that clear enough—but he knew enough to grasp that time changes everything unless institutions stepped in to keep things moving in the right direction.

Christianity Today's funding arrangements may have served the goal of permanence somewhat more firmly than Graham envisaged. Pew was skeptical of endowments. He believed that later generations often found ways to steer them away from their founders' intent—usually toward greater liberalism. So he favored periodic contributions for day-to-day operating expenses so that the faucet could be turned off if things went awry.

There are good reasons to believe that until Pew's funding dried up in the 1970s, the magazine remained more closely aligned with Pew's laissez-faire economic views, conservative political positions, and traditional theological outlook than Graham really wanted.

*   *   *

The second motive was identity for evangelicals such as Graham himself. Originally usually spelled "Evangelical," the word soon lost the capital *E* and went by the nearly generic term "evangelical." One journalist, looking at this burgeoning group of believers, said that their existence split the great river of American Protestantism into three recognizably distinct substreams: mainline Protestants on the left, fundamentalists on the right, and mainstream evangelicals in the middle.[2]

At the beginning of the 1950s, American Protestantism was by and large flowing in two channels, fundamentalist on the right and mainline on the left. Graham more than anyone else cut the center channel. At first he tried to avoid any label for it, preferring simply "Christian." But soon the label "Evangelical"—then "evangelical"—emerged and stuck.

Broadly conservative American Protestantism was much wider than these three steams, of course. It included confessional Lutherans, liturgical Episcopalians, peace-oriented Mennonites, noninstrumental (no musical instruments) Churches of Christ, and Calvinist Baptists, among others. Many made clear that they resented evangelicals' attempt to speak as if they represented all broadly orthodox Protestants. That being said, the evangelical stream dwarfed the numerical size of all the conservative nonevangelical Protestant streams combined.

Speaking broadly, the contrasts among the three substreams can be summed up in a few sentences. Fundamentalists insisted on God's direct hand in history, including supernatural miracles and the accuracy—or inerrancy, as it came to be called—of the Bible in matters of science and history as well as faith. Christ's death on the cross and bodily resurrection from the grave offered a substitute for sin and promise of a new birth. Born-again Christians were required to witness about their faith to non-Christians and seek to convert them.

More controversially, fundamentalists also affirmed that Christ would imminently and physically return to the earth and initiate a thousand years—or millennium—of peace, health, and spiritual prosperity. After that, the dead would be raised and all would be judged by the correctness of their belief as well as the holiness of their lives. The verdict would send them either to everlasting joy in heaven or everlasting separation in hell. From the very beginning to the very end of his career, Graham held this view of how history would end.[3]

Mainline Protestants on the left revered the Bible but emphasized its power to bring people to faith rather than its factual accuracy. Stories of supernatural events and personages were allegories at best, outdated myths at worst. Miracles in the modern world were changes internal to the heart, not external to the eye. Individual conversion to Christ as a model of selfless living was necessary but not sufficient to bring about social justice. Mainline Protestants sought to reform society's ills with structural solutions born of political action in the here and now. They downplayed arcane speculation about how history would end in favor of concrete discussions about how to live more moral and ethical lives now.

Evangelicals constituted the middle stream. They largely affirmed the tenets of Graham's *Peace with God*. Like him, they gave special emphasis to the authority of the Bible as the final rule of faith and practice. Most also affirmed its factual accuracy but preferred to focus on its authority, which is to say, its power to bring sinful men and women into the safe harbor of salvation by believing in the death and resurrection of Jesus Christ.

Evangelicals were closer to fundamentalists than they were to mainliners regarding miracles, and they saw Jesus returning to earth in person. But they did not want to get bogged down arguing about details of exactly when or how it would happen. All this was the good news (the gospel) that all Christians were privileged—not exactly required but certainly privileged—to share with others. Sharing involved proclamation of the gospel message, in words spoken and printed, works of mercy, and upright lives.

Graham was an astute reader of the surrounding religious culture. Whether he read it self-consciously or by instinct is a good question. Either way, he knew exactly which people he aimed to reach. The magazine should speak for at least three fairly distinct groups of evangelicals: those in mainline denominations who did not have an institutional voice, those in preponderantly evangelical denominations such as the Southern Baptist Convention, and those who were independent of any formal organization.

Sensing that evangelicalism was endlessly malleable, Graham wanted to turn it into something more substantial. Historian Elesha Coffman captured the aim succinctly: "to create a coherent, definable religious movement. This meant it would not represent any particular denomination or organization but rather serve as a theological center of gravity, or flag pole, for a set of ideas and practices. With definable and for all practical purposes enforceable boundaries, too." *Christianity Today* helped chisel out and maintain—some might say police—this identity partly by deciding who would and would not be published or advertised.

*   *   *

Besides permanence and identity, the third and final motive fueling the founding of *Christianity Today* was to win respectability. Though Graham used the word "respectability," the principals were shooting for something larger than their own prestige. Winning a voice in the culture meant gaining a permanent seat at the table of public discussion. It also meant that the views they taught in their seminaries would be given a fair shake—assessed on their merits—in the academy.

Until the 1950s, when Graham rose to prominence, fundamentalists (broadly defined to include both fundamentalists and pre-evangelicals) grudgingly accepted that they had lost the struggle for intellectual visibility in most seminaries and divinity schools. Events like the Scopes trial in 1925 had left them glum in their own circles and eclipsed in the larger culture.

But things did not have to stay that way. Evangelicals determined to project a serious theological/biblical/historical agenda of their own. This blueprint would boldly integrate the best of the new thinking, as they saw it, with the best of the old.

The respectability problem was compounded by the extraordinary influence of the rival *Christian Century*.[4] In 1908 Charles Clayton Morrison, a liberal Disciples of Christ minister, had rescued an earlier version of the *Christian Century* from bankruptcy and soon turned it into the flagship periodical of the Protestant mainline. The *Christian Century* projected a center-left or even left-left posture on the theological, political, and cultural concerns of the day. Graham was none too subtle about it: he intended to challenge the *Christian Century*'s monopoly, if not in mainline seminaries, at least in pastors' studies and on parlor tables in their parsonages.

Graham felt certain that another serious periodical—in this case, a biweekly—would help.[5] It is telling that in the beginning *Christianity Today*, like the *Christian Century*, featured small print and carried no pictures except in a handful of advertisements. Besides current religious news, several book reviews, and a clever satire column, the magazine mostly carried long, detailed articles about pressing theological and cultural issues of the day. Hoping to avoid arguments about subjects the editors deemed nonessential, *Christianity Today* steered clear of arcane talk about how history would end.[6]

Most readers, clergy and otherwise, probably viewed the magazine as ponderous and often simply dense. Indeed, the inaugural issue contained a plodding essay entitled "The Changing Climate of European Theology," by G. C. Berkouwer, and a weighty rumination, "Fragility of Freedom in the West," by Carl F. H. Henry. Graham told Henry, the first editor, that he thought his lead editorial represented "obscurity reaching for profundity." Graham later regretted saying it, but he did not retract the sentiment, and, true to form, rigorously critiqued his own contribution to the initial issue.

Though Graham was neither an academic nor an intellectual, he respected those who were. He brought to *Christianity Today* powerhouse minds from the evangelical world. The best known and most influential included Harold John Ockenga, L. Nelson Bell, and Carl F. H. Henry. We noted Ockenga's and Bell's academic credentials earlier; Henry was a journalist-turned-theologian, with doctorates from both Northern Baptist Theological Seminary and Boston University.

Of the three, Henry was the most progressive and Bell the least. Henry edited *Christianity Today* from its birth in 1956 until 1968. Ockenga served as chairman of the board until 1981 and functioned as a frequent contributor and behind-the-scenes force. Bell labored as executive editor until his death in 1973.

Bell swung a heavy bat. Though he was more conservative than Graham in pretty much every way, Graham gave him a free hand in shaping— not necessarily defining but at least shaping—the magazine's positions. Whether Bell influenced Graham and the magazine by virtue of his clear mind and forceful personality, or by virtue of his patriarchal role in the family, or both, is not clear.

*   *   *

The decade stretching from 1968 to 1978 saw significant shifts of personnel and of theological and social orientation. In 1968 Pew and Bell forced out Henry. They replaced him with associate editor Harold Lindsell, who was a more militant voice for biblical inerrancy and social conservatism. Lindsell oversaw the magazine for a decade.

Editors after Lindsell were, with important exceptions, less scholarly but more socially progressive and culturally attuned than the previous editor-leaders. The magazine gradually aligned itself more closely with Graham's irenic, inclusive, and increasingly moderate positions. With good reason, a later editor would privately say that everyone at *Christianity Today* always knew that it was "Billy's magazine."[7]

Big Apple

The year after *Christianity Today* started landing in pastors' mailboxes, Graham embarked on the most highly publicized crusade of his long career. The marathon meeting at Madison Square Garden in New York City started on May 15, 1957, and closed nearly sixteen weeks later on September 1, Labor Day Eve. If there had been any doubt about Graham's star status when the crusade began, none lingered by the time it ended. By then Graham ranked as the most famous evangelist since George Whitefield in the eighteenth century, and, by some measures, the most famous ever.

The New York story actually had a long prologue. In 1951 locals, known as the Billy Graham Breakfast Committee, started talking with him about visiting their city. Graham declined their proposal because it did not come from a broad enough base.

In 1954 the Protestant Council of the City of New York,[1] representing more than 1,700 congregations and thirty-one denominations, issued a new invitation. They set their sights on the summer of 1957. Graham took the new offer with utmost seriousness. His wife, Ruth, always a strong influence, thought he should say yes. After much prayer and reflection, he said, he agreed.

Graham freely admitted that he was sobered by the prospect of taking his crusade into the Big Apple, with its large Catholic, Jewish, and nonchurched population. Under the circumstances, it is not surprising that besides the usual regimen of Bible study and sermon preparation, he jogged the mountains around his house—training, he remembered, like a prizefighter going into the ring.

Meticulous preparation had distinguished Graham's crusades for years, but this one capped them all. It still stands as the largest and most intricately orchestrated undertaking of his career. Advance men (always men) and their families started moving to the city a full two years before the meetings began. As usual, they launched neighborhood prayer meetings and training sessions for the counselors.

But to an extent not seen before, advance men cultivated the media by arranging press conferences, talks with civic groups, and appearances on television shows, including *The Today Show* and *Meet the Press*. Their herculean advertising campaign gave new meaning to the word "mass," as they blanketed the city with handbills, billboards, bumper stickers, and banners on buses.

"Listen with your soul, tonight," Graham told the 18,500 people packing the Garden for the opening service. "Your heart also has ears." The *New York Times* printed the text of Graham's entire first-night sermon on an inside page. The titles of the sermons Graham preached night after night narrated the meetings' plotlines: "Conversion," "Christ Crucified," "Christian Discipline," "Power of the Gospel," "How to Live the Christian Life."

In every case Graham preached for a verdict, and he said so. Predictably, the very first night he preached on John 3:16: "For God so loved the world, that he gave his only begotten Son, that whosoever believeth in him should not perish, but have eternal life."[2] But he knew that the verdict— the decision—to choose Christ had to come from an underlying desire to do the right thing. The preacher's efforts that inaugural evening yielded 704 decision cards.

Graham invariably gave all the credit to God for results of that sort, but he made sure that he did his part too. At the beginning of July, *Life* magazine featured the crusade on its cover. Clearly Graham's close friend Henry Luce, owner of *Life*, played the key role in the cover choice. The BGEA broadcast one-hour segments of the meetings on local television nightly throughout. Beginning June 1, they broadcast the Saturday evening services live over the ABC television network, seventeen times altogether.

This venture took Graham into millions of homes around the country. Eventually, an estimated 96 million people reported that they had seen at least one of the meetings that way. He received a million and a half letters in three months. Television close-ups brought Graham face-to-face with his audience in a way that huge crusade venues and of course radio never could. After the meeting, the BGEA cut back the telecasts of live meetings to one series of two or three programs per quarter. The organization aimed to trim costs and not trivialize them by making them routine.[3]

*   *   *

Several features of the New York meeting linger in memory. First was Graham's effort to reach African Americans. The year before the crusade opened, Graham had published landmark articles in the mass-circulation magazines *Life* and *Ebony*.

In those articles Graham acknowledged that the races sometimes segregated themselves voluntarily, and he saw no problem as long as the pattern was truly optional and not prescribed by law or coerced by authorities. But it was a different story when the law or authorities forced races apart against their will. This practice was not merely unjust but manifestly *sinful*.

Recognizing that his audiences were mostly white but the city was not, Graham determined to make some changes. A few days into the crusade, he contacted his old friend Jack Wyrtzen and asked what he should do about it. Wyrtzen, who was white, and an influential youth ministries leader in the city, connected Graham with Howard Jones, who was black, and an influential pastor of a Christian and Missionary Alliance church in Cleveland. Jones advised Graham, do not wait for blacks to come to you, you have to go to them.

The subtext was clear: you and everything else about your crusade—music, choir, artists, associates, and congregation, not to mention your own Nordic face—shout one word: "white." If blacks are hesitant to come, what would you expect?

Graham responded with four moves. First and most publicized, he invited Martin Luther King Jr. to offer a "pastoral prayer" (not the invocation, as commonly reported) on July 18. King's words were affirming, albeit not ringing, and the same could be said for Graham's follow-up comments. But given the history of black/white relations, and the prejudices of the age, the wonder is not that the prayer and follow-up were less than resounding but that they were given at all. Afterward Graham received searing criticism from white fundamentalists.

Graham followed Jones's recommendations in several additional ways. He took the crusade out of the white precincts of the Garden and into preponderantly African American sections of Harlem and Brooklyn. Facilitated by Jones, he preached to audiences of eight thousand in Harlem and ten thousand blacks and other minorities in Brooklyn. In Brooklyn he acknowledged, perhaps for the first time publicly, that discrimination required antisegregation *legislation* as well as Christian love. He did not specify exactly what kind of legislation or policies.

Then too Graham and crusade leader Barrows diversified the roster of guest artists. When Barrows learned that, without his knowledge, the famed blues and gospel soloist Ethel Waters had joined the choir, he immediately invited her to center stage to sing her signature song, "His Eye Is on the Sparrow," backed by a choir of three thousand voices. She would sing it five times in the final eight weeks of the crusade. Graham also appeared on *The Steve Allen Show* with the African American actress and singer Pearl Bailey, who promised to attend the meetings.

Finally, at Graham's invitation Jones joined the Graham team in New York and sat on the platform. The solidly white image of the Graham revival was slowly beginning to crumble. Graham's least visible but in the long run most important move was to add Jones and, later, African Canadian Ralph Bell and (Asian) Indians Robert Cunville and Akbar Abdul-Haqq to the roster of trusted associates.

"In New York," Jones recalls, "Billy once and for all made it clear that his ministry would not be a slave to the culture's segregationist ways." Minority associates' occasional presence on the stage and behind the pulpit sent long-overdue yet powerful signals. By the end of the meetings, historian Edward Gilbreath has shown, "blacks made up 20 percent of the 18,000 people who attended each night."

*   *   *

Beyond outreach to the African American community, Graham deftly exploited the array of public relations opportunities the city offered him. That was a second striking—and strikingly memorable—legacy of the crusade. Critics dismissed them as stunts. However one evaluated these exploits, he clearly knew how to command the media and the public's attention.

The most notable example of deft PR was Graham's decision to move the meeting to Yankee Stadium on July 20—the day he had earlier targeted as the crusade's closing night. With one hundred thousand souls jammed into the stadium and another twenty thousand gathered outside the gates, Graham drew the largest crowd since Joe Louis knocked out Max Baer in 1935. Reporters drew parallels between Graham's bouts with the devil and Louis's with Baer. Though Graham had no way of knowing in advance, everyone sweltered in the heat, 96 degrees outside and 105 on the stage. The weather alone made the event stick in memory.

What Graham did know in advance was that Vice President Richard Nixon would attend and greet the faithful from the pulpit. Nixon even brought a word from President Eisenhower, whom he called "a good

friend of Dr. Graham." Nixon added that one of the reasons for the nation's progress was the "deep and abiding faith" of its people. Nixon's visit
marked two firsts: the first time a sitting vice president would participate
in a Graham meeting, and the first time Graham would mix the gospel
with partisan politics in such an unapologetic way.

Nixon made another comment that held large significance too. Walking into the stadium with Graham, the vice president complimented him
on the size of the crowd. Graham replied, "I didn't fill the stadium, God
did." Critics likely heard Graham's words as self-serving evangelical
boilerplate. Admirers heard Graham's words as self-deflections that reinforced the power of Graham's attraction to millions.

The New York crusade both embodied and portended one of the most
important strategic decisions of Graham's entire life. He determined that
he would work with any believers who would work with him if they accepted the deity of Christ and if they did not ask him to change his message.

In practice Graham quietly downplayed the "deity of Christ" provision. He accepted the help of mainline Protestants whose views of Jesus's
divine nature may have differed from his. Also a few Jews, who found
his emphasis on God, patriotism, and decency appealing. But the second
provision—if they do not expect him to change his message—proved absolutely nonnegotiable. No one tried.

Graham's inclusiveness worked—for the most part, anyway. The invitation to visit New York, we have seen, came from a majority of the
churches, including mainstream evangelical and mainline liberal ones.
While hard evidence about Catholic involvement is hard to come by, signs
abound that thousands of ordinary believers and many members of the
Catholic clergy supported him. At the same time, however, fundamentalists—the third stream on the Protestant landscape—wanted no part
of the crusade.

The crusade was sponsored and partly funded by leading figures in
the business community, such as George Champion, vice president (soon
president) of Chase Manhattan Bank, one of the largest in the nation.
The nightly meetings featured a retinue of testimonials from prominent
entertainers, politicians, and military men. Anecdotal evidence suggests
that thousands of ordinary people—readers of the *New York Post* more
than the *New York Times*—talked about the meetings on the subway and
in street corner diners.

Something else worked too. And that was how the entire endeavor
came together, night after night, creating something larger and more

lasting than the sum of its parts. The aggregate numbers spoke volumes: nearly 2,000,000 attenders at the regular meetings, 400,000 at miscellaneous and overflow meetings, more than 60,000 decision cards turned in, and 1,500,000 letters in response to the television broadcasts, in which 30,000 spoke of quiet decisions for Christ in their homes.[4]

As for Graham himself, he preached nightly for ten weeks with few breaks. At that point he began to spend most of the day in bed. Sometimes, he said, when he stepped forward to preach, he found himself "almost cling[ing] to the pulpit." "New York . . . took a toll on me physically," he remembered. "Something went out of me physically in the New York Crusade that I never fully recovered."

On the closing night, 125,000 souls crowded under the stars in Times Square and surrounding streets. Crusade organizers staged the event on September 1, the night before the Labor Day holiday, when many people would be off work. It was also a night that symbolized the closing of one season and the opening of another. For many who turned in decision cards that evening, it also undoubtedly symbolized the closing of one season of their lives and the opening of another.

Flesh Became Words

By the end of the New York crusade in September 1957, Graham's style of preaching—both what he said and how he said it—had settled into a pattern that remained remarkably fixed for the next three decades. Until the 1990s or so, his constant exposure in media—magazines, newspapers, radio, and television—helped make his manner of preaching normative for many others.

The sermon stood at the center. Sometimes Graham insisted that everything depended on the months of preparatory prayer by the organizing committee and sponsoring pastors. Other times he insisted with equal fervor that everything depended on the follow-up efforts of counselors and local churches after he left town. Or the spiritual power of the music during the meetings. Or the direct hand of the Holy Spirit. He surely believed every word he said. But at some level he also knew that the sermon stood at the center. Faith, after all, came by hearing.

The secular press and many historians have focused on Graham's activities in the realm of politics, but that focus reflects their interests more than Graham's. Close students of Graham's life quickly find that his heart lay elsewhere. The overwhelming part of all the words he ever spoke or wrote pertained to matters of salvation, not state. And that spiritual orientation emerged with particular force in his preaching.

Let's begin with the obvious. Graham was not a great preacher, if by great we mean eloquent. He knew it and almost everyone else did too, including his wife. "Homiletically," said W. E. Sangster, a leading cleric in England, "his sermons leave almost everything to be desired." Graham allowed as much about himself, admitting that he was a champion rambler, with as many as seventeen points in a single sermon. He told one biographer that the subject and the words of his first sermon were "mercifully lost to memory."

Still, he was a great preacher if by great we mean effective. Sometimes his sermons flopped, but far more often they did exactly what he hoped they would do: persuade men and women to stand up, walk to the front, and profess new or renewed faith in Christ. Or pull off to the side of the road, as the radio carried *Hour of Decision*, or bow their heads in their living rooms, as the television carried its version of *Hour of Decision*.

One story captures the difference between eloquence and effectiveness in Graham's preaching. When Graham spoke in Duke University Chapel in 1985, the university chaplain, Will Willimon, a renowned preacher himself, remembered the sermon as "a muddle—set pieces from Billy's work over the years, little biblical content, and no discernable theme. Nobody noticed. Just being among the crowd as Billy [preached was] sermon enough."

A 2010 poll of contributing editors of *Preaching*, a magazine of record in the field, asked them to list the most influential preachers in America in the past twenty-five years. They placed Graham—the grand muddler—at the top. The editors themselves went further. "Billy Graham," they judged, "simply stands in a category unto himself."

*   *   *

Graham's sermons followed a predictable pattern. The content, of course, changed with the times, audiences, and his own theological growth. But the mold that held the content remained remarkably stable year after year. One of Graham's associates drolly but accurately observed that if you heard ten of Billy's sermons, you heard them all.

First of all, Graham stepped to the podium when Barrows announced him, not before. That carefully choreographed pattern amplified the drama of his appearance. Graham invariably started off by complimenting the town or region as one of the finest he had ever seen. Then followed a gaggle of time-tested, perfectly honed warm-up jokes, mostly self-deprecating. Repeat attenders had already heard most of them, but that did not matter. They were funny every time around.

The menu of chestnuts was long. Take the woman who strolled over to his table in a restaurant and alleged, "You look exactly like Billy Graham." To which he drolly responded, "Yes, people often say that." And the time when a woman rushed up to him in an airport and blurted out, "I know exactly who you are! You're James Arness!" To the extended applause that greeted him in Charlotte's Ericsson Stadium in 1996, he dead-panned, "I have a lot of relatives here. . . . You all must be tired. So I'll talk for just a few hours." Preaching immediately after a long transatlantic flight, Graham warned the audience that he might end up resembling the pastor who dreamed he was preaching—then woke up and found he was.

Graham turned self-deprecation into an art form. So this man follows Graham into the restroom of a Howard Johnson. "You look so much like Billy Graham," he said. "Well, after seeing you close up, I realize that you are not." In 1973 a reporter asked the evangelist who would be the next Billy Graham. Without missing a beat Graham grinned, "I hope there will never be another one. I think you've had enough of me." By all accounts Graham really was a pretty good golfer but pretending otherwise worked well too. "The only time my prayers are never answered," he quipped, "is on the golf course."

And so it went. The preacher knew how to break the ice. He also knew his audiences.

Then the serious words. Graham's sermons followed the plotlines out-lined in *Peace with God* in 1953 but targeted some parts more than others. The messages regularly began with a biblical text, of course, but Graham rarely paused to exegete the text in depth. Whatever the stated passage, the actual one was always the one he used the first night at Madison Square Garden: John 3:16.[1]

Almost immediately Graham turned to a litany of crises. Interna-tional threats usually came first, then national ones, and then personal ones. The specifics changed with the decades, but underlying perennials included divorce, hopelessness, loneliness, immorality, and fear of death.

Natural disasters—earthquakes, floods, hurricanes—made occa-sional appearances too. Unlike his Puritan predecessors, Graham usually portrayed them as signs of the brokenness of creation, not direct pun-ishments from God for America's—or any other nation's—sins. But that was a distinction without much of a difference. They reminded folks of the precariousness of life.

Graham rehearsed these data with demonstrably wide reading of current newspapers and magazines, as well as the work of two or three trusted staff members and his wife, Ruth. He liked to quip that borrowing from one writer was plagiarism, borrowing from many was research.

Auditors might reasonably question whether Graham had actually read, or at least read in any serious way, the many authorities he routinely quoted—politicians, historians, theologians, philosophers, playwrights, musicians, sociologists, novelists—the list went on—and on. But no one doubted that he had read the Bible constantly and in depth.

For all the crises he named, there was one answer, and that answer was of course Christ. In Christ, people would find forgiveness and restoration. Again and again, he would say, "We need a new heart that will not have lust and greed and hate in it. We need a heart filled with love and peace and joy, and that is why Jesus came into the world . . . to make peace between us and God."

Graham gradually mastered the art of streamlining his sermons. Audiences did not hear deep theological discussions or debates about matters in dispute. Nor did they hear about misdemeanors like smoking and cussing, or tear-jerking deathbed tales, or attacks on individual persons. Pernicious movements like Communism, yes, but individuals, no. Graham saw no need to antagonize before he had a chance to share.

The timeless authority of Scripture reinforced the words that exploded at the beginning of countless sentences: "The *Bible* says . . ." Scripture, he said, turned the gospel into a "rapier."

Graham usually preached from the King James Version because he knew it contained the words people knew best.[2] His prodigious memory of the Bible kicked into gear in the first few minutes, as he fired passages rapidly and repeatedly, up to one hundred times in a single sermon. He rarely if ever tried to defend the truth or relevance of the Bible. Rather, he just proclaimed it as if everyone already accepted his working assumptions.

What audiences did hear was a message of hope. A litany of "re-" words—"reform," "rebirth," "renewal," "regeneration"—served as the pivot. Nothing had to stay the same. Everything could be changed. Others found new life, and so can you.

*   *   *

The sermons drew mixed reactions. Critics pounced for many reasons, and the bill of particulars ran long. They said that his preaching was simplistic. Or repetitive. Or premodern. Or disorganized. Or alarmist. Or all of the above.

But here it is crucial to note not only what Graham said but also, and perhaps more important, what people actually heard. Letters to Graham leave little doubt that many heard a message that seemed not simplistic but simple, not repetitive but reinforcing, not premodern but enduring, not disorganized but wide-ranging, not alarmist but timely.

Graham's listeners heard something even more direct. It might be called marching orders. Willimon rightly observed that whether the hearer was young or not, this was a young person's theology, a moment of closure that fit the other crucial moments of closure young people were expected to make as they reached maturity: choose a mate, choose a job, choose a path for your life. And choose Christ.

The main point rang out as clearly as any bell atop any steeple. Come as you are. "You don't have to straighten out your lives first," he told audience after audience. "You don't have to make yourself well before going to a doctor." The altar was a hospital for sinners, not a resort for saints.

SCENE 19

Preacher at Work

How Graham preached was just as important as what he preached. His authority lay in his words, but his words were inseparable from how he presented them.

The *how* started with his own preparation. We have seen that sustained Bible study and prayer were woven into his daily life routine. Those habits intensified as he geared up for crusades and during the meetings themselves. In the hours before he preached, he ran over his notes, which his secretary had typed up in sketchy outline form. Here and there he inserted cryptic handwritten comments about current events or illustrative stories or scriptural passages to weave in.

In the hotel room, Graham locked the door, pulled the shades, took a nap (with a baseball cap on to keep his long, wavy hair from crinkling up). He ate lightly if at all, reserving dinner for after the meeting. And fretted.

Though Graham spoke in public thousands of times, he never took his performance for granted. Before the opening night at Harringay, he remembered, he was so frightened of failure he almost turned back. At the end of a sermon, sometimes he was so exhausted associates had to help him, soaked with sweat, off the platform and directly into a waiting car.

No wonder. Tom Allen, an organizer of Graham's 1955 Scotland crusade, said that before Graham preached he saw in him "an inner and very finely controlled tension." But once the meeting started, "All the strain is gone, and from then on the man has forgotten himself."

If in Los Angeles in 1949 he had preached "fast and loud," by the time he got to New York in 1957 he had learned to dial down the speed and let the microphone do the heavy lifting. Yet his ability to hold listeners' attention remained, or even grew. Whatever he lost by reducing the pace and dropping decibels, he gained by intensifying the forcefulness of the words.

Reporters commented on three more aspects of Graham's preaching: his accent, his voice, and his energy. Earlier we saw that his particular accent—"Carolina stage English"—was just different enough to sound intriguing. It also told listeners where he came from. In the years when Graham was soaring into public prominence, the South had expanded culturally everywhere. Jim Crow was beginning to crack, and the Christian Right had not yet emerged as a polarizing stereotype of Southern religion. Southerners like the semimythical Colonel Sanders and avuncular Andy Griffith offered a vision of genteel civility.

This vision overlooked a great deal, of course, including racism, heat, and poverty, but it still rang true enough to seem attractive. Graham reminded folks of Mayberry, a receding world of small towns, summer nights, and stable values.

The preacher's voice, a timbered baritone, sounded remarkably like that of a professional newscaster. It proved crisp enough to capture attention yet mellow enough to feel inviting. Reporters compared it with that of the nation's most famous newscaster, Walter Cronkite. One journalist aptly called it "an instrument of vast range and power." Graham perhaps sensed that his voice was the most recognizable part of his calling card. He took care to protect it before he preached, and between meetings he practiced how he would use it.

Energy was part of Graham's calling card too. He never fell into the platform acrobatics of Billy Sunday, his high-profile predecessor on the revival circuit, but no one fell asleep during his sermons either. As noted, in the early days Graham prowled the platform, with Barrows furling and unfurling the microphone cord behind him. Graham rapidly bounced from standing ramrod straight behind the pulpit to crouching beside it. His right hand shot forward, fingers cocked like a man holding a pistol, while his left hand thrust aloft a large black leather Bible. In time these pyrotechnics mellowed to a more dignified style, forceful yet measured.

Graham spoke plainly and directly. Convinced that the average person had a working vocabulary of six hundred words, he made a point to stick with common words and short sentences. Though he never put it exactly this way, he instinctively grasped the import of Sister Aimee Semple McPherson's recipe for rabbit stew: first "you have to catch the rabbit."

If plain words formed half of Graham's repertoire, direct ones formed the other half. In his early work with Youth for Christ, he later remembered, he used "every modern means to catch the ear of the unconverted and then we punched them straight between the eyes with the gospel." To the end of his preaching career, qualifications such as "I think" or "on the whole" or "in general" rarely softened the rhetoric, and abstractions rarely inflated it. Illustrations drawn from ordinary life turned up constantly. Graham knew the perils of ambiguity.[1]

Everything Graham said and did behind the pulpit pointed toward one goal: the invitation at the end of the sermon to stand up, walk to the front, and *decide* to follow Christ. "No matter how large the crowd," said journalist Laurie Goodstein, he knew that "he had to move each man and woman there personally."

Night after night the words took a familiar pattern. "Are you prepared to meet God? Does he have first place in your life? Is he the Lord of your life?" Graham assured people he would stay as long as it took. "The buses will wait." "Come. You come. We will wait." And wait he did.

In Graham's mind, potential inquirers had to turn inclination into concrete action. Quietly accepting Christ in one's heart was not good enough. It was too easy to back out when the euphoria melted into the ups and downs of everyday life.

The preacher understood the importance of perfectly spaced pauses of precise duration. He also understood the power of stillness in the audience. Standing ramrod straight, right fist tucked under his chin, right elbow cupped in his left hand, he called for absolute silence. Even in a stadium packed with a hundred thousand people, he insisted that the slightest noise or movement might thwart the Holy Spirit's work.

A big part of Graham's reputation—and legacy—rested on the response to the invitation. Admittedly, sometimes—especially early on—few people came forward. Occasionally no one did. But usually the response proved encouraging. Even Chuck Templeton, Graham's early rival for superstardom in the pulpit, knew when he was beaten. "We would travel together and preach on consecutive nights," Templeton remembered. "He would get 41 (people to answer the altar call); I would get 32."

At the height of Graham's career, people streamed forward by the hundreds and sometimes by the thousands. If Billy just stood there and read a telephone directory, one associate said, people still would come. When Graham died, megachurch pastor Rick Warren captured Graham's pulpit art in five words: he knew "how to draw the net."

But there was more. Critics charged that the seemingly endless streams of inquirers showed that the masses succumbed to the power of suggestion at best, that they were gullible at worst. Yet critics—and admirers too for that matter—often missed the subtleties. Anthropologist Susan Harding discerned the inner texture of the process. "At first," she said, "you don't get it. He seems so ordinary and accessible. He doesn't make you think instantly that he is going to change your life. You are taken in gradually. You get captured. . . . [He] made Christianity come true."

Graham knew perfectly well that inquirers came for a variety of reasons, some superficial, some profound, and some undoubtedly both at once. But the main point held. Publicly declaring a new direction for one's life implicitly acknowledged that things had gone astray and it was time to set them right.

Visiting journalists repeatedly said that inquirers showed little overt emotion. Photographs show that some descended the steep concrete steps in the great stadiums of the world with moist eyes. Yet the emotion likely came from the hymns, not his preaching. Graham never suggested that emotion was bad, just secondary to the business at hand.

The preacher's own tearless conversion experience, back when he was fifteen, set the precedent. And so did his deportment in the pulpit. Unlike many evangelical revivalists, he never cried. In the 1980s audiences started applauding when inquirers stood to walk forward. Graham did not like it (just as Shea did not like applause when he sang), but eventually he accepted it as a sign of the times that he could do little to change.

Also, too many inquirers—likely a majority—were already church members who had grown lax in their faith or former church members who had dropped out altogether. For some the decision represented a radical transformation from nonbelief to belief. One writer called transformations of that sort "sky-blue" conversions, as though they had tumbled from realms above as a sacred meteor. BGEA publicists sometimes implied that the sky-blue conversions were the only ones that really counted. Not Graham. In God's eyes, he affirmed, new birth and renewed birth were the same.

How many inquirers stayed with their decision for five or more years? Though the evidence is both sketchy and inconsistent, it seems safe to say that for a majority the decision marked a permanent turning point in their lives.

For a sizable minority, however, it did not. Few took to the streets to renounce their decisions. They simply drifted away. Graham often compared this pattern to Jesus's parable of the seed and the sower. Not every seed that was sowed sprouted or grew to maturity. Even so, for many the long walk to the front surely lingered in memory.

In sum, Graham possessed the gift. With a dash of dramatic flourish, we might call it "The Gift." *Newsweek*'s veteran religion writer Kenneth

Woodward captured it precisely: Graham, he said, could make "the simplest sentence sound like Sacred Scripture." He combined accent, voice, animation, vocabulary, humor, timing, and, above all, authority, in a manner that proved inimitable.

The evangelist knew that the point was not to impress but to connect. Reading Graham's sermons could be a test of endurance. But hearing them, preached live in front of one hundred thousand people, was entirely different. The message pulsed with energy as flesh became words. If numbers can be taken as an index of accomplishment, he was easily the best in the world at what he did. Maybe the best ever.

SCENE 20

Art of the Crusade

Over six decades Graham shouldered more than four hundred distinct crusades or preaching events, ranging in duration from a single afternoon to sixteen weeks. On average he held three to five extended meetings per year (plus those in which one of his associates preached under his auspices). He accepted invitations only if they came from a majority of local pastors spread across a spectrum of denominations. Graham received hundreds of invitations each year—one year more than 8,500—so he could accept only a tiny fraction.[1]

In later years the crusades grew shorter in duration, partly because the organizers found that stadiums were harder to book for longer stays, and partly because Graham's stamina for those ordeals diminished with age. Anaheim in 1985 and Denver in 1987, when Graham was approaching age seventy, ran ten days apiece. Those were the final extended ones.

Graham believed, of course, that the success of every meeting ultimately depended on the Lord, but he determined to remove needless obstacles. He initially focused his energies on venues that yielded as many attenders as possible. The crusades of the 1950s usually took place in outdoor stadiums and indoor arenas in large metropolitan sites.

But after 1970, the crusades shifted to smaller cities such as Indianapolis and Fresno. With high-speed technology, slighter venues, with lower overhead costs, proved more attractive for the bottom line. Moreover, he believed that the big cities of the nation—New York, Chicago, Los Angeles—already had been saturated with his presentation of the gospel, whereas many of the smaller ones had not.

Like his most successful predecessors—Dwight L. Moody, Billy Sunday, and Aimee Semple McPherson—Graham well understood the power of advertising. So when a Graham crusade headed into town, the BGEA paved the way with blanket advertising, typically by means of handbills (in the thousands), bumper stickers, billboards, ads on radio and television, banners on buses, live interviews on local radio and television, and stories in newspapers. Much of the advertising focused on Graham's name and image. He appreciated the power of repetition. He once remarked that the quality of the words and colors on a billboard was less important than the number of billboards a motorist passed.

Occasional disappointments aside, the results were eye-popping. Numerous stadium records were broken or near records achieved, including 110,000 in Yankee Stadium in New York City, 116,000 in Soldier Field in Chicago, 120,000 in Wembley Stadium in London, 130,000 in the Rose Bowl in Pasadena, 250,000 in New York City's Central Park, and 250,000 in Maracana Soccer Stadium in Rio. The peak event occurred in Seoul in 1973, with 1,120,000 attenders (more on this later).[2] In many instances thousands more visitors, unable to gain admission, crowded outside the gates and listened over loudspeakers.

What did those numbers mean? Graham repeatedly said that quantity was not the point. If just one person gave their life to Christ, that would make everything worthwhile.

But sometimes the preacher slipped up and let big numbers slip through his lips as if they somehow documented God's favor. And so did the BGEA—far more often than Graham himself did. After all, wasn't the point of evangelism to draw as many people as possible into the faith?

Attenders heard testimonies from an array of athletes, politicians, entertainers, military heroes, and other celebrities about their spiritual journeys. Almost always the testifiers had enjoyed successful careers, but at some point their lives had run off the rails. An experience with the Lord—often through a Graham book or crusade or broadcast—got them back on track again.

The evidence leaves little doubt, however, that except for Graham's sermon, the music exercised more influence and lingered longer in memory than any other aspect of the meeting. It sometimes even outshined Graham's sermon. As far back as Graham's first itinerant preaching ventures as a student at Florida Bible Institute, the preacher had made a point to team up with soloists and other musicians. He understood the power of music to win converts to Christ and, even more, back to Christ. Nostalgia played no small role.

Graham had no ear for music himself, and certainly no talent for it either. Shea joshed that Graham suffered from the "malady of no melody." But he knew about—and appreciated—the role that songsters had played in the great urban revivals of the late nineteenth and early twentieth centuries. Dwight L. Moody and Ira Sankey loomed as the best-known pair. Indeed, for many decades Graham kept figurines of Moody *and* Sankey in his personal study.

Other pairs that Graham undoubtedly knew about included J. Wilbur Chapman and Charles Alexander, Billy Sunday and Homer Rodeheaver, and Graham's contemporaries, Kathryn Kuhlman and pianist Dino Kartsonakis. The Graham team was however the first to feature two—and, if one counts pianist Tedd Smith, three—musicians integral to the unit.

The choirs and guest artists became a draw in themselves. A few visitors admitted that they attended mainly to hear the choir and, in some cases, because they hoped that being onsite would boost their chances for getting into the choir.

One of Barrows's most important duties lay in his oversight of the guest artists. In a forthcoming work, historian Edith Blumhofer shows that he was acutely sensitive to regional tastes and ethnic and racial diversity. Latino, Korean, Hawaiian, Swedish, Native American, and, of course, African American artists were featured. Besides Ethel Waters, notable figures from the last group included Mahalia Jackson, Leontyne Price, Kathleen Battle, Andraé Crouch, and the Montreal Jubilation Gospel Choir. Barrows also paid attention to musical genres, embracing pop, classical, western, country, inspirational, and Christian rock.

Altogether, Blumhofer writes, Shea, Barrows, pianist Tedd Smith, favored guests, and the distinctive arrangements of the (typically) massive choirs, created a "signature sound."

Finally, why did people come? Letters and interviews show that many came for the simple and often overlooked reason that someone invited them. Knowing the power of the person-to-person invitation, Graham deftly exploited what might be called the "buddy system." As noted, the 1954 London crusade saw the implementation of an outreach program called Operation Andrew, in which participants brought a friend without a church home.

In New York, however, crusade planners encouraged entire congregations to sponsor buses to carry actual and potential members to the crusade. The idea was shrewd, for it capitalized on the conviviality of a long bus ride, free from the hassles of driving and parking, and the promise of reserved seating—with one's friends—once they got there.

Besides being invited, visitors gave reporters and counselors a variety of reasons for going. For some, going to church in the middle of the week was a good way to spend an evening out with the family. Others went so that they could someday tell their grandchildren they had seen Billy Graham up close. And some went with a premonition that at the end they would walk to the front and try to start their lives all over again.

At least two more reasons came into play. Visitors rarely stated these reasons explicitly, but they are easy to infer from the letters they sent afterward. The first was the comfort of predictability. People had a good idea what would take place. Indeed, the very predictability of everything—all the way down to Graham's jokes—actually worried some BGEA insiders. Where was the Holy Spirit in all this? Had Graham and Barrows swapped their own ideas for the Holy Spirit's?

The second implied reason was the thrill of a spectacle. The meetings' predictability promised that things would be exciting—but not too exciting. Historian Michael Hamilton aptly notes that the event promised traffic, crowds, tickets, ushers, music, testifiers, choir, guest artists, and the magnificence of the arena itself. It offered the glamor and excitement that their own churches lacked.

And no one asked for a refund.

SCENE 21

Other Players

Historian Garth Rosell rightly said that Graham emerged on the midcentury revival scene not alone but from an extensive "band of brothers." Actually Rosell might well have called them an "army of brothers."

These men—almost all were male—facilitated Graham's success by the excellence of their work and by their willingness to blend their careers with his. They shared goals, worked together smoothly, and clearly felt affection for one another. Being human, they undoubtedly felt a stab of envy once in a while. But there is little public evidence of it. The band had three distinct parts: the "Platform Team," the "Backstage Team," and the board.

The Platform Team has been underplayed or even ignored in treatments of Graham's success, but it would be hard to overstate its importance. Graham later said that without the team, "burnout would have left me nothing but a charred cylinder within five years of the 1949 Los Angeles Crusade." The Platform Team consisted of three men: George Beverly Shea, Cliff Barrows, and Leighton Ford. Shea and Barrows appeared almost every time Graham did, whether live in crusade meetings or recorded on radio and television. Ford showed up less often, but when he did, he was more front and center.

Graham, Shea, and Barrows together constituted one of the closest and longest-running evangelistic teams in the history of American revivalism. The first time Graham conducted a crusade entirely on his own—independent of Youth for Christ auspices—both Shea and Barrows were on hand to help out. That was in Charlotte in 1947.[1]

When the trio traveled to Los Angeles in 1949, local billboards showed them standing together. Graham appeared simply as one of the three. Granted, by the end of the meetings eight weeks later, Graham without question ranked as the leader. Even so, as late as 1951 *Life* magazine would say that Shea and Barrows were as well-known as Graham. To the end of

Graham's public ministry in 2005, the three men saw their relationship foreshadowed in Ecclesiastes 4:12: "a threefold cord is not quickly broken."

Earlier we saw that Graham tapped Shea to join him at the very beginning of his ministry, inviting Shea to be the regular vocalist on his weekly Sunday radio program, *Songs in the Night*. Their professional relationship soon turned into a close friendship that would last till the end of both men's lives seven decades later.

In 1947 Graham invited Shea to join him in itinerant ministry. Shea asked if he would be expected to talk, too. Graham grinned and replied, "I hope not." Shea said the same about Graham's singing: he hoped not. The crooner caroled two or three vocals in every crusade meeting and one or two in every radio or television program.

Shea's sonorous baritone was reverential, even ponderous, which set the tone for everything else. He discouraged applause, tried not to entertain, and consistently sought to boost Graham's ministry, not his own. Shea also was understandable. He wanted the people readily to grasp the lyrics' straightforward meaning, not marvel at the poetic allusions they might hold.

Soon esteemed as "America's beloved gospel singer," Shea offered a predictable lineup of beloved hymns, including "The Love of God," "I Love to Tell the Story," "I'd Rather Have Jesus," "The Old Rugged Cross," "How Great Thou Art," and, of course, "Just as I Am." With good reason, one early journalist wrote that Shea was "the golden voice of the decade . . . thrilling his listeners while melting their heart with God."

Shea's commitment to gospel classics was as shrewd as it was heartfelt. The mainline Lutheran historian/theologian Martin Marty visited a New York crusade meeting in 1957. He observed that he and Catholic attenders did not know the songs, while the majority of worshipers lustily sang along without sheet music. They knew them by heart. Year after year "To God Be the Glory"—usually sung with the congregation—ranked as one of the crusade favorites.

Just as Graham and Shea immediately forged a close friendship that lasted their entire lives, so did Graham and Barrows—and Shea and Barrows with each other. Barrows was best known for his high-energy leading of audiences in song and for directing the crusade choirs. "He is enthusiastic—vital—dramatic!" wrote one reporter about Barrows during the Los Angeles revival. "He combines the high spirit of a college cheer leader with the quiet dignity of an expert choral director."

Barrows served as the announcer for both the radio and television versions of *Hour of Decision*, as well as the worship service in the crusade meetings. He not only selected the choir members but also led the mass choirs, which numbered as many as five thousand voices and totaled more than one million over the course of his career.

Less visible to audiences was Barrows's role as the final orchestrator of all of Graham's public outings. Historian Edith Blumhofer wryly notes that Barrows was totally in charge but took care never to upstage the boss. He selected the guest artists, approved the music they presented, and decided who would testify. He managed all the other specifics of the broadcasts and meetings too, down to the operation of the sound system and the parking arrangements. If the little things didn't work, nothing worked. Barrows was, in short, the one who *did* sweat the details, and he did it with such efficiency and reliability that Graham left everything except the sermon up to him.

Leighton Ford played a very different yet equally important role. Born in 1931 in Toronto, Ontario, he attended Wheaton College, where he met and, after graduation, married Graham's younger sister Jean. He completed formal seminary training at Columbia Theological Seminary in Georgia, making him by far the best formally educated person on Graham's Platform Team.

Ordained in the (Southern) Presbyterian Church in the United States, Ford became an associate evangelist in 1955. Between 1969 and 1985 he served as a frequent alternate speaker on the radio version of *Hour of Decision*. He was gifted with Graham's crisp baritone voice and forceful speaking style—but without the Southern accent. And though his preaching came across as less crises-oriented and more pastoral than Graham's, the similarities of style and content were close enough that many listeners thought they were hearing Graham himself.

Since Ford was blessed with a commanding presence much as Graham and Shea were, many people expected him to take over the BGEA when Graham retired. As things turned out, however, Ford left the organization in 1986 to form Leighton Ford Ministries, an independent program designed to train young leaders in mentoring skills and to confront problems of racism, hunger, and poverty. Besides leading the Lausanne Continuation Committee from 1976 to 1992 (as we will see), Ford wrote numerous books of serious theological reflection, including, most notably, *Transforming Leadership* (1991) and *The Attentive Life* (2014).

As early as the 1970s reporters started wondering if a person with Graham's unique combination of "gifts and graces" would ever come around again. Though few seemed to realize it, that question was only half the puzzle. The other half was whether the Platform Team's unique combination of "gifts and graces" would ever come around again.

Five men formed the Backstage Team. The Ontario-born Tedd Smith played the piano. Graham's childhood friend T. W. Wilson served as public relations adviser and fill-in preacher. Wilson also played a vital if largely unseen role as Graham's executive assistant, handling everything from travel arrangements to security. T. W.'s burly brother Grady Wilson, another childhood friend, served similar roles—and unfailingly functioned as an ever-affable sounding board. His quick wit lightened Graham's skies. As noted, when Graham founded the BGEA in 1950, he tapped Northwestern Schools' business manager, George W. Wilson (no relation), to run the financial side of things. By all accounts, he did so expertly—and with an iron hand.[2]

It didn't hurt that Graham never took a bad picture. His photographer, Russ Busby, saw to that. Busby joined Graham in 1956 and stayed to the end of the preacher's career. "I've seen most of the world with one eye closed," Busby quipped. Rumor held that he was the only person who could tell Graham where to sit. A fair number of the 1.1 million negatives archived in the BGEA photography vaults stand as a testament to Busby's industriousness.

If everything ran remarkably smoothly, year after year, decade after decade, which it did, the two teams—Platform and Backstage—could take much of the credit. Larry Ross, Graham's long-term public relations guru, said that Graham functioned with his team like a jazz leader and his band, setting the tone but then turning them loose to riff as they would.

The story was a bit more complicated than this, however. Graham was never an entirely hands-off administrator. He gave his crew plenty of rope to work with, but they also knew that at the end of the day he held the end of the rope firmly in his hands. Wherever he was in the world, he called in daily to see how things were going. Moreover, a big part of Graham's genius was that he did not delegate everything. He kept for himself the job that he felt he did best: headline preacher.

The BGEA Board of Directors, about fifteen in number, formed an additional "team" indispensable to Graham. Graham frequently sought counsel from the board in general and from individual members in particular. They added credibility to the BGEA's decisions (George F. Bennett, for example, was treasurer of Harvard). Graham often sought their advice on spiritual matters too.

The role of counselors started to take shape under Ruth's leadership in the 1949 Los Angeles meeting, but the program was not fully developed until the 1951 crusade in Fort Worth.[3] Counselors undertook systematic training months before crusade meetings, usually six. Eventually counselor training was offered in twelve languages, along with special training for counseling with children, the elderly, and the deaf. Counselors performed multiple tasks. During the meetings, when an inquirer stood to walk forward, a counselor "captain" assigned a counselor of the same age and gender to accompany the inquirer to the front.[4]

In a typical meeting the counselors constituted many—sometimes upwards of half—of the people moving forward. After Graham prayed with them as a group, each counselor would talk with their inquirer about the meaning of faith, give them a copy of the Gospel of John, a decision card to fill out, and urge them to join or rejoin a local church (usually but not always evangelical). For two to six weeks after the meeting ended, counselors would follow up by phone or by personal visits to see how they were doing in their "Christian walk." Crusade and telephone counselors ranked among the most understudied yet most important people in Graham's entire ministry.

And women? Notwithstanding Graham's early indebtedness to Henrietta Mears, women rarely preached and never held any of the main platform positions. Perhaps Graham sensed that his constituencies just were not ready for women preachers. Perhaps he was not ready either.

In one sense the eclipse of women at the very top was ironic. From beginning to end, the male/female ratio in his crusades remained unchanged, with females predominating at about 60 percent or more. Ruth was a charter founder of the BGEA board. Graham frequently touted his daughter Anne Graham Lotz as the best speaker in the family, and the one who knew the Bible best.[5] Women often graced the platform as testifiers and guest performing artists. At least half of the crusade counselors were women, and women constituted a solid majority of the telephone responders. Graham routinely interacted with women in the media, entertainment, and political worlds—Katie Couric, Hillary Clinton, Kathie Lee Gifford, and Dale Evans Rogers, among many others.

Then too not a few women felt that Graham's fidelity to his marriage, without a trace of compromise, affirmed women's rights as much as any public political position he might take.

A quick glance at Graham's view of women's ordination and of the Equal Rights Amendment (ERA) helps put their virtual absence from preaching positions in the crusades—and minimal representation on the board of the BGEA—in perspective. On women's ordination, Graham refused to take a position, insisting that ordination was a matter for individual denominations to decide for themselves. Even so, I have found no evidence that Graham ever took a public stand on this question, up or down, among his own fellow Southern Baptists, either.[6]

Did Graham's reluctance to wade into the women's ordination debate help or hurt the cause? It is hard to say, but common sense suggests that energetic support from the most famous and influential figure in the denomination might—just might—have carried the day.

Graham's reticence on women's ordination was entirely consistent with his reticence on many controversial topics, including the Equal Rights Amendment. This amendment, which was designed to guarantee equal legal rights for women, was ratified by the US House of Representatives in 1971 and the US Senate in 1972 but never received approval from thirty-eight states, the number needed to add an amendment to the Constitution. Graham's position on the ERA was predictably evasive. "I won't endorse it publicly," he said, "but personally I have no problem with it."

A final matter should be noted. The press rarely recognized how much stress Graham placed on winning the support of neighborhood pastors and churches. Both were vital for his goals. He started reading local papers six months before he got to town and arranged regular breakfast meetings for local pastors. A large and enduring part of his legacy, journalist Laurie Goodstein astutely observed, lay in his recognition of the centrality of the parsons who cared for the spiritual rhythms of daily life and the worshiping communities they nurtured.

By making sure that representatives from individual congregations were on hand to meet inquirers as they walked to the front, and by funneling inquirers back into those families of believers, Graham exerted "a huge impact" on building up not just his own movement but on Christianity itself.

Journalists sometimes wondered why local pastors worked so hard to bring his crusades to town. On the face of things, Graham's meetings competed for the same finite resources. Yet the answer is not all that hard to find. When Graham came to town, everybody won.

Critics in the Pulpit

If the Madison Square Garden crusade offered Graham one of the signal triumphs of his long ministry, it also engulfed him in a firestorm of criticism. And the criticism came from all sides, both then and later. Nearly everyone who met Graham in person found him witty, charming, and utterly—disarmingly—unimpressed with himself. Yet he also polarized people. If many thought he could do no wrong, a smaller though not negligible number thought he could do no right. And this latter group took the time and effort to make sure he clearly understood the magnitude and severity of his shortcomings. Why?

Enough criticism, even hatred, persisted to keep him and his managers perpetually on edge. At the extreme end of the opposition came threats of physical violence against him and even Ruth and the children. Death warnings filled a fat folder. Graham wrote off the senders of such threats as mentally unbalanced, and they probably were, but that fact did not erase the reality of the menace. At the urging of FBI director J. Edgar Hoover, Graham erected a tall iron fence around his house in Montreat. He also posted guard dogs. After 9/11, BGEA workers lined his newly built portable pulpit with a bulletproof shield.[1]

Fundamentalists—partisans of the wide river flowing on Graham's theological right—assailed him without mercy. This group included gladiators such as John R. Rice, long-term editor of the *Sword of the Lord* and also at one time a close friend. Better known was Bob Jones Sr., founder and president of Bob Jones College. A decade after the New York crusade ended, Jones was still seething. "I think that Dr. Graham is doing more harm in the cause of Jesus Christ than any living man," he judged.

Rice, Jones, and other fundamentalists objected less to anything Graham explicitly said than to his willingness to work with mainline Protestants and Catholics who said things fundamentalists found abhorrent. To them, Graham's association with people who had chosen to defy the plain teachings of Scripture implicitly condoned their errors. Graham's actions raised pragmatism over principle. And principle counted, supremely. After all, the eternal destiny of souls was at stake.

This split between Graham and his former fundamentalist friends was more like a divorce than a friendly disagreement. Most historians have not treated fundamentalists very well. Fundamentalists usually come off looking like bigots. But it is important to see the world through their eyes too. Fundamentalists felt that Graham had betrayed them. Once he had been one of them, but now he was crossing sacred boundaries, they thought, just in order to gain fame and success.

Graham too was stung. He expected opposition from liberals and secular pundits, but he did not see an attack coming from the right. After all, fundamentalists had been family. He had gone to their schools, recommended their newspapers, publicly affirmed their doctrines (albeit some more than others), and attributed his spiritual conversion to one of their stalwarts, Mordecai Ham. This was not a humdrum disagreement about fine points of theology or jealousy about priority in the spotlight. Rather, it ran deep in the river of disillusioned love.

*   *   *

Opposition also came from mainline Protestants, the wide river on Graham's theological left. Here we must be careful. Many voices from that side, such as John Sutherland Bonnell, pastor of Fifth Avenue Presbyterian Church—sometimes called "the cathedral of Presbyterianism"—supported him wholeheartedly. Others, such as Henry Pitney Van Dusen, president of Union Theological Seminary, embraced Graham's larger aims, though not all his methods. And some, such as John Mackay, president of Princeton Theological Seminary, felt that their mainline colleagues were asking more of Graham than they asked of themselves. "It is unfair to demand that Billy Graham should have offered a blueprint for the solution of complicated social issues in our highly industrialized mass society," Mackay averred.

It is important to remember, too, that some mainline allies seemed to transcend their own theological principles in order to stand behind Graham in support of a broader notion of evangelism. They took fire from their own colleagues for doing so.

And finally, it is easy to forget that many mainline partisans simply remained quiet. They did not buy one or another aspect of Graham's ministry, but they did not think his mistakes were grievous enough to warrant public rebuke. And some found him and his message irrelevant to their lives and just ignored him.

Still, many—likely a large minority—of mainliners felt Graham was doing so much harm that they needed to call him on it. Examples of all sorts tumble from the record. Typical was a smack-down from the *Christian Century*, the normative voice of the mainline. When Graham visited India in 1956, for example, he popped off that the United States might do better with a symbolic gesture—such as giving Indian prime minister Nehru a white air-conditioned Cadillac—than with outright financial foreign aid. Outraged, the *Century* shot back: Graham "hasn't a glimmer of a notion about what is really going on in the world."

A year later, as Graham descended on New York City, the *Century* once again descended on him: "The Graham procedure . . . does its mechanical best to 'succeed' whether or not the Holy Spirit is in attendance. At this strange new junction of Madison Avenue and Bible Belt, the Holy Spirit is not overworked; He is overlooked."

Reinhold Niebuhr, professor of Christian ethics at Union Theological Seminary in New York, appraised him harshly, too. The professor's withering judgment received a wide hearing. Niebuhr starred as the most influential serious academic theologian in America. His critique may or may not have been fair, but no one doubted that it was forcefully argued.

A Niebuhr biographer tells us that Niebuhr was "angry" when the Protestant Council of New York invited Graham to hold meetings. Writing in *Life* in March 1957, he acknowledged that Graham was a "personable, modest and appealing young man," but he dreaded Graham's "rather obscurantist version of the Christian faith."

Niebuhr did not change his mind when Graham actually came to town and attracted thousands—by then an aggregate of more than one million—to his nightly meetings. Mass evangelism's success, Niebuhr judged in the July 1 issue of *Life*, "depends upon oversimplifying every issue." Graham's version "offers . . . even less complicated answers than it has ever before provided."

Niebuhr concluded that Graham's bland message "promises a new life, not through painful religious experience but merely by signing a decision card. . . . A miracle of regeneration is promised at a painless price by an obviously sincere evangelist. It is a bargain." Niebuhr allowed that Graham himself had posted a good record on civil rights, but his preaching said too little about the problem. He also thought that Graham did not talk enough about how consumer capitalism harmed Americans' lives.

True to form, Graham asked George Champion to arrange a visit with Niebuhr in Niebuhr's office at Union Theological Seminary. Champion was not only chair of the New York crusade committee but also vice president of the Chase Manhattan National Bank. Champion later said that he called Niebuhr, but Niebuhr turned him down. Champion then called Ben Strong, chair of the Union board and also chair of the US Trust Company. Strong assured Champion he could arrange it, "no question." Strong soon came back, Champion remembered, "with his tail between his legs." Niebuhr had refused Strong's request too.

We do not know the rest of the story. As far as I know, Niebuhr never admitted that Champion and Strong had called him, let alone why he declined to see Graham. The reason may have been mundane—perhaps he wasn't feeling well that day. Maybe he feared that Graham's legendary charm with critics might dull his edge.

Whatever the reason, it is important to remember that Niebuhr represented a cluster of assumptions far removed from Graham's. Granted, at that time the professor and the preacher were on the same page in their fear of Communism. And Niebuhr's understanding of sin—loosely defined as incorrigible selfishness—was not all that far from Graham's.

But in other ways the chasm was deep. Niebuhr embraced a historical-critical understanding of Scripture. He handled talk of God, miracles, and all things supernatural very gingerly—largely with a vocabulary of myth, allegory, and metaphor. And he judged economic and racial injustice not as an aberration of American-style capitalism but endemic to it. To a significant extent Niebuhr and Graham were talking past each other.

Such reproach was hardly new. Over the course of Graham's ministry, it had come in waves, rising and falling according to things he said—or failed to say when others thought he should have spoken up. We have seen that pundits started to challenge his message and methods as soon as he stepped onto British soil in 1946. The disaster with Truman in 1950 marked another low point. Southern fundamentalists assailed his growing sympathy with racial integration in 1953. Harringay unleashed another series of attacks in 1954. Then New York.

Graham aimed to save a world broken by sin, but clearly thousands disliked the way he was trying to do it, or even that he was trying to do it. And that too was part of Graham's story.

Critics in the Crowd

While theologians on both sides of Graham found plenty to censure, a greater number of critical letters came from grassroots readers, listeners, and viewers. Whether these grassroots critics took glee in highlighting his shortcomings no one can say, but they certainly took time, as a striking number of these letters were lengthy and detailed. They targeted Graham's surface mistakes along with deep-running character flaws.

Letters about the lousy things Graham had done formed a small part of the total now housed in the Billy Graham Archives, but they were large enough in number, and sharp enough in tone, to make clear that thousands of people believed that "America's pastor" was not much of a pastor at all. Critics rarely if ever charged him with sexual immorality, which was not surprising, since no shred of evidence ever suggested that Graham had strayed.

But a litany of real or perceived personal flaws of other sorts unfolded with considerable regularity. One long missive, posted from the West Coast in 1958, for example, lacerated him for being inconsiderate of his wife. The problem was the menagerie of animals, mostly large ones, that the family kept, including sheep, goats, and, especially, Graham's beloved Great Pyrenees, Belshazzar. Just who cleans up after all those creatures, the writer demanded? You?

Suspicions about Graham's finances ran deep. One Midwestern woman smacked Graham for living high on the hog when he was out on the road. In the Southwest, another woman wondered if he really was, as people alleged, "a fake & a hypocrite." The problem was that he "commercialize[d] off of his words" instead of "going to God for his needs." Of course, she added, "I am not one to judge you."

But the brunt of the letters targeted Graham's theology. These attackers fell into roughly three groups: those who thought he was too liberal, or too conservative, or distorted the Bible's plain meaning.

For the first group, loosely labeled fundamentalists, Graham played fast and loose with passages he happened not to like. His cavalier style, they charged, led him to downplay nonnegotiable doctrines like the deity of Christ, the inerrancy of the Bible, and the inescapable destination of non-Christians in hell.

Along with his perceived doctrinal laxity came his willingness to consort with well-known enemies of the true faith, especially modernists and, not far behind, Catholics. "You seem to stress . . . that the modern day clergyman is in The Faith," one Southern zealot charged. "If he is, then the Bible and God are liars. . . . Just how stupid do you think people are?" By his modernist and Catholic friends, they alleged, Graham was known.

The second group of critics—those who found his reading of the Bible and his theology too conservative—was actually quite small in number. Folks holding this view likely thought his ideas were just too antiquated to merit serious criticism. Yet incredulousness did not stop all of it. One Southerner thought that Graham's cosmology was simply not credible in the modern world. "I don't really expect an answer to these questions," the author sniffed, "since you . . . can simply sidestep unanswerable questions by consigning them to file thirteen." Scoffers could not imagine how Graham could, with a straight face, ignore the kind of critique Charles Templeton had leveled against him in the 1940s.

The final group of critics was the most telling for what they said about the breadth, variety, and intensity of feelings among broadly evangelical Christians. Neither fundamentalist nor liberal, these folks found fault with how Graham read—or more precisely, misread—the Bible. The problem was not that he failed to take it literally enough, as fundamentalists would have it, or that he took it too literally, as liberals would, but rather that he *twisted* the plain meaning of Scripture to suit his purposes.

Most letters along this line were larded with a dense array of proof texts from the Bible. Typical was that of a premillennialist who challenged Graham's rendering of the fiery furnace story in the book of Daniel. "I'll be waiting for your answer," he signed off, then added, ominously: "Note: For Mr. Graham's Personal Answer Not His Counselors Please!!!"

Two men from the Northwest challenged Graham's preaching about the Trinity for the same reason: he distorted the Bible's plain meaning. "Is the word Trinity in the Bible?" they demanded. "We sincerely pray that you might see the light." A Midwestern man felt that Graham played fast and loose with the Bible when he talked too compassionately about suicide. "To tell the truth," the writer shot back, "your answer is not correct according to the Word of God."

If Graham was guilty of a misreading of the Bible, he was also guilty of miscounting. According to one earnest soul, living in the South, Graham said Jesus used the word "hell" seventy-five times, but that was not right. Jesus used it only sixteen times. "Your teaching on hell is repulsive to one who knows the facts of God's word." Still, there were no hard feelings. "May God bless you!" the writer concluded.

For some, Graham's fault lay not in a twisted reading of the Bible but in something deeper. A bad attitude, ignorance born of pride. Another Southerner assured Graham that he read Graham's columns every day, hoping to see evidence that he would acknowledge his limitations. But he never did. "Why do you write so expertly on subjects you know little about?" Lest there be any doubt, the writer grimly added: "Never more sincere in my life." One woman wondered: "Are you vitally interested in preserving life on this Planet? Or are you more interested in preserving Billy Graham's prestige?"

Other correspondents felt Graham's missteps grew not so much from pride as from willful negligence. One of his earliest followers, writing sometime between 1948 and 1950, appreciated his work, especially the music, but then sharply challenged him: "Do you ever preach on our Lord's return? Or the Rapture? If not why not? . . . Think it over."

The perceived incompetence of Graham's staff took some of the heat off him. For a woman in the Northwest, Graham's statement that "There will be no 'perfection' until we get to heaven" brought grief. "I do not know whether you personally believe this or if the staff which works under you phrased it." The author, like so many others, felt enough of a personal connection to Graham to write him—but couldn't tell whether she would encounter Billy Graham the person or Billy Graham the institution. But she had to try.

Man in the Arena

How did Graham handle all this censure? Clearly he had the moxie and verbal ability to punch back. But he didn't. Across the years countless evangelists had interpreted opposition as persecution. They believed that persecution gave them license to retaliate, for they were defending God's interests, not their own. But again, Graham didn't. Why?[1]

Graham gave two reasons. The first and more obvious was that he just did not have time for it. If he tried to answer all his critics, he said, he would not have time for anything else. Besides, Graham shrewdly understood that if he responded to his judges, he would be letting them set his agenda.

And Christians were not supposed to fight; that was a second reason. Graham never deemed himself a pacifist, but he consistently showed more interest in persuading people to hear his message than in hitting back. He often tried to talk with his critics in person.

The story of Graham inviting a clever but acidic London journalist who went by the pen name of Cassandra to meet him has acquired mythic status in Graham lore. As historian William Martin tells the story, Cassandra chose a pub ironically called the Baptist's Head. As far as we know, the journalist never came around to Graham's style of evangelical Christianity, but he did come away from the meeting with a different view of the preacher. "I never thought that simplicity could cudgel a sinner so damned hard," he said later. "The bloke means everything he says."

Beyond those two reasons—practical and theological—stood two more. First, face-to-face combat of any sort was just not his style. He hardly ever engaged critics in a point-by-point debate about theology or politics or anything else. "I have really never been a fighter at heart," he once remarked, perhaps revealing more about himself than he realized.

With rare exceptions—and those were early on, when he was in foreign countries—he tried not to criticize any aspect of a culture, including the religion. His message was a positive proclamation of the Christian faith and the benefits of personal and social peace it provided.

Graham's weightiest critic was undoubtedly Reinhold Niebuhr. We have seen how he handled Niebuhr's attack. Rather than firing back, Graham offered him an olive branch, first with an unsuccessful handshake and then with irenic words: "When Dr. Niebuhr makes his criticisms about me, I study them for I have respect for them. I think he has helped me to apply Christianity to the social problems we face."

These words may have been strategic, but they were also sincere. After his Northwestern Schools days in the late 1940s and early 1950s, he began to pull away from the hard hitters on his right. He led more moderate believers like himself to a more open-minded attitude toward other traditions and toward the surrounding culture. Working ecumenically with fundamentalists, Graham found, was pretty much a lost cause, but working ecumenically with mainline Protestants was not. Religious rivals did not create Graham's irenic attitude so much as uncovered it.

In an essay bearing the revealing title "What Ten Years Have Taught Me," published in the *Christian Century* in 1960, Graham would say: "In groups which in my ignorant piousness I formerly 'frowned upon' I have found men so dedicated to Christ and so in love with the truth that I have felt unworthy to be in their presence . . . although Christians do not always agree . . . what is most needed in the church today is for us to show an unbelieving world that we love one another."

That willingness was mutual. A surprising number of mainline Protestants proved open to labor with Graham and Graham-style evangelicals in the larger cause of the moral reform of society. Indeed, a surprising number proved open to soft-sell and sometimes even hard-sell evangelism. The theological liberalism that effectively defined the mainline in the final decades of the century was still molten enough in the middle decades that Graham could find plenty of friends—or at least cobelligerents.

But the most important reason Graham chose not to fight may have been one that he simply sensed without formally stating. He discerned that refusing to respond elevated him in the public's esteem. He looked good when he entered the ring of public conversation, took a few blows, and then walked away as if it didn't hurt. It did hurt, of course, but it also turned criticism into public relations gold.

Wounded Souls

Who were Graham's followers? What can we say about those who trekked across town to hear him speak in a crusade? Or listened to him on the radio, or watched him on television, or read his words in his magazine and newspaper columns? Who were the earnest givers who sent a few dollars each month to Minneapolis?

The answer breaks into two large categories: the demographic and the spiritual. The demographic includes features such as age, class, race, gender, and region. Sociologists of religion have looked into the demographics and come up with a fairly consistent profile. Later on we will briefly scan it and try to see what it was and how it changed (and did not change) over the years.

At this point, however, I wish to focus on the other category, the spiritual. What were the inner needs and the inner joys that attracted millions of Americans and others around the world to share their lives with Graham? Many were wounded, and they came to him for answers. Many others were joyful, and they wanted to share their thankfulness with him.

One of the best ways to view both groups—the wounded and the joyful—is to look at the letters that folks sent Graham. The BGEA did not keep track of the numbers, but between 1950 and 2005 millions poured in. A small but systematic sampling of this rich resource shines a bright light on the inner spiritual lives of Graham's followers.[1]

In this Scene we will try to understand the first group, the wounded, what those wounds were, and how they thought Graham might help. In the following Scene we will turn to the second group, the joyful, and how they thought the encounter with Graham had brought new or renewed peace to their lives.

* * *

People were brutally candid about the ordeals they had brought on themselves. A dominant theme was addictions, especially to alcohol and drugs. A man from the Chesapeake Bay region, who had gone four weeks without a cocaine hit, wrote that he had been on the verge of a relapse. Reading Graham's newsletter had saved his life. "I know I've got a long way to go but I'm going to make it." He signed the missive—significantly—"A lost soul back on track."

No one—literally *no one*—spoke of addictions as diseases, let alone as habits of the flesh beyond their control. But that did not diminish the overwhelming sense that addictions were powerful demons, forces that not only controlled the authors' lives but also landed them in danger of damnation.

Senders worried too about smoking and swearing. They knew that smoking harmed the body—the temple of the Holy Ghost—which of course placed them way ahead of most Americans at that time.

But of the two addictions, swearing seemed to create greater guilt, perhaps because believers saw it as a more significant spiritual problem. In the language of one Southern woman, "I do not say curse words out loud but they cross my mind and I try very hard to keep from doing this but it just happens." Both vulgarity—barnyard language—and profanity—taking the Lord's name in vain—proved that the tongue was enslaved by a practice God abhorred.

The self-inflicted actions for which people especially condemned themselves were abortion and masturbation. The epistles uniformly spoke of abortion as the snuffing out of an innocent life. One Southwestern woman spoke for many. "I hope God can forgive me." No one portrayed abortion as the lesser of two evils. All writers regretted it and, more ominously, feared that God would condemn them.

Masturbation was a frequent topic, too. "I hate masturbating almost every night but I can't help it," wrote a Canadian woman. "It's stupid [to ask God for forgiveness] when you know you are just going to do it again." A few saw masturbation as the natural expression of a God-given sexual drive, implying that the practice was an acceptable alternative to unsanctioned sex. But most framed it as a sin and sought both forgiveness and some means for conquering the vice.

Sex drives fueled many of the sins people confessed to Graham. Topping the list was illicit sex—both pre- and extramarital—as well as lust and homosexuality. Fornicators regretted both past lapses and ongoing ones. A few, not surprisingly, wondered if it was all that wrong for singles if they planned to marry. Letters about the real or suspected sexual treachery of a spouse turned up especially often. When the husband of a woman from the Northwest left for a younger woman, she wrote, her "world fell apart." The story was almost typical: straying husband, younger woman, often a coworker, and devastating consequences for the spouse at home.

Any form of sex outside marriage raised troubling questions. Wrote one woman from the Chesapeake Bay area: "My husband left me and then died and then a good Christian man moved in with me and we are living on my husband's pension. Does God understand?" The writer needed a nod from Graham to put her mind at ease.

Some placed lust for the opposite sex in the crosshairs. A seaman, tormented with desire for the daughter of missionaries, saw no hope for himself. "It seems as though I have an 'incurable disease' in me that must be cured," he told Graham. The letter contained no hint that the seaman hoped that Graham would excuse him. He just needed to tell someone, as though Graham were an evangelical priest in a confessional booth.

Homosexuality was more complicated. No one drew a distinction between inclinations and practices. Both were bad, not only in God's eyes but also in the eyes of nature itself. One writer, a lesbian, told Graham that her life was "in shambles." She had attempted suicide many times. At the end of the letter, she scrawled, in big capital letters: "PLEASE SOME ONE HELP ME! NOW!"

Not a few hoped not only for forgiveness but also for the power to resist temptation down the road. After reading Graham's book *The Four Horsemen*, a man from the Northeast surrendered himself and his sexuality to Christ. "I no longer see myself as 'gay,'" he wrote, "but as a dear child of God forgiven." As with most letter writers, the rest of his story we do not know.

No one claimed to have been delivered from same-sex desires, yet a tiny few did not see them as sinful. One author spoke of her conviction that her condition was absolutely natural. She and her partner had been active in their church for many years. They lived together and had "relations" with each other. "I cannot feel that I will be doomed to eternal suffering because of . . . something I honestly believe is congenital with me."

Letters spoke poignantly of guilt. Many felt it for failing "to witness," as evangelicals put it, to their faith on the job. One Midwestern woman struggled over her inability to win an atheist coworker to Christ. "I feel like I have failed God. Any advice?"

One senses a special poignancy in the guilt of the failed parent. "I am heavy laden for something I did in my earlier years," a Northeastern man confessed. "[I] have tried to rectify, a situation which I feel is my fault for failing to bring my children up as Christians and have Jesus in their lives." These opportunities seemed forever lost.

The wrongs that writers had inflicted on themselves marched alongside the wrongs that *other* people had inflicted on them. Abusive fathers ranked high. Night after night, recalled one Midwestern woman, she and her sister and mother would "sneak out of house when dad came home in middle of night drunk and chase after us with a rifle." Others spoke of jobs lost, crimes committed, and family members in prison because of alcohol.

More often than not, fathers posed the problem, but mothers were not exempt, less for imbibing themselves than for tolerating it in their family. "My whole life is in a mess," said one woman from the South. "My son died . . . in a car accident. He was drunk just 18 years old. . . . Its all my fault." This mother's anguish was not unique.

Letters named additional sources of pain coming from the outside. One nurse had to put up with smutty stories from coworkers. The fear of debt loomed large, too. Partisans saw declaring bankruptcy as unethical at best, sinful at worst. For people of this middle- or lower-middle-class social stratum, seeking a legal loophole for debt was simply not in the cards.

The sorry behavior of other church members accounted for many missives. Other church members showed that they were no better than most folks, gossiping, backbiting, telling lies, running around with "loose women." One Southern correspondent nailed the problem dead-on. "What do you think of people in the church who lie, slander, gossip and talk about Jesus Christ, all at the same time and call themselves Christians?" Stained glass shards cut deep.

Fragmented homes inflicted hurt, too. A few writers saw themselves as at least partly to blame. But for most, the problem stemmed from other people, usually a straying spouse or adult children gone off the rails. Several asked for prayers for children in prison.

Most surprising, perhaps, was the number of letters that spoke of molestation. Sometimes the victims described those events taking place in the distant past but festering in present memory. More often, however, letters spoke of the vice in the present tense. One mother—no name, no date, no place—explained that her daughter, age twelve, had been molested by her father ever since she was five. "I would appreciate your prayers to help her."

And yet even here appearances could be deceiving. One wife admitted that her husband had molested their daughter, but he did it, she said, because he was possessed by a demon. Since then, the demon had been cast out, yet the court remained skeptical. She wanted him home again.

And then there were the more or less routine injuries to body and soul that came simply by living. The list ranged from cancer, with a prognosis of weeks to live, to the chronic aches and pains of old age, to dark clouds of loneliness. Graham once said that, with one exception (which he did not name), people wrote him about loneliness more often than anything else. The elderly especially talked about going for long stretches without their children visiting or calling or writing, or of any friend stopping by.

Closely related to loneliness were grief and depression. Heartache for a departed spouse cropped up from beginning to end. Typical was a note from a Southern woman. "Missing my husband of thirteen years," she told Graham. "I am seventy now and live alone. . . . The nights are the worst." Many others struggled with acute melancholy, a loss of desire to live. A Southern woman boiled it down as forcefully as words permitted: "How may I build my faith so that I may more ably combat this hell?"

Letters spoke surprisingly often about suicide. A middle-aged son had taken his life long ago, wrote a grieving Plains State parent. "We ask your prayers for his soul and request any materials you might have that might help us through this pain."

Equally dark was fear for themselves. "Life means nothing to me," grieved a man in the Upper Midwest. "I found my wife was having an affair." Aiming to end his misery, he picked up his "special military weapon." But then for some reason he turned on the radio. Graham's message helped him through. "THANK YOU! THANK YOU! THANK YOU!"

Perhaps most surprising of all was the disquiet fostered by the "blessed hope of Christ's return." This phrase referred to a notion held by millions of evangelicals that Christ would "rapture" his saints back to heaven before the cataclysmic events at the end of time.

The "blessed hope" sometimes shattered on the anvil of a mother's love. One listed her fourteen children by name and then invoked the Lord's protection for each of them, both in this life and in the life to come. Another mother agonized about the possibility that one of her six children might not make the rapture. One Midwestern woman wondered, "How . . . can I have a real heaven, knowing that even one of them is cut off from the love of God?"

Running through many of these letters, which detailed pilgrimages of sorrow, was an element of confession. The writers often said Graham was the only one they could tell. They felt he knew them, even when he didn't.

Grateful Friends

A second broad group of letter-writers detailed the good things that life, and especially the Christian life, had brought their way. A few talked about ordinary joys, such as the gift of a loving husband or responsible teenagers or even the comforts of a nice home. But these were rare. Most writers focused on something else: their conversion to Christ. And for most of them Graham was the messenger. They wanted him to know, and to thank him.

Contrary to the conventional narrative offered by the BGEA, most people who came to Christ under Graham's ministry described their path as one of renewal, not a sudden turn from nonbelief to belief. A Northeastern woman exemplified the pattern. "I was once close to the Lord but my life turned into a mess. . . . I saw your program and I started to feel close to the Lord again."

As these stories usually ran, the writers had been reared in a Christian home, embraced Christ as a teenager—very often at a church youth camp—and then went off to the service or to college. On discharge or graduation they married and settled down. But then life happened. They stopped going to church. When Graham came to town or preached over the radio or on television, they remembered the Christian life they had once lived and the joy it brought. Now it was time to make things right.

Though renewal stories of this sort predominated, narratives of about-face conversions were not rare either. Many were remarkably specific about the time and place the conversion happened. Writers often detailed the bad habits they had left behind and the soaring sense of freedom they now felt.

One researcher asked converts what differences they saw in their lives after finding Christ at a Graham meeting. A woman in the Northwest found the question easy to answer. "My life was completely changed. Things that I thought were so important lost their meaning, new things took their place." A Southern woman remembered "growing up in a home with an alcoholic daddy and a hysterical, manipulating mother. . . . There was always, always confusion." Those three words—"always, always confusion"—told the story for her and many others.

Yet both kinds of narratives—renewed faith and new faith—bore similarities in how they described the process before, during and after their pilgrimages. The state of mind and heart that most often set the stage for going to a meeting, or tuning in Graham on the radio or television, is also the most difficult to describe.

Converts—inquirers—used similar words over and over again. "Hopelessness," "despair," "futility," "pointlessness." A Midwestern man put it as concisely as any. "I can still remember the turmoil I suffered, the emptiness inside. . . . After giving my life to Jesus two years ago, I received the help you preach about; forgiveness, peace, love, meaning for existence."

Writers typically pointed to one or more specific triggers in the background—being fired, losing a parent, hitting rock bottom with alcohol—but at the end of the day most came to the same thing. People found themselves backed into a corner, and they did not know how to find their way out again.

Figuring out why inquirers went to a meeting is one thing, but knowing why they would leave their seats in the great stadiums, descend steep flights of stairs, make the long trek across the playing field bow their heads, and then sign a decision card is quite another.

Converts gave a variety of reasons. A few said, without evident embarrassment, that they had no specific reason, just felt like doing it. Some admitted that they wanted to get a closer look at Graham. One said he hoped it might get him into the choir. Some admitted to group pressure; they did not want to stand out by sitting back when their friends were going. Some wanted to show Graham they appreciated him for coming. Others respected his authority born of long experience in the spiritual trenches.

Thoughts about the life to come played a role too. Fear of hell cropped up surprisingly often in the letters. One inquirer at the 1963 Chicago crusade spoke for many others. "Really [I don't] know [why]. Just didn't want to die and go to worse place than this." Surprisingly few identified the flip side, the assurance of going to heaven.

Many said they were motivated by the music, which took them back to times gone by when they had walked more closely with the Lord. When counselors asked inquirers what prompted them to go forward on the night they made their decision for Christ, they repeatedly named specific songs, especially "How Great Thou Art," "Just as I Am," and "This Is My Story."

The events that unfolded during, or at the time of, the conversion were described in many ways as well. Letter-writers alluded to warm feelings pulsing through their bodies. A Catholic convert in a Northeastern city put it this way: "I feel the great love that God has for me and it makes me feel so warm inside." Writers often mentioned healing of their spirits, though never a miraculous event, as Pentecostals commonly did in their meetings.

For some the entire service and especially the invitation and response period seemed like another time zone—a time out of time. "I have made every service, wish [it] could go on forever," said one. In a way time did stand still, for the writer gave no name, no place, no date; his "letter" was just a scrap of paper mailed in.

The feelings that followed the conversion ran from nothing to everything. At one extreme were those who said nothing changed at all. When asked if any significant transformations had come into his life after he made his decision for Christ, one inquirer—who was far from unique—responded: "Can't say there has. Same person since as was before. . . . I go to church but really don't get anything out of it."

But some said that everything had changed. They never or virtually never meant acquiring commodities like a new car. Few prosperity preachers prowled the revival circuit in those days, and the handful that did—usually billed as deliverance evangelists—had little influence among Graham's people.

For some writers, in fact, conversion under Graham's ministry seemed to produce the opposite results. After giving his life to Christ, a man in the Southwest wrote that he had lost everything, including his wife, children, and business. All that he had left was "God and a few friends." Even so, through it all, he had "gained strength in the Lord," and for that he was grateful.

For some the import of the conversion experience was simply a better life. A factory worker could not pinpoint the motivation for giving his life to Christ— "Don't know what the heck it was—I really don't"—but whatever the cause, the result was solid: less temper, better personal relationships, and better understanding of the Bible. For other inquirers, the results were eminently practical. "I began wood-carving and selling what I made," one attested.

We might reasonably guess that Graham was happy with reports of practical results like this but that he also hoped for something more. And he surely finished reading any given batch with a smile.

Many talked about the restoration of broken relationships, separated spouses coming home again, or wayward adult children finally gaining a grip on their lives. One retiree put it as simply and plainly as the language permitted: "got good home now." A New England Catholic, who judged Graham on a par with Saint Teresa and other saints, said that during the lowest point of his life *Hour of Decision* had started his "journey back to God."

For others, the best results still lay ahead. A Southwestern husband wrote that his wife was blind, yet she saw in the way that most counted. Most people shunned her or even pretended that she did not exist, he grieved. "But your message on spiritual blindness was even more meaningful. . . . I promise you we will meet you in Heaven." One senses that some authors just could not find the words they needed. At the end of the broadcast, a Midwestern woman rhapsodized: "I wept but I do not know why."

The letters leave no doubt that for many writers hopelessness became hope, and despair, confidence. Yet here again we must be careful. A Southern woman wrote that she had been molested as a child, divorced four times, and now suffered from depression. The woman did not say that under Graham's ministry she had found Christ and peace. Rather, she simply asked Graham to pray for her and her family. What Graham offered was less a message to be believed than a pastor to be trusted.

These considerations bring us, finally, to letters of outright praise. For a few writers, the person they mainly wanted to praise was not Graham but his wife, Ruth. "Does Mrs. Graham correspond with anyone?" asked a woman in the Northwest. "I would like to write her to tell her how much I love her and admire her for being such a wonderful Lady."

But of course, the main attraction was Billy. No one used the word "charismatic," but that is what they saw in him. For many people Graham's charisma began not with some ethereal spiritual gift but with good looks.

For a female teenager in New England, just hearing him on the radio was enough for her to know that he was "very handsome and charming." Besides that, he embodied "all the fine qualities" she wanted her own father to have. That attitude was "immature," she admitted. Still, "every young person needs a hero to look up to."

Only a tiny sliver of the millions who encountered him in crusades or over media had ever actually met him in person, yet a remarkable number of the letters were crafted as if they had. A seaman allowed, in a four-page, very carefully handwritten letter, that Graham probably would not remember him, but he was the "bold one" who stuck his hand through a limo window and introduced himself. After all, the sailor said, "I feel as though you are one of my closest friends."

Though most addressed Graham as "Reverend" or "Doctor," a surprising number started out with a simple "Dear Billy." They rehearsed the most mundane details of their lives, unfolding stories about their kids, or they invited him to drop by their houses for lunch or just coffee and dessert the next time he was in town.

And then some letters of appreciation—affection—can only be called sweet. One elderly woman wrote: "Dear Bro and Sister Graham, I am writing you a line or two to let you know I am still here. But not feeling very well today. . . . So I will write you and tell you I love you both very much."

Gentle quips abounded. A salesman said that his job was very much like Graham's, except that Graham sold "higher quality" merchandise. The writer then added—"I've followed your TV ministry and read your newspaper column for many years; not passionately mind you, but more or less on a casual basis." We can almost see the twinkle in the eye.

And some told Graham stories that almost certainly were spoofs. One woman explained that just before Christmas her husband had left her and their three children; her rent was three months overdue; her car had broken down four times in the past month; she had to walk three miles each way to work; her gas heating bill was three months late; her father had abandoned her mother, who was in a nursing home; and she was four months pregnant. "And you think you have problems?"

Many letters showed concern for Graham's personal welfare. Somehow people learned about his spider bite, his hurt toe, the trouble with his eyes. In every case they promised to keep him in their prayers. Many thought he needed to take better care of himself. Rest more. "You and Ruth need some time to just walk along the beach and smell the ocean."

Authors compared their own lives with his, identifying themselves with him at a deep level. As one woman put it, she too had "5 children . . . and 15 grands plus 2 with the Lord and 10 greats." The details did not quite match up, but the main point held. Like so many others, she saw in Graham not only a confessor but also someone who could empathize with their joys and victories. Somehow he managed to convince millions of people that he wanted to know about the good things too.

PART 3

Priestly Prophet

Cross and Crucifix

Two tightly entwined stories defined Graham's public influence in 1960, one of the most momentous years of his entire career. The first involved his relationship with Roman Catholics, the second his relationship with the presidential election. In real life the narratives were inseparable, but it is easier to track his career if we take them one at a time.

Graham's connection with Catholics was both complicated and controversial. However we tell it, we need to begin with the backstory, the links that were forged during the previous decade. The short of it is that from at least 1950, Graham had managed good, working relationships with Catholics. The fundamental source of that amicability was his temperament. Deep down he wanted to build bridges, not dig ditches.

Moreover, Graham grew up in North Carolina, which had the fewest number of Catholics per capita of any state. The absence of Protestant interaction with Catholics could have fostered stereotypes about Catholics, unhindered by the reality check of personal interaction. But for many Southerners, the process worked in the opposite direction. Catholics were just rare enough to seem like an exotic plant: interesting but not a threat. Graham never said this, but historians of Southern religion, such as Andrew Stern, have found plenty of Southerners who did.

We remember that as early as January 1950 Graham fashioned good relations with Archbishop (later Cardinal) Richard Cushing in Boston. In light of four centuries of bitter and sometimes lethal hostility between Protestants and Catholics, it would be difficult to exaggerate the importance of this warm and highly unusual tie. Soon enough Graham's fundamentalist critics would assail him for consorting with "papists."

Graham's openness to Catholics ran deeper than this, however. Unlike most evangelicals, he insisted that Catholicism enjoyed a perfect right to flourish as a *religion* on the wide open religious landscape. He even fudged that line when he promised President Harry Truman that he would not oppose Truman's announced intention to send General Mark Clark as an ambassador to the Vatican, which was technically a sovereign nation. As it happened, Congress thwarted that appointment, which was not filled until President Ronald Reagan filled it in 1984. The delay signaled residual power of cultural Protestant fear of Catholics. It also signaled just how unusual Graham's openness was.

But there were limits, including for Graham. Like virtually all evangelicals and most non-Catholic Americans, Graham was deeply skeptical of a Catholic in the White House. He—and they—saw that arrangement as altogether different from Catholics exercising their constitutional right simply to worship. What if a conflict of interest between the Vatican and the United States should arise? Whose side would a loyal Catholic president take? And wouldn't Catholics vote as a solid and powerful religious bloc? This concern came to a head in the presidential election of 1960, which pitted the Protestant Nixon against the Catholic Kennedy.

In August of that year, about twenty-five evangelical leaders joined Graham at a chateau in Montreux, Switzerland. The lineup included heavyweights such as Carl F. H. Henry, the movement's house intellectual; Harold John Ockenga, a pugnacious foe of Catholicism; L. Nelson Bell, another pugnacious foe of Catholicism; and Norman Vincent Peale, pastor of the influential Marble Collegiate Church in central Manhattan and author of one of the best-selling religious books in American history, *The Power of Positive Thinking*. Peale was more a fellow traveler than a card-carrying evangelical, but in this setting he seemed to fit right in.

At this distance the initial purpose of the meeting is not entirely clear. Was it to discuss strategies for evangelizing Europe? Or for blocking the election of the Catholic Kennedy? Or both at once? Though the evidence is scarce and inconsistent, no one denied that thwarting Kennedy soon became the overriding aim.

The group agreed to meet again in early September at the Mayflower Hotel, the site of the first National Prayer Breakfast, in Washington, DC. At the Mayflower they joined another anti-Catholic troupe, Citizens for Religious Freedom, which had connections with the National Association of Evangelicals. And this time the purpose was absolutely clear: stop Kennedy.

The Mayflower gathering included about 150 partisans representing thirty-seven denominations but excluded visitors and journalists. (Two reporters slipped in anyway.) Graham himself did not join the group, as he was vacationing in Europe with Ruth. But he clearly had a hand—

likely the primary one—in planning the event and encouraging Peale to participate.

The fearful band discussed a document, drawn up earlier, that detailed the peril of a Catholic in the White House. The text did not explicitly endorse Nixon, and it affirmed Catholics' right to worship freely. But it also stressed the danger that Catholics posed for American democracy because they (purportedly) refused to separate church and state. Though Ockenga was the principal architect of the document, Peale was better known, so the group commissioned Peale to take main responsibility for releasing a statement to a hungry press corps outside.

Peale walked into one of the most agonizing ordeals of his life. Though he later insisted that the Mayflower discussion pertained solely to the political threat that Catholics posed, the press and many Americans heard it as a blanket condemnation of all things Catholic. The result was outrage toward the cabal and especially their hired gun, Peale. Wounded, Peale apologized, tried to explain himself, offered (unsuccessfully) to resign his pulpit, and tumbled into a period of depression. "I was not duped," he later lamented. "I was just stupid."

Graham did not come to Peale's defense. Peale himself never publicly said that Graham had deserted him. Yet many wondered why Graham did not wade in, given his views on the risk of a Catholic in the White House, and given his long-standing comradeship with Peale.

Even so, Graham's behavior surely fit a pattern. First off, he feared being tarnished as a bigot. Moreover, some of his advisers had urged him to stay out of the fray lest he imperil his chances for crusades in Catholic countries. And open confrontation was never his style.

The story bristled with ironies. Both men claimed to value Catholics in American life, but both also feared them in the Oval Office and other high posts. Both had prospered mightily in their careers, and both spoke from positions of power. And both knew what it was like to be pummeled in the public forum. ("I find the Apostle Paul appealing and the Apostle Peale appalling"—a line attributed to various people—surely stung.)[1]

And so it was that the relationship between Graham and Peale hit choppy waters. On one hand, in 1965 Graham gave Peale a copy of his best seller *World Aflame*. He inscribed warm words on the fly leaf: "To Norman Vincent Peale . . . My Much Beloved Friend—How I Thank God for You and Your Ministry—And Your Friendship . . . Billy . . . Phil 1:6."[2]

On the other hand, both men later intimated that a measure of hard feelings remained. During the Watergate scandal Peale privately smacked

Graham in a letter, and smacked him hard, for being disloyal to their mutual close friend Nixon. And he defensively rehearsed the Washington fiasco—albeit without naming Graham—in his 1984 autobiography, *The True Joy of Positive Living*. Graham, for his part, gave Peale only a few fleeting lines in his own 1997 memoir, hastily apologizing for "inadvertently" encouraging Peale to attend the Mayflower Hotel meeting.

Viewed whole, the friendship between the two giants seemed real enough, yet vulnerable to the storms of controversy that arose when Protestants tried to dictate Catholics' proper role in public life.

Sharon High School Graduation

Within twenty years Graham would rank as one of the most influential preachers in the United States and other parts of the world. But hardly anyone saw that trajectory ahead when he graduated from high school in 1937 at age seventeen. He was both an average student and an average adolescent male with predictable interests in sports, fast cars, and young women. Even so, he was being shaped for a larger destiny by the strict disciplines of his (Scottish) Presbyterian Church, his mother's fundamentalist convictions, his own exuberant personality, and a life-defining conversion experience shortly before his sixteenth birthday.

Photo courtesy of Jean Graham Ford

Home from College

One semester at Bob Jones College, in Cleveland, Tennessee, led to five more at Florida Bible Institute near Tampa, Florida. This shot, taken in Graham's parents' backyard near Charlotte when he was about twenty, intimated a young man who would, for the rest of his life, remain at ease with the informal way of life of his native South.

Photo courtesy of Jean Graham Ford

Youth for Christ Meeting

Graham, age twenty-seven, preaching at a Youth for Christ "rally" in Grand Rapids, Michigan. This frequently reproduced photograph of his first citywide revival in September 1947 well illustrates the youthful Graham's electrifying style, reminiscent of Billy Sunday, his famed predecessor on the revival circuit. Graham soon left YFC to conduct meetings around the world under his own auspices.

Photo used by courtesy of Commercial Photo Company, Grand Rapids, Michigan. Reproduction courtesy of the Billy Graham Center Archives, Wheaton College

Boston Common

On Sunday afternoon, April 23, 1950, Graham held a one-day follow-up to the land-mark crusade that he had conducted in Boston in the first two weeks of January. In this spring meeting, he famously called for a national day of repentance to help fight communism, but he also—less famously—called for personal and political peace. Despite rain and cold, the event drew from forty to fifty thousand attenders, making it the largest assemblage Graham had yet preached for and the largest in the history of the Common.

Photo courtesy of Jean Graham Ford

Billy at Bat

Though Billy batted left-handed, for all other activities he was right-handed. The setting was the Youth for Christ Summer Camp at Mound, Minnesota, September 1950. As an adolescent, he had aspired to become a professional baseball player but eventually found that he lacked the requisite skills. Even so, for most of his active years, including days on the road, he maintained a rigorous regimen of daily exercise. Graham counted many professional athletes and coaches as close friends and ministry supporters.

Photo copyright 1950, Star Tribune. Reproduction courtesy of the Billy Graham Center Archives, Wheaton College

Outdoor Crusade Meeting

One of hundreds of outdoor services, many of them held in rain, snow, heat, or cold. Notable features in this unidentified but representative photo, probably from the mid-1950s, include the Christian and United States flags, the middle-class (or better) dress of the attenders, and the visible mix of races, ages, and genders. Song leader Cliff Barrows and pianist Tedd Smith were predictably on duty. Graham especially liked football stadiums because visitors could stand on the field as well as sit on the bleachers.

Photo courtesy of Jean Graham Ford

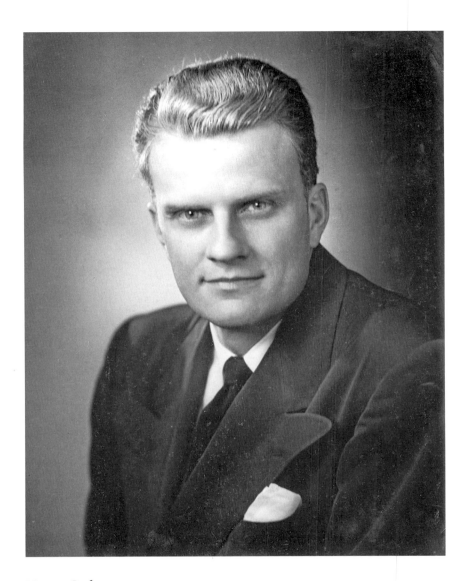

Mature Graham

Graham was strikingly handsome, and everyone—including the press, the BGEA, and Graham himself—knew it. With his square jaw, wavy hair, perennially trim physique, and million-dollar smile, he fit the conventional Hollywood image of the ideal (white) American male. No one claimed that successful proclamation required good looks, but no one doubted that good looks reduced resistance to the message.

Photo courtesy of Jean Graham Ford

Billy and Ruth Graham

Billy and Ruth Bell Graham were married nearly sixty-four years. The date and site of the photo are unknown, though it was probably taken in the early 1960s, when they would have been in their early forties. A snowbird, Graham was especially fond of vacationing on sunny beaches in Florida or California. Though a sedulous worker, he understood the *re*-creative power of time off.

Photo courtesy of Jean Graham Ford

Golf Enthusiast

Billy Graham's sports outings provided good ccpy for newspapers eager to sell copies by rounding out the preacher's image. The countless photographs of Graham on the golf links playing with rich friends, famous celebrities, and prominent politicians, including many US presidents, signaled his access to the pinnacle of cultural power. But in the 1990s he largely gave up the game because he did not like that image—and because it took too much time.

Photo courtesy of MOHAI, Seattle Post-Intelligencer collection, 1986.5.26631.2. Reproduction courtesy of the Billy Graham Center Archives, Wheaton College

Way, the Truth, and the Life

At Work

The date and site are not stated, but the event probably took place in the 1970s at the height of Graham's fame. The photo shows his classic preaching posture: ramrod straight, Bible firmly and prominently displayed, index finger thrust out like a cocked pistol. And classic attire: black suit, starched white collar, silver cuff links, and stylishly long hair. Though Graham suffered many critics, few underestimated the charismatic power of his platform presence.

Photo by Mike Maple

Alma Mater

Graham on the platform of Edman Chapel at Wheaton College in the late 1970s. He graduated from the college in 1943 and in the following six decades returned to speak at least forty-four times, including four commencement addresses. The college awarded him an honorary doctorate in 1957. The Billy Graham Evangelistic Association partly funded the 60,000-square-foot Billy Graham Center (and Museum) at Wheaton, completed in 1980.

Photo courtesy of Wheaton College Archives

Graham and Muhammad Ali

Graham and Muhammad Ali at Graham's mountaintop home, "Little Piney Cove," near Montreat, North Carolina, in September 1979. This was the first of (at least) two times the preacher and the prizefighter would visit casually. Afterward, Ali, who was Muslim, said that if he were Christian, he would like to be "a Christian like [Graham]," and Graham said, "Ali's primary beliefs are something we could all believe." Reportedly neither man tried to convert the other.

Photo by Bill Scott, gifted by Leighton Ford and John Sullivan

Preacher for Educators

Graham preaching for a Board of Trustees meeting at Gordon-Conwell Theological Seminary, late 1970s or early 1980s. He helped cofound the institution in 1969 by merging Conwell School of Theology in Philadelphia with Gordon Divinity School in Wenham, Massachusetts. Graham spoke at GCTS at least seventeen times, including multiple commencement addresses. The seminary awarded him an honorary doctorate in 1974.

Photo copyright Gordon-Conwell Theological Seminary and used by permission

Listener

Graham at the lectern in Kerr Chapel at Gordon-Conwell Theological Seminary in the late 1980s, when he chaired the seminary's Board of Trustees. The photograph—almost certainly spontaneous—reveals a side of Graham that the press often missed: his willingness not only to proclaim but also carefully to listen, especially in Christian and evangelical settings.

Photo copyright Gordon-Conwell Theological Seminary and used by permission

Graham at Ease

Graham at a family event at the home of his brother, Melvin Graham, in Charlotte, North Carolina, in 1998. Graham once quipped that he liked Montreat for the repose and Charlotte for the food. His culinary tastes were decidedly "down home," including cheeseburgers and lemon pound cake.

Photo courtesy of Jean Graham Ford

Graham and Leighton Ford

A Canadian (later US) citizen, Leighton Ford was ordained in the (Southern) Presbyterian Church in the United States. He served as an associate evangelist, and frequent main preacher, in BGEA radio and television programs from 1955 until 1986, when he left to form Leighton Ford Ministries. Ford was married to Graham's younger sister Jean Graham Ford. The photo was snapped at a party celebrating Graham's ninetieth birthday at Graham's home in 2008. A picture of Ruth Graham, taken some years earlier, graces the back wall.

Photo courtesy of Jean Graham Ford

Kennedy versus Nixon

The second strand twisting through Graham's life in 1960 was his curiously intense friendship with Nixon, which was already nearly a decade old. They had met in the US Senate dining room in 1952, when Nixon was still a callow senator from California.

The comradeship rested on two foundations. The first and insufficiently appreciated one was old-fashioned camaraderie. They would golf together more than one hundred times. And they both saw the advantages of cultivating the other, though Nixon probably saw it first. And Billy and Ruth Graham and Richard and Pat Nixon were all friends with each other.

Granted, the personal bond between Graham and Nixon defies easy explanation. The two men's personalities were very different. In one-on-one situations Nixon was reserved and awkward. In every situation Graham was outgoing and, in the words of journalists Nancy Gibbs and Michael Duffy, "all liquid charm." Still, the differences somehow proved more complementary than inhibiting.

The other foundation was a broad similarity of political orientations. Briefly put, both were center-right on the political spectrum. Though Graham remained, as noted, a lifelong registered Democrat, more often than not his inclinations ran moderately right of center. Or, in the memorable words of the journalist Murray Kempton, he "prayed Republican."

Deeper political similarities marked their relationship too. Both Graham and Nixon started out fiercely anti-Communist but gradually embraced more tempered views. Both believed in law and order. Propriety mattered. Moreover, Graham admired Nixon's intelligence and grasp of world affairs. He once compared Nixon with Winston Churchill. When Nixon and Kennedy challenged each other for the Oval Office, the wonder is not that Graham supported Nixon but that he did it with as much restraint as he did.

Here the twists and turns in the story grow obscure, but the broad outlines are clear enough. In August 1960 Graham privately told Kennedy that he would vote for Nixon. Nonetheless, Graham promised Kennedy that if he won the election Graham would wholeheartedly support him and try to unify the American people behind him. He also promised that he would not drag Kennedy's Roman Catholic religion into the campaign.

In one sense Graham kept his promise. He never said a word in public about Kennedy's Catholicism. And Graham urged Nixon not to do so either, lest it boomerang. More Catholic voters would turn out for Kennedy because he was Catholic, Graham reasoned, than Protestants would turn out for Nixon because he was Protestant.

Then another twist: Graham sent a letter to the two million people on his mailing list urging them to vote, knowing exactly how they would vote. He also privately told Nixon that if Nixon would associate with him in Graham's home state of North Carolina, it would affirm Nixon's religious identity as a Protestant. Graham was trying to have it both ways: publicly maintaining a nonpartisan stance but working behind the scenes, using religion as a tool, to get Nixon elected. In other words, he was doing exactly what he promised not to do.

As the presidential campaign of 1960 ground forward, Graham's admiration for Nixon continued to grow. In October he plunged in, head first. He wrote an article for *Life* magazine effectively endorsing Nixon on the grounds that he was simply better qualified. Hours before the article was scheduled to go to press, *Life*'s editor, Henry R. Luce, stepped in. Kennedy's father, Joseph Kennedy, had caught wind of the article and implored Luce to pull it. Then too Luce undoubtedly sensed that Graham would irreparably harm himself if he broke his own rule about remaining nonpartisan, at least in a manner so flagrantly partisan.

So Graham whipped up a substitute article simply urging folks to vote. Luce published the substitute. Graham was relieved, and so was Ruth. He later admitted that his ministry had been helped by the proverbial—or was it providential?—bell in the night. Graham thanked Luce for ringing it.

After the election Graham warmly congratulated the young president. He seemed truly to mean it, too. Both Graham and Kennedy were politicians in their own way. The president's politico father, still worried, immediately arranged a photo op for the two men. Four days before the inauguration, photographers captured them riding in Kennedy's white Lincoln convertible at the Seminole Golf Club in Palm Beach, Florida. Kennedy was driving, Graham riding shotgun, and both were cheerfully smiling at the camera as the car passed by.

Graham said that on the way to the clubhouse, Kennedy stopped the car and asked if he believed in the second coming of Christ. Kennedy said that his church did not preach about the subject very much. So Graham rehearsed his views on the topic. Finding Graham's notions "very interesting," Kennedy invited Graham to talk more about them someday.

No one explicitly detailed the purpose of the convertible outing, but they did not need to. Clearly the aim was twofold. It was first to assure Protestants in general, and evangelical Protestants in particular, that they had nothing to worry about with the first Catholic president.

This was a big deal. Anecdotal evidence abounds that many Americans, including Graham's supporters, believed that Soviet premier Nikita Khrushchev and Pope John XXIII had conspired to help the allegedly socialist-leaning Catholic Kennedy grab the reins of power. Yet Graham trusted him, and that carried weight.

The second aim was equally clear. Joyriding with Kennedy gave Graham legitimation he could use, especially among the nation's Catholics, by far the largest denomination. The glamorous young incoming president showed that he trusted Graham, and that too mattered.

When Kennedy took office, Graham's relationship with the president might be described as cordial but not close. According to a staffer, Kennedy said that Graham made him grit his teeth. According to Graham, Kennedy said he was the only clergyman he trusted. The stories were not necessarily incompatible.

Graham also told of the time the two men were golfing together before the inauguration. When Graham failed to hit the ball very far and ended up with a double bogey, Kennedy joked that he thought the preacher played better than that. "Well, sir," Graham said, "when I'm not playing with the President-elect, I usually do." After Kennedy had been in office a few months, Graham wrote Nixon, applauding Kennedy's talk of "sacrifice and dedication."

Kennedy was assassinated in Dallas, Texas, shortly after noon on Friday, November 22, 1963. The president had left Washington the day before, on Thursday, November 21, for political rallies in other Texas cities. In his 1997 memoir Graham said that Wednesday night, just before Kennedy departed the city, he nearly phoned the president to urge him not to go. Graham felt he had inexcusably resisted the Holy Spirit's bidding. He never explained why.

Enter LBJ

Next to Graham's closest associates in the ministry, Bev Shea and Cliff Barrows, President Lyndon B. Johnson—to millions, just LBJ—may well have been the closest friend he ever had.

Johnson had been baptized as a teenager at a revival meeting in a Christian Church (Disciples of Christ) in east Texas. One great-grandfather had been a well-known Baptist preacher in Texas. Lady Bird was Episcopal. LBJ often worshiped with her and sometimes moonlighted in other denominational churches, including Catholic ones. Like Graham, he was no stranger to Christian ecumenism.

Graham's memoir and correspondence with Johnson are revealing. They tell of skinny-dipping in the White House pool (with two other friends), repeated ventures on the links, joyriding in Johnson's convertible, praying on their knees by Johnson's bed in the president's White House bedroom, and talking about the Bible and the state of Johnson's soul as Johnson approached his end.

Little noticed but very important, too, was the close friendship between their wives, Lady Bird Johnson and Ruth Bell Graham. One unheralded event was more significant than it seemed at the time. When the president and first lady attended the closing service of Graham's 1965 Houston crusade—which had attracted nearly four hundred thousand attenders over ten nights—Graham introduced the couple as "dear personal friends." This occasion marked not only the first time a sitting president of the United States would visit a Graham meeting but also the first time a first couple would receive this kind of very public attention from the preacher.

The letters between Johnson and Graham when Johnson was president reveal a quality of friendship that defies any utilitarian explanation. Graham's letters observed the time-honored precedent of addressing the president of the United States as "Mr. President," yet Johnson addressed him as "Billy," and they routinely signed off as "Billy" and as "lbj."

Even more telling are the contents of Johnson's letters to Graham after he left the presidency. The former chief executive told Graham how much the friendship meant to him. "No one will ever fully know how you helped to lighten my load or how much warmth you brought into our house. . . . My mind went back to those lonely occasions at the White House: when your prayers and your friendship helped to sustain a President in an hour of trial." Graham felt the same. After Nixon came into office in 1968, he wrote Lyndon: "I hope you will always remember that there is one country Baptist preacher from North Carolina who loves you, appreciates you, and hopes to see you often."

In the winter of 1973, Johnson sensed that his end was near. He was no stranger to heart attacks. Like most people, Johnson feared death, but he evidently feared it more than most. Under the circumstances, it is not surprising that this notoriously profane, rough-hewn, philandering president would quiz Graham about how he could know for sure that he was saved and headed for heaven.

Johnson asked Graham to preach his funeral sermon. When Johnson's end came on January 22, 1973, at the untimely age of sixty-four, Graham delivered the funeral homily with simple eloquence and manifest emotion. Johnson had asked him to talk about "some of the things I tried to do." And so the preacher did.

Graham called LBJ "history in motion." "To him the Great Society was not a wild dream but a realistic hope. The thing nearest to his heart was to harness the wealth and knowledge of a mighty nation to assist the plight of the poor." Graham said it was LBJ's unwelcome fate to be confronted with a war he did not want.

The preacher concluded with the words Johnson had used for Kennedy when Kennedy was assassinated. "A great leader is dead. A great nation must move on. Yesterday is not ours to recover but tomorrow is ours to win or lose." Like Moses allowed to view but not enter the promised land, Johnson did not live quite long enough to witness the peace he earnestly desired.

At first glance the comradeship between Graham and Johnson was an odd one. In some respects, they showed dramatically different personalities. The president was, in Graham's discreetly oblique word, "rough." Nor was he above lying to the public if he felt it served a larger purpose. The preacher fit none of those categories. Yet the friendship flourished. Why?

Trying to divine the inside of any close friendship is risky, but we can make some informed guesses. Journalists Nancy Gibbs and Michael Duffy

astutely noted that Graham and Johnson actually bore significant similarities. Both were born and grew up in the rural/small-town South. Though
neither was bookish or highly educated, both rose to the very top of their
professions by virtue of ambition, hard work, and gritty determination.

The resemblances continued. Both manifested a relentless work ethic,
running huge organizations successfully, not least by placing their vocations ahead of their wives and children. And both were immensely persuasive. Johnson knew how to strong-arm colleagues into going along.
Graham achieved the same goals, not with strong-arm tactics but with a
ready handshake, an easy grin, and a prodigious memory for names. And
both loved golf.

The improbable but deep friendship between Graham and Johnson
grew from factors besides similarities in their backgrounds and personalities. They shared many political views. Graham claimed that he and
Johnson rarely talked about politics or military strategy, but given the
number of hours they spent together, that claim is hard to believe. We
know for example that Graham urged Johnson to choose Graham's good
friend Senator Hubert Humphrey for his vice-presidential running mate
in 1964.

More important, Graham and Johnson found themselves largely in
agreement on the three great social issues of the day: the need for massive
federal action to fight poverty, racial injustice, and Communist aggression. Each of those causes was a crusade. And each demanded meticulous
preparation, unprecedented levels of financing, and sustained commitment from all levels of government, most especially the federal level.

And all three struggles loomed large in both men's legacies. For Johnson, the poverty and civil rights crusades were positive—indeed, by most
measures, overwhelmingly so in intent if not fully so in execution. The
war crusade eventually toppled his presidency and irreparably tarnished
his memory.

Graham's legacy would mainly rest on his evangelistic efforts, not
his forays into politics. But when he did venture into politics before the
Nixon presidency, he usually did so in lockstep with his hard-driving fellow Southerner. His legacy would win approval for his participation in the
war on poverty, mixed approval for his contribution to the struggle for
civil rights, and disapproval for his role in the Vietnam War.

SCENE 30

Racial Justice

The late 1950s and the 1960s showed Graham moving forward on questions of racial justice, but they also showed him shuffling his feet along the way.

When a bomb exploded in a newly integrated public high school in the east Tennessee town of Clinton in October 1958, the columnist Drew Pearson launched a campaign to raise funds to rebuild the school. Pearson and Tennessee senator Estes Kefauver challenged Graham to join them.

In the face of strenuous opposition from the town's White Citizens Council, including death threats, Graham accepted their challenge. He not only came and held a meeting—part civic, part revival—but also served on the executive committee of Americans against Bombs of Bigotry.

In September of the following year, 1959, Graham held a crusade in Little Rock, Arkansas. Again, over the strenuous objections of the White Citizens Council as well as the Ku Klux Klan, he came on the condition that the meeting would be integrated. His pressure bore fruit, as the races sat together without incident.

A thirteen-year-old boy from the small town of Hope, Arkansas, saved up his weekly allowance to go with his Sunday school class to the Little Rock revival. Though Graham did not explicitly address race that night, the young Bill Clinton grasped the import of the setting: thousands of people of both races quietly sitting together in a public meeting for the first time in the state's history.

In 1960 Graham published one of the most influential articles of his career. The venue was *Reader's Digest*. This monthly boasted a circulation of twelve million, with a strong appeal to preponderantly white middle-class Americans. In the essay, Graham repeated the phrase, usually attributed to Martin Luther King but by then common currency, that eleven o'clock on Sunday morning was still the most segregated hour of the week.

Yet Graham's response to race in the late 1950s took some reverse steps, too. In July 1958 he asked Texas governor Price Daniel to offer a greeting at his crusade in San Antonio. There was nothing unusual about Graham inviting the governor of a state or mayor of a big city to drop by and say a few words. The problem was that Daniel had recently gone on record with a vigorous defense of segregation.

Many people held segregationist sentiments privately, but Daniel held them publicly. Moreover, he was scheduled to speak the evening before the state's Democratic primary election for governor. In Texas the primary election was effectively the same as the general election. This meant that Daniel seemed to carry Graham's partisan endorsement.

Local African American pastors were incensed. They asked King to try to persuade Graham to rescind the invitation. King tried but failed, and Daniel spoke as planned. Graham never explained his actions, except to say that everyone already knew his position on segregation.

Not helping matters in those years was Graham's decision to join Dallas's First Baptist Church, even though he rarely worshiped there. Indeed, he would remain a member for fifty-four years, from 1953 to 2008. He saw Dallas First Baptist as the "national" church of the Southern Baptist Convention.

But in 1954 the church's visible and prolific pastor, W. A. Criswell, publicly criticized the Supreme Court's *Brown v. Board of Education* decision prohibiting segregation in public schools. Criswell maintained this position until 1968, when he became president of the Southern Baptist Convention and repented of his declaration and retracted it. Throughout Criswell's segregationist phase, Graham repeatedly said that he differed with his close friend on this matter, but some wondered why he did not differ enough to pull out of the church.

In the fall of 1958 Graham seemed to step forward again. At his crusade in Charlotte in September, black counselors met with white inquirers. The next crusade was scheduled for October in Columbia, South Carolina, on the state capitol grounds. But South Carolina governor George B. Timmerman Jr. caught wind of what had taken place in Charlotte. He rescinded Graham's permit to use the grounds because he was a "well-known integrationist." The commanding general of nearby Fort Jackson offered the base to Graham. The sixty thousand attenders constituted the first integrated mass meeting in the state's history.

Then backward again in the spring and summer of 1963. His response to the march for racial justice that King led in Birmingham, Alabama, in April 1963 proved to be a literary as well as a political landmark. Immediately after the march, King was arrested for parading without a permit.

While he was in jail, he crafted his milestone "Letter from a Birmingham Jail." This seven-thousand-word manifesto targeted well-meaning white liberals more than openly racist conservatives.

Liberals, King said, called for gradual integration in order to let everyone get used to the idea. White conservatives, on the other hand played no games. They didn't like integration and openly said so. Yet liberals actually did more harm, precisely because they marched under the flag of friendly forces. They failed to see that justice delayed was justice denied.

Graham viewed King's tactics in general and his letter in particular as counterproductive. He thought they were likely to provoke generally supportive whites to dig in and fight back. He publicly urged King to "put the brakes on a little bit." Graham never retracted those words, and they lived to haunt him.

The March on Washington, where King delivered his memorable "I Have a Dream" speech, unfolded three months later, on Wednesday, August 28, 1963. A quarter million people showed up, packing the mall in front of the Lincoln Memorial.

But not Graham. He was holding a crusade in Los Angeles at the time. Since events of that size required a year or more of preparation on the ground, canceling was not realistic (although wedging in a couple of days away might have been possible). In any event, Graham hardly could have foreseen the magnitude of the meeting, or the power of King's speech, or the symbolic significance the meeting and the speech would acquire later on. And protocol would have required him to sit on the platform. One suspects that would have been too much for him and, for that matter, for King.

The plain truth is that Graham was never comfortable with the increasingly confrontational tactics King espoused, and King almost certainly found Graham's approach both timid and ineffective. Despite Graham's sunny claims to the contrary, the relationship between the two giants was always unsteady.

Shortly after the march Graham opined: "Only when Christ comes again will the little white children of Alabama walk hand in hand with the little black children." The comment was entirely consistent with Graham's evangelical theology, simultaneously expressing dismay about the intractability of human sin and hope about its ultimate resolution. But as with many of Graham's offhand remarks in those muscular midcareer years, it was simply the wrong thing to say at the time.

But with Graham and race nothing stayed fixed for long One month later, September 1963, four Ku Klux Klansmen bombed the African American Sixteenth Street Baptist Church in Birmingham, taking the lives of four young black women (one eleven and the others fourteen years old). Once again, over the strenuous protests of the White Citizens Council, including death threats, Graham agreed to hold a crusade in Birmingham on Sunday afternoon, March 20, 1964.

At the March service, Graham preached to the first fully integrated major meeting in Alabama's history. The choir, featured in a front-page photograph in the *New York Times*, was fully integrated too. Pictures show no signs of even self-segregation. A rarely noticed aspect of the Birmingham story is that local white-owned businesses that supported the integrated service were subjected to vandalism, and their owners threatened.

In short, in those years we see Graham feeling his way along the edges of a new world.

*   *   *

People close to Graham—friends he admired and family members he both admired and loved—complicated his journey. On one hand, he did not enjoy much support on the home front. Through 1966 Graham's father-in-law, L. Nelson Bell, explicitly opposed legally "coerced" integration, condemned civil disobedience, and resisted the civil rights movement in the pages of the *Southern Presbyterian Journal*.

As noted, Graham acknowledged Bell's strong influence on him, which was not surprising, given Bell's superior formal education and, unlike Graham, eagerness to go to the mat with theological foes.[1] Moreover, the two families lived only a few miles apart in Montreat for nearly a quarter century. The content of dinner table conversations is not known, but it seems reasonable to guess that when the two men "retired to the drawing room," the question of race came up. In the words of historian Anne Blue Wills, Bell was Graham's North Star, but not on everything.

Then too Carl F. H. Henry, a formidable influence in midcentury evangelical circles, certainly condemned racism. Yet he worried that most civil rights legislation would make things move too fast. Historians differ about the uniformity of other white evangelical leaders' views of race in those days, but there can be little doubt that on the whole they resisted integration more than they supported it.

On the other hand, countervailing forces tugged Graham in a different direction. Two of Graham's associate evangelists, Howard Jones and Canadian brother-in-law Leighton Ford, broadened his vision. They helped him see—and publicly acknowledge—that American racism was impeding his proclamation of the gospel, both at home and abroad.

Though it is impossible to know another person's mind and heart, Graham's evident struggle suggests that the pull of conscience played a role too. A. Larry Ross, Graham's long-term public relations agent, argued that "integrity (doing the right thing, beyond doing things right)" marked his life throughout.

Given Graham's roots, social location, instinctive conservatism, irenic temperament, and the conflicting pressures he experienced through the 1960s, we should not be surprised that finding a sure grip on race would elude him for another decade or more.

Civil Rights and Civil Order

When an assassin's bullet felled President John F. Kennedy on November 22, 1963, Vice President Lyndon B. Johnson took office, and the real 1960s began. The turmoil of that decade, which the violent change of presidents forever symbolized, shook the nation to its foundations. The turmoil involved more than race, but race impacted every part of it.

With considerable arm twisting, the new president pushed through a reluctant Congress the Voting Rights Act of 1964 and the Housing and Accommodations Act of 1965. Together, they came to be known simply as the Civil Rights Acts. Graham endorsed them. As we have seen, starting in Brooklyn in 1957, he publicly and repeatedly declared that such legislation was a necessary—though never sufficient—means for winning racial justice. He also repeatedly declared that whites too must obey the law of the land.

Even so, at the same time, Graham, like most white and some black evangelicals, began to call for more rigorous enforcement of laws against crime. Historian Aaron Griffith has shown that many of the sermons that Graham preached in those midcareer years mentioned crime, including at least two dozen at the Madison Square Garden meeting in 1957. Graham also urged public school teachers to read Bible passages in classrooms to combat teen delinquency. But the threats of the 1960s seemed to require more muscular measures.

In principle the campaign for "law and order" was color-blind, for it applied to white and black crime alike. But for many whites, street violence was the main problem, and blacks were the main perpetrators. "Congress should immediately drop all other legislation and devise new laws to deal with riots and violence such as we have witnessed in Los Angeles," Graham preached in August 1965, while the Watts riot was still in progress.

In Griffith's words, "The evangelist who had previously proclaimed personal conversion as the ideal response to crime had himself had a change of heart: laws were indeed necessary in order to address the widespread disorder that was rampant on America's streets."[1]

Granted, Graham was hardly alone. Soon enough, in the 1970s and 1980s progressive African American leaders such as Jesse Jackson were calling for tougher measures to deal with drugs and guns. But coming from a white preacher, who had long championed the power of individual conversion to change toxic social trends, it just sounded different. It made him sound as if he was part of the problem.

*   *   *

Despite Graham's (unverified) claim that King once asked Graham to call him Mike—a nickname reserved for King's close friends—the cracks in their fragile relationship grew deeper when King began targeting the Vietnam War in addition to racial injustice. Graham snapped that King's actions constituted "an affront to thousands of loyal Negro troops." Graham echoed others. King's speech drew condemnation from other civil rights leaders, parts of the black press, the *Washington Post*, and the *New York Times*, which called King's remarks "facile" and "slander."

Graham was holding a crusade in Australia when King was assassinated in April 1968. Graham said that the killing left him "almost in a state of shock." The organization sent telegrams and flowers. "Many people who have not agreed with Dr. King can admire him for his non-violent policies," he stated, "and in the eyes of the world he has become one of the greatest Americans." Five weeks later Graham was back in the United States, where he publicly described the murder as "one of the greatest tragedies in American history."

Though both King and Graham were acutely aware of the toxic results of social as well as personal sin, King emphasized the former, Graham the latter. Perhaps both men sported egos too large to accommodate the other one's. Perhaps both felt that the other one just missed too much of what the gospel called earnest Christians to do.

Then too King may have felt that Graham squandered his potential influence with presidents, while Graham may have known about grave failings in King's private life. However one evaluates these variables, many people dreamed about what might have been accomplished if the two titans had worked together.

*   *   *

No part of Graham's career has divided historians and journalists more sharply and more persistently than his record on race in the late 1960s and early 1970s. Was he a regressive or a progressive voice? Few have argued that he was as reluctant about integration as L. Nelson Bell, let alone as opposed to it as his longtime pastor in Dallas, W. A. Criswell. At the same time, few have argued that he was a forceful integrationist such as his associates Howard Jones and Leighton Ford.

Recently historian Darren Dochuk has argued that Graham's record on race should not be placed on a conservative-liberal continuum at all. For one thing, Dochuk notes, he grappled with race at the *local* level, working with pastors and businessmen face-to-face, one-on-one. In those relationships, Graham continued to insist racial reconciliation started with spiritual regeneration of individuals. Better results required better people.

But there was more to Graham's approach. It included a conviction that lasting reconciliation required commitment from civic leaders, especially the business community. This meant boosting employment opportunities and fair compensation for black workers. It also meant a strong dose of the Protestant work ethic for everyone, the victims and the perpetrators of injustice alike. And it included unstinting Christian charity for those unable to get back on their feet on their own.

Dochuk calls this package of convictions "an alternative brand of civil rights." He points to Graham's long crusade in Houston in November of 1965 as a good example. There, Graham enlisted the support of not only President and Lady Bird Johnson but also powerful black pastors in the city, such as N. C. Crain and E. V. Hill.[2]

Viewed as a whole, Graham's record on civil rights in those influential middle decades of his career revealed blind spots. Most obviously, notes historian Curtis Evans, he never explained why born-again people showed so little remorse about their racism. Nor did he address the plain fact that the South—the part of the nation that claimed the highest percentage of born-again Christians—was also the part of the nation that most stoutly resisted racial justice. Nor did he explain why he fulminated more about blacks who marched and sometimes looted in the streets than about whites who flouted civil rights laws by keeping their schools, businesses, restaurants, hotels, and neighborhoods segregated.

In these years Graham's record on race is perhaps best described as two steps forward, one step back. Or, in the words of Graham's biographer

William Martin, the preacher was "typically ahead of his own unit, but never at the head of the parade." Once again, we see him working both sides of the aisle, partly for practical reasons, partly because his instincts just ran that way, and partly because he saw the good, or what he perceived to be the good, in most of the players' points of view.

SCENE 32

Great Society

Two constants marked Graham's thinking about poverty and how Christians might help. The first was the conviction, which he held from beginning to end, that around the world and across the centuries people had mistreated each other for many reasons, but the fundamental one—the one that lay at the root of all the others—was the corrupt heart. And since the corrupt heart spewed the poison of greed, the only permanent solution was to attack the problem at its root, where it started, on the inside.

The second constant, also running from the beginning to the end, was that the message of God's redeeming love for humans must show itself in the reform of society. That meant not only compassion for the needy but also a willingness to roll up one's sleeves, open one's wallet, and try to do something about it.

Historian David P. King offers two incidents that nicely bookend the evolution of Graham's social reform views. In 1950, just after the founding of the evangelical humanitarian organization World Vision (for which he served as an early chair), Graham announced that he was canceling his order for a new Chevrolet in order to give that money to World Vision. By itself, this was not a big deal, but it was an important signal from a man so strongly identified with evangelistic preaching and individual decisions for Christ.

A half century later, just after the final major crusade of his career in 2005, the *New York Times*'s religion editor, Laurie Goodstein, asked Graham if he thought the "clash of civilizations" was the most grievous problem facing the modern world. Goodstein and her readers might have expected Graham to point to the rise of militant Islam, as his son Franklin Graham had done. But he did not. The senior Graham simply said that the main problem was "hunger and starvation and poverty."

*   *   *

Until the 1970s Graham's evangelical humanitarianism expressed itself more forcefully when he looked abroad than at home. This inclination proved especially visible when he saw the living conditions in the developing world. And he was more prone to think that structural solutions worked better overseas than at home. In 1950s trips to India and Africa, for example, the realities of destitution, particularly among children, turned an intellectual grasp of poverty into an emotional reality.

Graham's acute awareness of poverty, especially abroad, started early and ran late. One reason he supported World Vision from the outset grew from his conviction that the organization's methods worked: direct relief, no questions asked, especially to orphans in war-torn regions. Soon, Graham was providing both rhetorical and financial backing for other direct-relief ministries abroad, including the National Association of Evangelicals' World Relief Commission, Compassion International, the BGEA's own World Emergency Fund, and, later on, Samaritan's Purse.

Back home, in contrast, Graham seemed more worried about the dire results of American affluence and materialism. He excoriated Americans for their indifference to the world's suffering, noting that "substandard conditions" in Appalachia hardly compared to the level of abject poverty abroad.

This comment was a sword with two edges. One cut against grim conditions in other parts of the world—which called for American evangelicals' help. The other edge highlighted the comparative security of the most impoverished regions in the United States. Though Graham did not explicitly say so, of course, one might infer that evangelicals' help was better spent abroad.

*   *   *

By 1967, however, Graham counted himself a convert to Johnson's War on Poverty at home. He had reread his Bible and found more than one hundred passages calling believers to shoulder the burden of caring for the poor.

Graham publicly allied himself with the work of Sargent Shriver, head of the Office of Economic Opportunity. He accompanied Shriver on a tour of a federally funded irrigation project in Appalachia and later appeared with Shriver in a PBS documentary film, *Beyond These Hills*, designed to win support for the government's antipoverty measures. Graham spoke before Congress in favor of the program, making clear that it was not a giveaway but a critically needed measure to assist the working poor.

Even so, such gestures toward a structural response to poverty, especially at home in the United States, appeared inconsistently. His comments at the Billy Graham Day celebration of his career in Charlotte in 1971 (discussed later) were telling. In a public address there he boasted that his parents had survived the Great Depression by their scrappy determination to take care of themselves, come what may. They killed their own rats, he said, and they did it without government help. Though Graham later apologized for the line and never used it again, the damage was done. If people were confused about where Graham really stood, they had good reason.

Graham's critics attacked him for being not only inconsistent but also vague about the exact causes of social ills, and even more vague about the solutions. In a rare gesture of defiance, he fought back. He felt that the problems he targeted were too widespread to be reduced to the specifics of time and place and that, more to the point, the origin of the problem was universal. He also expressed irritation at mainline clergy who, he asserted, paraded as experts on political and economic problems they actually knew little about.

And yet, Graham was "a man still in process," as he later said of himself. His thinking about the mechanisms for solving social justice dilemmas was moving from a substantially compassion-oriented program, designed to provide immediate relief, to an awareness of the need for deeper reconstruction of the structures of societies.

*   *   *

In January 1974 the preacher affirmed most parts of the "Chicago Declaration of Evangelical Social Concern," issued two months earlier. This landmark document, crafted by young firebrands such as Jim Wallis, Richard Mouw, and Sharon Gallagher, called for economic justice, peacemaking, racial reconciliation, and gender equality.[1]

One of the most important steps in Graham's humanitarian evolution emerged in his comments to nearly 2,500 evangelical delegates from 150 countries at the International Congress on World Evangelization in Lausanne, Switzerland, in the summer of 1974. The BGEA had largely planned and funded the congress. There Graham heralded his support for social justice movements, including economic parity among nations.

By then, Graham was moving from a tight focus on the alleviation of the symptoms of poverty, disease, and hunger to addressing their causes. For example, in *Approaching Hoofbeats: The Four Horsemen of the Apocalypse*, published in 1983, and one of his best-selling books, Graham specified the looming specters of war, famine, death, and false religion as signs of the imminent coming of the Lord.

Even so, his solutions, as historian King notes, now lay not simply in personal conversion but in "structural readjustments" such as debt forgiveness to reduce the grinding disparities between rich and poor nations. He even encouraged Americans to see the necessity of a "simpler life style . . . for the sake of others."[2]

Three years later—in 1986—Graham would open the United States Senate with a prayer that ended with a pastoral word: "Give us a new passion for justice, a new zeal for peace, a commitment to compassion and integrity, and a new vision of what You desire of us and this Nation." Such words may have shown that he had not only heard those newer voices from the developing world but also had taken them to heart.

To the end, most of Graham's critics remained unpersuaded. They felt that he embedded his remarks about social justice in arcane speculations about the second coming of the Lord and in lurid descriptions of Armageddon ahead. By focusing attention on the world to come, Graham deflected constructive attention to solving the problems at hand, critics argued.

Graham heard the criticism but insisted that the *expectation* of the end times should inspire Christians to roll up their sleeves and put their faith to work, not only in conversion-oriented missions but also in social reform efforts here and now. Thoughtful Christians could do both.

*   *   *

As Graham grew older, and as he saw more and more of the world's problems firsthand, Americans' self-centeredness fell in the crosshairs too. "I think Vietnam has taught us," Graham told a Houston press conference in 1973, "that we are not all-powerful and that America is not the Kingdom of God. We can go into [other nations] with a lot more humility. We have a lot to be proud of in the past; we have a lot to be ashamed of in the past."

Looking back at himself in the 1950s from the perspective of 1980, he would admit that he "used to make the mistake of almost identifying the Kingdom of God with the American Way of Life." No longer. "I've come to see that other cultures have their own way of life that may be of just as great a value to them as our way of life [is] to us."

Graham's vision of the world's needs continued to deepen and widen as he grew older. In 1998 he suggested that Canada, "a peace-loving country," might be a model for Americans. It is "looked upon as a country that doesn't get involved in other people's affairs around the world. . . . We seem to have our people everywhere telling other people what to do."

Playing both sides of the aisle—or perhaps it is more accurate to say all sides of all aisles—came naturally. That strategy surely grew from multiple motivations: peacefulness, evasiveness, pragmatism, fairness, and conscience, all wrapped up in one. Some contemporaries had a hard time figuring out how someone so close to LBJ could also be so close to Ronald Reagan, both personally and in terms of their social and political outlooks.

"Many people saw Graham," historian Sarah Johnson Ruble observed, "but it also is true that he saw many people." Taking their multiple, diverse, and complex mental worlds to heart all at once was easy for Graham. All he had to do was look in the mirror.

Endless War

After race and poverty, the Vietnam War loomed large as the third social crisis that marked Graham's relationship with Johnson. For Graham's
generation, which came to maturity during World War II, patriotism was
measured by obedience to the government's call. And that call was unam-
biguous. Through the late 1960s, both President Johnson and President
Nixon (following in the steps of Presidents Truman, Eisenhower, and
Kennedy) forcefully insisted that the core problem in Southeast Asia was
Communist aggression: a vicious war of conquest by North Vietnamese
troops invading South Vietnam.

Johnson and Nixon were not alone. Most—certainly not all but most—
leading public figures, such as National Security Adviser McGeorge Bundy,
National Security Adviser (later Secretary of State) Henry Kissinger, and
Secretary of Defense Robert McNamara, embraced the "domino theory"
without reservation: if we do not stop Communist aggressors over there,
they reasoned, the invaders will not quit until they overrun the rest of the
world. Sooner or later, and probably sooner, they will overtake Hawaii,
and then the island nation of Cuba, right on America's doorstep, and then
they will win the allegiance of wavering nations such as India.

Graham agreed, but with a twist. He not only feared North Vietnamese
Communist aggression but also trusted President Johnson, just as he had
trusted Eisenhower before him and would trust Nixon after him. Which
motive was stronger is impossible to say, for they reinforced each other.

We have already explored Graham's thinking about Communism, but
his thinking about trusting presidents in general and Johnson in particular also merits a word. For one thing, Graham believed, presidents were
smart men. They would not be where they were if they were not. More
important, they were privy to diplomatic and geopolitical secrets most
people knew nothing about. But most important, the institution of the

presidency deserved the benefit of the doubt. Absent clear evidence of malfeasance, citizens owed presidents their loyalty.

And why not? For most people, the military and political details of the conflict were above their pay grade, and certainly above his. Besides, both presidents were close personal friends. Disentangling public principle from personal loyalty was never easy.

*   *   *

In the late 1960s Graham made comments to the press that seemed extraordinarily ill-considered. They might have been apt in another context, but they carried the wrong message at the time. Preaching in 1966, for example, he took pains to point out that fewer than 2,500 soldiers had been killed in Vietnam. Though tragic, the number of combat fatalities should be put in perspective. That many people were killed on American highways every two weeks. Who protested?

In 1970 Lieutenant William Calley was court-martialed for his role in a massacre of some five hundred unarmed civilians, including women and children, in the village of My Lai two years before. Graham retorted that the officers above him should be held responsible too. He also said that in a sense everyone was guilty because of the universality of human sinfulness. Though clearly not his intent, his words were taken to excuse Calley.

Altogether, the enduring menace of Communist aggression, along with the authority of a president committed to thwarting that aggression, left Graham with few doubts about the war's justification. Moreover, Graham made clear his dismay for protestors' libertine lifestyle, ill-groomed demeanor, disregard of the rules of lawful protest, and ingratitude for the gift of American democratic institutions.

So it is not surprising that he supported Nixon's enormously controversial decision to extend the war into Cambodia in 1970 and bomb Hanoi, the North Vietnam capital, on Christmas Day 1970. Or more precisely, perhaps, he supported President Nixon, who authorized those bombing campaigns.

On May 4, 1970, the tragic drama took lethal form on the rolling green campus of Kent State University in Ohio. When a student protest against the war seemed to be spiraling out of hand, Ohio National Guardsmen shot and killed four students and wounded nine others (including one who suffered lifelong paralysis).

Less than one month after the shootings—on May 28—Graham invited Nixon to offer a few words at his crusade at the University of Tennessee at Knoxville. Nixon accepted, undoubtedly grateful for the legitimation it would provide him and his administration. Graham evidently had no doubts about the propriety of inviting the president in the midst of such turmoil. And he stoutly denied that the invitation was partisan since, he said, Nixon was not actively running for office.

For the seventy-five thousand souls gathered in Neyland Stadium that night, the contrasts were startling. Before Graham spoke, part of the 1,500 protesters sang John Lennon's song "Give Peace a Chance," as they filed out of the stadium. When Graham proceeded to introduce the president, some 300 remaining protestors chanted "Politics! Politics!" Soon antiwar slogans mixed with pro-Nixon retorts.

Nixon's remarks were brief but filled with praise for Graham and for the good he was doing for the nation. Graham tried to quiet the marchers with diplomatic appeals to decorum. Protest, he declared, fell within the American democratic tradition but not when it disrupted others' lives.

The protestors eventually dispersed without incident, but the repercussions rumbled long. The student newspaper ragged the event as a circus, complete with a (Republican) elephant. With few exceptions, the secular press found Graham's judgment deplorable. He not only politicized the gospel but also showed insensitivity to the suffering engendered by the Kent State shootings. How a man so astute in so many ways could be so naive when it came to Nixon left many people scratching their heads.[1]

* * *

This is the context in which we should view the Honor America Day proceedings, conducted a few weeks later, on July 4, 1970, on the lawn of the National Mall in Washington, DC. Before the event Graham insisted that the day aimed to give a "super-salute to God and country."[2]

Graham's desire to win religious and political support across the religious and political spectrum won at least a measure of success. Mormon hotel magnate J. Willard Marriott was the main organizer. Honorary members of the sponsoring committee included people as diverse as Mamie Eisenhower, Hubert Humphrey, Lyndon Johnson, and Harry Truman. Nelson Rockefeller and H. Ross Perot endorsed it, and so did President Richard Nixon.

Funding came from a host of corporate sponsors as well as reliable Graham supporters such as J. Howard Pew, *Reader's Digest* founder DeWitt Wallace, and *Reader's Digest* long-term editor Hobart D. Lewis.

The celebration unfolded in two parts. The morning event, which featured Graham as the keynote speaker, took place at the Lincoln Memorial, while the evening event, which featured Bob Hope as the emcee, progressed halfway up the Mall at the Washington Monument.

The crowds tallied 15,000 and 350,000, respectively. National television coverage added millions. The sea of visitors looked like a page torn from a *Heartland America* coffee-table book. "Despite organizers' insistence that the attendees would be diverse," historian Kevin Kruse writes, "they turned out to be overwhelmingly white, middle-class, and middle-aged." In the memorable words of a *Baltimore Sun* journalist, Kruse goes on, "There were fewer black faces than one might have expected in Alaska."

Pat Boone opened the morning's festivities by leading the crowd in the national anthem, Kate Smith sang "God Bless America," Rabbi Marc Tanenbaum read from Leviticus chapter 25, and E. V. Hill, the influential African American pastor noted earlier, led in prayer. After Graham's address, Monsignor Fulton J. Sheen offered the benediction. He called for a West Coast version of the Statue of Liberty, a "Statue of Responsibility."

In the evening Red Skelton recited the Pledge of Allegiance, Dinah Shore sang "America the Beautiful," and the New Christy Minstrels intoned "This Land Is Your Land." Other celebrities included Jack Benny, Glen Campbell, black performer Teresa Graves, and Graham's close friend Johnny Cash. Afterward, Graham's longtime friend Jimmy Stewart narrated a collector's disc of the festivities.

Playing off Martin Luther King's "I Have a Dream" speech, given seven years before at the same site, Graham called his talk "The Unfinished Dream." Though he seemed more worried about the excesses of the radical Left than the radical Right, he focused on the need for unity: "Today we call upon all Americans to stop this polarization before it is too late." He urged the "overwhelming majority of concerned Americans—white and black, hawks and doves, parents and students, Republicans and Democrats"—to honor the nation and support its fundamental institutions.

*   *   *

Graham's prominent role in the allegedly bipartisan Honor America Day celebration actually fueled the feeling that he had thrown the power of his pulpit squarely behind the war. That belief started long before the summer of 1970 and persisted long after it. The number of invitations to

Graham to speak at secular colleges and universities dropped dramatically between 1967 and 1973, and he ran into stout headwinds when he tried to take his message to left-leaning New Zealand in 1969.

Dismay grew from the grass roots, too. One example speaks for countless others. A spring 1972 issue of *Christianity Today* carried a letter to the editor that blasted Graham for failing to use his influence in Washington to end the war. The letter was signed by an unknown student at Harvard Divinity School named Grant Wacker. With the passing of years, I have come to see that the issues in Vietnam and in Graham's own mind were not as simple as I once thought. Even so, Graham's support for a conflict that had taken thousands of lives and inflicted untold suffering for increasingly obscure reasons stained his record.

Sharp criticism also emerged from both mainline Protestants and left-leaning evangelicals. In 1972 Ernest T. Campbell, for example, the pastor of the eminently mainline Riverside Church in New York City, released an "Open Letter to Billy Graham." Though the tone was respectful—one clergyman to another—it deplored Graham for failing to use his singular access to the president for prophetic purposes. Campbell was far from alone.

To such critics, Graham invariably gave the same response. Presidents and I do not talk about politics. I am their friend and pastor, not their military and political adviser. Besides, you do not know what I say to presidents in private. My conversations with all presidents are totally confidential. If I did not keep them that way (remember Truman), I would never be invited back. Graham's critics remained unpersuaded, but Graham never budged.

It is hard to say whether Graham caught more criticism from Protestant and Catholic liberals or from the evangelical Left. Radical evangelical periodicals such as the *Other Side* and the *Post-American*—later *Sojourners*—carried article after article calling Graham to account.

The response to Graham from the evangelical Left resembled fundamentalists' response to him in the late 1950s: disillusioned love. Your loyalty to Johnson and Nixon, they effectively said, reeks of complicity in their lies. At the deepest level you are one of us, so it is hard to see how you can be so blind to the folly of this war.

SCENE 34

Twisted Path to Peace

In the early 1970s Graham, like millions of Americans, began to harbor second thoughts about the war. They were never enough to prompt him to come right out and say he had been wrong, but he did admit that both antiwar and prowar sides had good arguments. He just was not sure, he said. The issues were too complex for a preacher to untangle, so he would try to remain neutral and stay out of it.

This development may have been cooking in the back of Graham's mind for some time. In 1968 he had urged presidential candidate Nixon to select Mark Hatfield, the antiwar senator from Oregon, as his running mate.[1] Of course, Spiro Agnew, the stridently prowar governor of Maryland, eventually won the nod. But Nixon led Graham to think that his choice of Agnew was not a foregone conclusion—and that he wanted the preacher's advice.

How much Graham's support for Hatfield grew from the senator's antiwar position and how much from Hatfield's strong evangelical-Baptist faith is not clear. What is clear is that Graham's repeated claim that he did not talk with presidents about politics was at best misleading.[2]

Graham's waffling on the war proved highly damaging for his legacy. It produced a widespread feeling that he was pitching his sails wherever the wind was blowing. Altering one's mind on the war, as respected newscasters Walter Cronkite and Eric Sevareid had done, was one thing. People change in the face of changing evidence. But waffling—a posture Graham excoriated in the spiritual realm—was another.

The Paris Peace Accords were initiated in 1968, then sputtered because of Nixon's distrust of the Viet Cong's promise to return American prisoners of war. The accords started up again in 1973 when Nixon twisted the screws by threatening to throw massive military force into the fray. Graham backed Nixon at every step.

Graham also insisted that the United States bore a moral obligation to stand behind South Vietnam in order to bring a safe and honorable conclusion to that bitter conflict. The South had committed itself to the war, confident that the United States would back it. To abandon it now would signal moral weakness. Who could trust us?

When Nixon and Kissinger finally signed the treaty in March 1973 that formally ended the war, Graham predictably heralded Nixon's statesmanship. As American withdrawal unfolded, he said little more about the war, except that he had moved from hawkishness to neutrality. He never offered much of an explanation for why, except that the geopolitical issues were complex and beyond his knowledge.

*   *   *

In 1989 Graham's reputation took another hit. That year documents obtained via the Freedom of Information Act showed that Graham and President Nixon most definitely had communicated about war policy on at least one occasion.

Back in 1969 Graham had sent a thirteen-page typed letter to the president. The missive detailed the results of a conference of veteran American missionaries in Southeast Asia about how to end the war. They agreed that the United States must prosecute the conflict more strategically by de-Americanizing it, withdrawing one hundred thousand troops, cracking down on corruption, and beefing up propaganda, air power, and special forces.

Their recommendations included using North Vietnamese defectors "to bomb and invade the North." But then Graham continued: "Especially let them bomb the dikes which could overnight destroy the economy of North Vietnam." Graham's report on the conference almost certainly reflected his own views too.

Critics were aghast. They claimed that if Nixon had acted on Graham's advice about bombing the dikes—which he did not—the move would have killed a million people. True or not, bombing the dikes certainly would have violated the Geneva Conventions of War by targeting civilians.

It is not clear how well Graham understood the ramifications of his recommendation, for it occupied only fifteen words in a document of more than three thousand words. Some of Graham's supporters undoubtedly hoped that this was another instance of his lifelong propensity for popping off ideas without serious knowledge of the issues at hand. But he had given his critics plenty of ammunition.

By the 1990s, in any event, Graham would say he regretted that he had not come out and forthrightly opposed the war. Yet that confession may not have been as prophetic as it appeared. Though Nixon's smashing victory in 1972 suggests that most Americans still supported it, by the end of the century Graham proved no different from the majority. They too had come to regret the conflict and the terrible human cost on both sides.

Myth and Icon

The peak years of Graham's visibility—roughly from the mid-1960s through the mid-1980s—offer a good place to pause the story for a few minutes and think about how the public saw him.

By the 1960s Graham had turned into a mythic figure, larger than life. He became the benchmark by whom many people—including ones outside Christian ministry—were measured. Examples turned up everywhere, and in unexpected places. Libyan dictator Muammar Gaddafi, said one reporter, was "sounding at times like a Moslem Billy Graham." In 2008 a PBS *American Experience* special cast the Transcendentalist Ralph Waldo Emerson as something like a combination of Oprah Winfrey and Billy Graham.

At the same time, some figures made acrobatic efforts to distance themselves from Graham. The witch Sybil Leek, for example, disavowed any desire to convert anyone else to witchcraft: "I'm not the Billy Graham of the witchcraft world," she stressed.

In these midcareer years Graham displayed a celebrity-like status rather like a Hollywood star. With good reason a London newspaper called him "Charles Atlas with a halo." One family member recalled that during a single meal at a restaurant in Asheville, more than a dozen different people walked up and asked for an autograph. He once said that not being able to go out for dinner or even walk down a street without being hailed was the hardest part of his job. Graham started wearing sunglasses and floppy hats to disguise himself. Every word he uttered behind the pulpit—or otherwise—was examined by the press and prompted a response from someone somewhere. By the 1970s anonymity had soared entirely out of reach.

*　　　*　　　*

Good looks were part of it. At the time of Graham's death, a retrospective essay by *Newsweek*'s venerable religion writer Kenneth Woodward began, "His face was Hollywood handsome." Writing for the Associated Press, Rachel Zoll and Jonathan Drew started their retrospective essay the same way: "The Rev. Billy Graham, the magnetic movie-star handsome preacher..."

And so he was. Graham knew the marketing value of his God-given visage. The chiseled jaw, azure eyes, and usually-too-long sandy hair came with the six-feet-two-inch physique of a seasoned athlete. He carefully maintained a rigorous personal regimen for staying in shape—swimming, weight lifting, and, of course, golfing.

Television played a large role in boosting Graham's status by taking the ever-present winsome smile into heartland America's living rooms. Though few people knew him in person, television made him seem warmly accessible, everybody's friend. If millions simply liked him—and polls leave little doubt that they did—a big part of that appeal clearly grew from the real and perceived image of affability he conveyed.

Graham's front men were careful to say that God judges the heart, not the face. At the same time, they were stone-cold realistic about the marketing value of Graham's image. One associate quipped that good looks "reduce resistance." Another was asked how things would have turned out if Graham had been pudgy and scrappy of hair. The aide responded—presumably with a grin—"Well, but he wasn't, was he? The Lord worked it out so that he wouldn't be."

Graham fit the reigning definition of the virile (white) American male magnificently. "Straight from central casting" is how one reporter described him. It was not accidental that the mature, midcareer Graham bore a striking resemblance to Warner Sallman's iconic *Head of Christ*. Released in 1940, just when Graham started itinerant preaching, the picture eventually netted more than 500 million reproductions. Americans—or at least white middle-class ones—evidently found that particular configuration of features appealing.

Graham knew how to dress the part, too. In the early days, rocketing around the country for Youth for Christ, he had distinguished himself with a flamboyant wardrobe of pastel suits and flashy ties. But by the mid-1950s, he looked more like a smartly dressed banker, invariably outfitted in dark suit, subdued tie, wing-tipped black shoes, starched white collar, and the ever-present cufflinks. One reporter called him "a walking Arrow collar man."

*   *   *

Manliness formed part of the image too. Of course, manliness, no less than attractiveness, was culturally defined. In the immediate postwar era, macho figures such as actor Marlon Brando and General George S. Patton exemplified the conventional profile, in which manliness was equated with tough-guy swagger. And for Hollywood, at least, manliness also included sexual prowess, more often outside than inside the boundaries of marriage.

Graham never embraced tough-guy swagger, let alone sexual overtones, in his personal deportment, but his early doctrinal positions came with a hard edge, preached with jut-jawed certainty. So did his public policy pronouncements, especially on Communism. Along the way Graham spoke admiringly of men he deemed the real deal, "men's men," Prince Philip, General Mark Clark, and even his dear friend Bev Shea, who boasted a square jaw and straight shoulders.

Photo-ops of Graham posing with celebrity athletes such as Arnold Palmer and Muhammad Ali graced the shelves of his display cases. He often quoted soldiers and athletes in his sermons, and they figured prominently among his platform guests. His preaching gestures fit the image too, with the stabbing finger, chopping hands, and steel soldier posture.

The cover of Graham's second book, *I Saw Your Sons at War*, based on his 1952 trip to the Korean battle zone, bore an image of two helmeted soldiers charging up a hill, rifles in hand, ready for action. Graham never extolled war itself, but he did extol the disciplined character that war fostered.

Yet historian Seth Dowland has shown how Graham also deepened the definition of true manliness. To some extent that redefinition had been there all along, and to some extent it reflected the changing curve of the culture. From the beginning he affirmed that true manhood did not lie in macho bravura. Rather it lay in the ability to say no to temptation, especially sexual lures. He freely acknowledged that he himself had been tempted on those lines, especially when he was far from home for long stretches of time, but he also made clear—perhaps a bit too often—that he never came close to succumbing.

Later we will see that over time Graham also took more malleable positions on many aspects of evangelical doctrine and American public policy. He was not afraid to show a pastoral side, presenting himself as a gentle patriarch, embracing mediating stands, the kind stereotypically associated with women. Graham legitimized these malleable positions for men in evangelical subculture.

Drawing fast and shooting straight from the hip, he eventually realized, won enemies, not allies, and certainly not converts.

Man for All Seasons

In 2006, A. Larry Ross, Graham's long-term media consultant, told this story in New York. "So Moses turns for advice to his public-relations man as he's wondering how to cross the Red Sea. . . . And the guy says . . . , 'Stand at the water's edge and raise your staff and the sea will part.' . . . And Moses asks, 'Is that really going to work?' And the PR guy says, 'I don't know, but if it does, I can guarantee you two pages in the Old Testament.'"

This wisp of a story reveals not only Ross's flair for his job but also Graham's. Between 1949 and 2013, historian Elesha Coffman writes, "Graham became one of the most recognized, televised, photographed, published, and quoted figures in America—and abroad—owing in large part to his adept engagement with media." Coffman rightly notes that this skill stretched across his entire career.

* * *

Graham grasped the power of television to market his "product." With radio he had jumped on a locomotive set in motion long before. But with television he ranked among the first to seize the opportunity in the 1950s. He could not have known that in the first five years of the decade, television use in American households would grow by 700 percent, but his instincts ran that way.

Like his Catholic counterpart Monsignor Fulton J. Sheen, Graham shrewdly understood that television commanded an elusive power to project him into America's living rooms. Catholic journalist Jon M. Sweeney spoke for many: "For Mr. Graham, intangibles like personal humility and kindness translated across the television screen."

But television did something else for Graham that it could not do for Charles Fuller, who worked only on radio, or Fulton Sheen, who worked only in a studio. It conveyed the magnitude of the stadium crowds as well as the scale of the lines of inquirers streaming forward at the end. The sheer size of these events, captured on the screen, normalized them, making it harder for critics to dismiss them as the aberrations of the fundamentalist fringe.

Graham used television as no other evangelist had done, not only by mounting his own nationally syndicated broadcast, but also and perhaps more important by regularly appearing on secular talk shows. He filled guest spots on the Woody Allen, William F. Buckley, Johnny Carson, Phil Donahue, David Frost, Merv Griffin, Jack Paar, Dinah Shore, and Larry King programs, among others. Indeed, when Graham retired, he may have held the record for the most appearances—at least twenty-five—of any guest on King's program.

Allen and King were forthright about being secular themselves, but that did not cramp Graham's style. In one now-classic performance, Graham masterfully countered Allen's friendly jabs and got in a few of his own. When Allen challenged Graham to name which of the Ten Commandments he liked best, Graham, without missing a beat, shot back that as the father of five children still at home, he was especially fond of the fifth: honor your father and mother.

Sporting his trademark grin, Graham came across on television as relaxed and often just as witty as the host. King and Graham in particular bantered with manifest mutual affection, which played well in an increasingly pluralistic society. Graham never fell into the kind of tabloid stories and off-color innuendos that many guests traded on such programs. For that matter, the preacher invariably managed to slip in the substance of the gospel. But he did it in a way so winsome that no one seemed to take offense.

*   *   *

Graham mastered the secular magazine culture with equal aplomb. He wrote for periodicals as diverse as *Cosmopolitan*, *Family Circle*, and *National Enquirer*. Newspapers routinely reported on the content of sermons he preached in their cities. As we have seen, the *New York Times* carried the entire text of his first Madison Square Garden sermon.

Besides writing for magazines himself, Graham readily cooperated with the reporters writing about him. Historian Anne Blue Wills has tracked down more than sixty periodicals featuring the preacher. That Graham appeared in recognized newsmagazines such as *Time*, *Newsweek*, and *US News and World Report* was predictable. His appearance in general-interest magazines such as *Life, Look, TV Guide,* and *Saturday Evening Post* was perhaps equally predictable.

Less predictable was his visibility in trade publications catering to niche markets. A handful of examples, drawn from a range of constituencies, includes *African Challenge, California Parent-Teacher, Fotorama, Frontier Airlines, Golf Illustrated, Golf Canada, Greeting Card Magazine, Guns & Ammo Magazine, IGA Grocergram, Insurance Salesman Magazine, Milling and Baking News, Motion Picture, Mr. America, My Baby, National Candy Wholesaler,* and even *Playboy* (to which Graham gave only testy cooperation). The stories testify to the public's avaricious capacity for trivia about his daily life—and to Graham's willingness to oblige.

*　　　*　　　*

The Graham publicity machine also mastered the art of capturing photos of him with celebrities from many walks of life. Some that appeared (or, more often, reappeared) in the memorial commemorative edition of *Decision* included Graham hobnobbing with sports stars such as Muhammad Ali, Jack Nicklaus, Joe Namath, "Bear" Bryant, Arnold Palmer, and Jeff Gordon; entertainment celebrities Cecil B. DeMille, Woody Allen, Dinah Shore, George Burns, Roy Rogers, Dale Evans, Johnny Carson, Walt Disney, Sir Cliff Richard, and Bob Hope; and media celebrities John F. Kennedy Jr. and Carolyn Bessette-Kennedy, Diane Sawyer, Larry King, Greta Van Susteren, Paul Harvey, Peter Jennings, Katie Couric, and David Frost.

Graham's family was a special favorite of the media. The children appeared in sappy poses, lined up in their Sunday best, coming across as the normative white middle-class American family. Ruth captured special attention. In those stories and photos Billy emerged, in Wills's words, "as a reassuringly strong patriarch, and Ruth as lovely to behold and resourceful (rather than resentful) at home."

The magazine press knew a good dollar when they saw one. Editors were not above juxtaposing a picture of the preacher on one page with a picture of a glamorous actress on the other. The drumbeat repetition of photographs of Graham in all imaginable settings and poses—especially ones of him playing golf with celebrities or presidents—documented his easy connection to the power elite. There is no evidence that Graham profited materially from these outings, but he was astute enough to know that such exposure would enhance his ministry and ultimately the BGEA's ledger sheet. And, like most people, at some level he surely relished being the center of so much attention.

* * *

Unlike many of his predecessors—and successors—on the itinerant trail, Graham enjoyed a good relationship with the press. With the exception of his controversial trip to Moscow in 1982 (which we will examine later), he rarely saw himself as a victim. He said that journalists almost always treated him fairly and quoted him accurately. Indeed, he said that sometimes he wished they had *not* quoted him quite so accurately.

Graham freely acknowledged that Hearst and Luce had catapulted his career into its orbit. He liked journalists, whom he took seriously as professionals trying to do a job, and they liked him for the same reason. The transcripts of the scores of press conferences that Graham held with them brim with notations of "laughter" and show a good deal of lively and almost always friendly banter.

Typical was one press conference in which Graham told the photographers and television crews that he hoped he would see them in heaven. And "bring your cameras," he wisecracked. In the few instances in which we see testiness (either way), Graham invariably defused the situation with a quip or personal story. He grasped the importance of free publicity, and journalists grasped the importance of stories about—and with—a real-life celebrity.

* * *

Another form of media outreach—much less noticed—was Graham's interaction with academics, especially in the most visible years of his career. In those situations he drew on a surprising reservoir of factual information gained from biographies, including scholarly ones; a wide variety of newspapers and newsmagazines; and, of course, constant study of his Bible.

Granted, the famed Columbia University historian Richard Hofstadter featured him as a key example of "anti-intellectualism in American life" in his Pulitzer Prize-winning book of that title. There was some truth to Hofstadter's jab. Graham never went to seminary and held no advanced degrees. His wife, Ruth, and his research assistants evidently supplied him with a steady stream of names and factoids about famous intellectuals, which he sprinkled through the text of his sermons and books, but with few signs of serious engagement.

That being said, over the course of six decades—going back to his first visit to Boston in 1950 when he was but thirty-one years old—Graham accepted dozens of invitations from all sectors of the academy—colleges, seminaries, and universities, secular and religious, Protestant and Catholic, mainline and evangelical.

Historian Andrew Finstuen has shown that the list includes many of the most prestigious institutions in the world, including old Ivies such as Harvard, Yale, Princeton, Brown, and Columbia; powerhouse research universities outside the Northeast such as Chicago, Berkeley, Duke, and the University of North Carolina; the two oldest and most distinguished schools in the Anglophone world, Oxford and Cambridge; and political action groups such as Students for a Democratic Society at Columbia University. He was the first evangelist since George Whitefield in the eighteenth century to grace the pulpit of Memorial Church in Harvard Yard.

Granted, some engagements went better than others. In the fall of 1951 Graham was holding a meeting in Greensboro, North Carolina. A student group at nearby Duke Divinity School wanted to invite him to drive over and speak about evangelism. When the leader of the group asked the dean for permission, the dean punted to a called meeting of the faculty. The vote was hardly resounding, with only nine of sixteen agreeing.

There is no evidence that Graham ever declined an invitation because he feared audiences would be skeptical or hostile. He seemed willing to stride into any ring, undeterred. To some extent he was, undoubtedly, simply naive, not really grasping how much he did not know about critical scholarship. But his repeated admissions that he was not a theologian, let alone an intellectual, suggest that he knew himself pretty well.

Graham did not try to match wits with academics on the turf of their specialties. Rather, he deftly brought them onto his turf by talking about things he knew he *could* talk about: dilemmas of human life and the need for a higher power to rescue them. This was good news—Good News—which merited sharing with everyone everywhere, regardless of their training or background.

Without question, Graham occasionally mistook derisive snickers for sympathetic laughter, and many pundits remained skeptical at best. One charged him with setting back the cause of Christianity by a hundred years. (To this Graham quipped that he hoped to set it back exactly nineteen hundred years.) Another—John C. Bennett, renowned professor of social ethics at Union Seminary in New York—heard him address the students and faculty in his school and found him "better than expected, or not as bad as feared." Bennett said that Graham succeeded because "he knew where to say what."

Yet the record of positive interactions between the preacher and the teachers is impressive. Finstuen's sedulous research in rarely consulted resources has shown that numerous prominent academics, including Karl Barth, Helmut Thielicke, Harvey Cox, Krister Stendahl, Paul Tillich, Henry Pitney Van Dusen, and even John Bennett, approached him with surprising openness before they met him in person—or came around after they did.

Disarmed by Graham's manifest sincerity and humility, and impressed by his wit and winsomeness, Christian academics recognized that he could do things they could not. Graham's humor was a big part of it. In such settings he liked to tell of the farmer who entered his mule in the Kentucky Derby. When a friend asked what chance the mule had, the farmer said, "None, but look at the company he'll be keeping." That was, Graham said with his trademark grin, the way he felt when he was the speaker for a meeting of scholars.

A common photo of Graham addressing faculty members and students at the Harvard Law Forum in 1962 is revealing. It shows a packed room, Graham up front casually standing behind the lectern, arms casually folded, dressed to the nines in a natty sport coat and black trousers, laughing, and the audience smiling broadly. We see a man clearly at ease with himself and in control of his situation.[1]

Far more often than not, then, Graham emerged from these encounters with the press and academics neither bloodied nor bowed but energized. His refusal to get into verbal combat with any audience anywhere projected an image of a Christian statesman simply standing above the fray. More important, he gave the impression that the message he proclaimed had nothing to fear from forthright engagement with modern thinking.

Billy Graham, Inc.

Graham's far-flung mission ran on the tracks of a highly developed organizational infrastructure. When the preacher thought about the BGEA, "Inc." may not have been the first term that popped into his mind, but it fits. Outsiders did not have to embrace his theology in order to admire his entrepreneurial skills.

The admiration started early and ran late. It may have been most conspicuous to the public in the same midcareer decades in which Graham's image in the media also was most conspicuous. This Scene focuses on that period, the twenty or so years stretching from the mid-1960s to the mid-1980s. But the story actually started in 1950 with the incorporation of the BGEA and continued essentially unchanged into (and past) the years of Graham's retirement in 2005.

From the beginning the BGEA proved to be not only scrupulously honest but also a model of streamlined efficiency. It managed Graham's continually expanding empire of books, magazines, movies, radio programs, television shows, media appearances, press conferences, civic talks, and, of course, crusade appearances. Representatives of nonreligious organizations routinely made the hike to Minneapolis to see how the BGEA operated.

As far back as 1957, William G. McLoughlin, Graham's first academic biographer—and sharp critic—saluted the BGEA's effectiveness. To this day both outsider and insider historians and journalists have (with rare exceptions) consistently agreed.

The creation of the BGEA regularized Graham's affairs with the IRS and kept the business side of things in order, and also set in motion other productive consequences surely not evident at the time. Since BGEA director George W. Wilson hailed from Minneapolis, for example, he naturally headquartered the organization there rather than in Montreat. The miles between Minneapolis and Graham's home in Montreat were enough to dampen any temptation to micromanage. Locating the BGEA in the

Twin Cities also gave it the image of a national (and soon international) rather than regional organization.

The BGEA moved its roughly five hundred employees to Charlotte, North Carolina, in 2003, because it needed more space and wanted to be closer to its cousin organization, Samaritan's Purse, in Boone, North Carolina.[1] But intended or not, that move did not come about until long after business routines were firmly established and the public image was firmly in place.

All of Graham's outreach endeavors required money, which the BGEA handled efficiently and with little fanfare. Radio and television broadcasts kept the gospel message front and center, mentioning money relatively rarely. A 1996 study of television programs found that Graham spent 2 percent of his airtime asking for money, compared with 17 percent for Jerry Falwell and 13 percent for Robert Schuller.

The fund-raising emphasis fell rather on the thousands of names on the BGEA mailing list, who received regular letters. The letters were cast in the same format as Graham's sermons. World, national, and personal crises loomed everywhere, but Christ offered an answer for every one of them. "We need your prayers and support." Less was more.

*   *   *

A word about Graham's personal financial arrangements is in order too. In the fall of 1950, Graham returned to the region of his roots for a five-week crusade in Atlanta. The press coverage of those meetings inadvertently triggered one of the most valuable strategies he ever devised.

When Graham left the city in early December, the *Atlanta Constitution* splashed two big photos on the second page. One was of a grinning Graham hopping into a car, waiting to whisk him to the airport. The second photo, positioned next to the first, showed ushers holding four sacks bulging with money from the crusade's offerings. Though both photos were authentic, placing them together like that left the bogus impression that this was Graham's personal haul.

Graham took two steps. First, he directed the freshly minted BGEA to make its audited financial records public. From then on, anyone who cared enough to check could know exactly how much money they took in, how much they spent, and where. Second, in January 1952 he placed himself and his top associates on a publicly stated salary.[2] For him the amount was pegged to that of a successful urban pastor—at that time, $15,000.

Several points merit notice here. First, fixing the salary meant that it was disconnected from the generosity of donors sitting in the audience who might be swayed by the emotion of the moment. Second, Graham's personal compensation in 1952 was in fact generous. In 2018 dollars, it would amount to nearly $140,000—a handsome sum for any pastor thirty-four years old. He lived comfortably. He also freely accepted gifts and favors, such as expense-paid vacations to sunny beaches, limousine rides, greens fees, and worldwide passes to Holiday Inns and Marriott hotels, courtesy of their owners, who were close friends. He never pretended to be abstemious, let alone deprived. He felt, in line with biblical precedent, that the servant was "worthy of his hire."

Yet those benefits were not remotely close to what prosperity preachers today take in. He refused the offer of a private jet and pilot and declined to stay in opulent suites, free or not. Eventually he gave up limousine rides and playing golf entirely because he did not like the country-club image (and golf took too much time anyway). Indeed, Ruth Graham once commented that "Bill"— she always called him Bill because she thought it was sort of silly to call a grown man Billy— "literally spends hours, *hours,* trying to figure out how not to make money."

Finally and most important, Graham's compensation remained open to scrutiny by the public. Critics targeted Graham on many fronts, but rarely for mishandling funds for personal gain, or for a luxurious lifestyle. Young as he was, Graham understood from the outset that transparency about money, like transparency about pretty much everything else, counted.

*   *   *

The enterprise brought Graham into frequent, close contact with highly successful entrepreneurs in the business and finance worlds.[3] They came from diverse lines of work. A disproportionate number had found their fortune in oil, especially in Texas, including Sid Richardson, Glenn Mc-Carthy, and Earl Hankamer. Others included advertiser Walter Bennett, grocer Howard E. Butt Jr., home decorator Mary C. Crowley, silver miner H. L. Hunt, heavy equipment developer R. G. LeTourneau, hotel magnate J. W. Marriott, insurance mogul John D. MacArthur, gun maker Russell McGuire, shoe manufacturer W. Maxey Jarman, ServiceMaster CEO C. William "Bill" Pollard, *Reader's Digest* founder DeWitt Wallace, and, of course, *Time/Life* founder/owner Henry Luce.

Graham also forged strong bonds with finance experts such as Chase Manhattan president George Champion and Harvard University treasurer George Bennett. He brought many of these and other successful people on to the board of the BGEA. He respected their business acumen.

Beyond admiration, Graham simply enjoyed their company, and they enjoyed his. In many ways, they were much alike. Most were self-made, rising not from poverty but from middling roots. All were men of strong will, soaring vision, and a savvy sense of how to get things done in the real world. Frequent golfing outings with Graham and his ultrarich friends suggest that something like a (mostly) male-bonded, sports-centered camaraderie was in play as well.

But something else, less recognized, was present too. Graham gravitated toward tycoons with strong philanthropic interests, especially ones committed to funding Christian enterprises with a social conscience.

Graham largely turned down offers of major contributions, except for specific causes such as hurricane relief. There were no deep-running revenue streams such as the ones Andrew Carnegie provided for libraries or John D. Rockefeller for liberal Protestant endeavors. More than once Graham said that he really did not want them, lest they discourage mom and pop donors.

The main revenue came from middle- and working-class people, not exceptionally wealthy friends and supporters. Though exact figures are hard to come by, in 1976 Graham said that the average contribution was seven dollars (roughly forty-five dollars in 2017 values), usually tucked in one of the untold number of letters that streamed into the BGEA decade after decade.[4]

A steady revenue stream from the general population undoubtedly yielded a greater and more reliable return, decade after decade, than a handful of large contributions. Relevant sermons suggest too that Graham believed that giving was simply part of a Christian's walk with Christ. Converted men and women voted with their wallets as well as their hands.

Trust rested at the heart of everything. Financial mistakes befell the BGEA, but scandals—efforts deliberately to scam givers or the law in order to line anyone's personal pockets—never cropped up.[5]

The widespread image of Elmer Gantry with his fingers in the cookie jar formed a perennial challenge. But Graham met the challenge partly by keeping his personal bookkeeping straight, and partly by keeping the affairs of his enterprise straight. In the words of one benefactor to the BGEA, contributions to Graham paid reliable dividends. Grace was no less amazing for being dependable.

SCENE 37

Perils of Power

By the late 1960s and early 1970s, the farm boy from Charlotte was on a roll. In January of 1971, Graham served as the grand marshal of the iconic Tournament of Roses Parade in Pasadena, California. Photos show him broadly smiling and waving at the crowds, pretty much as any glamorous Hollywood celebrity would do.

Nine months later Graham's hometown honored him by setting aside an entire day and dubbing it Billy Graham Day. Charlotte dismissed public schools, hosted President Richard Nixon, named a major road Billy Graham Parkway, and sponsored a big parade in which Graham rode in a caravan, along with the president, as an honored guest of the city.

Telegrams poured in from Hollywood celebrities including Bob Hope, Ronald Reagan, Jimmy Stewart, Robert Stack, and Lawrence Welk. Heads of state Prince Rainier and Haile Selassie, General William Westmoreland, and Graham's old friend Arnold Palmer sent telegrams too. Political leaders John Connally, Sam Ervin, and Strom Thurmond came in person. President Nixon capped off the event with a glowing tribute. Graham gave an acceptance speech in which he said that he didn't deserve all this hoopla. But the press noted that he was not too bashful to accept it anyway.

Graham's appearances in such venues intimated a sense of being utterly at ease with American life. To be sure, in those appearances he almost always worked in a reference to his fundamental calling as a preacher of the gospel. As with his media appearances, especially television talk shows, he never fell into smutty stories, and the integrity of his personal life remained above reproach. And throughout these years he articulated a constant refrain of prophetic judgment on Americans' sins, both personal and social, including America's racism, materialism, militarism, crime, and sexual immorality.

Even so, the press and probably millions of followers perceived him more as a symbol of the American good life than as a prophetic critic of it. With good reason, the media began to slam Graham less for his purportedly premodern theology than for his smug accommodation to the comforts and power of twentieth-century America.

Historians have not treated Graham very kindly regarding his tenacious support for Nixon. Yet it is important to remember that if Nixon "snookered" Graham, as one of his friends put it, he also snookered the entire nation. The president won the 1972 election by the fourth widest popular vote margin in American history. In the electoral college, Nixon won every state except Massachusetts (and District of Columbia). And Nixon implemented reform legislation and actions that progressives would later applaud, including the establishment of the Environmental Protection Agency and the opening of diplomatic doors to the (Communist) People's Republic of China.

The Watergate scandal, as it has come to be called, precipitated Nixon's downfall, and it almost undid Graham too. The particulars of the Watergate episode have been told many times, and we do not need to rehearse them here. The relevant point is that in the summer of 1973 the details of the Watergate break-in soon implicated Nixon himself. The president's critics started to call for his impeachment. The president's admirers stoutly resisted all such talk as premature at best and outrageous at worst. Graham fell into the latter camp and stayed there long after most folks had given up on the cause.

Multiple factors came into play. We have seen that Graham admired Nixon's mind, sagacity, and knowledge. He touted the president's high moral values too. He appreciated Nixon's Quaker upbringing and especially the faith of his evangelical mother. Though he wished that Nixon would be more forthright about his faith, he forgave the president's reticence on the ground that Nixon was just shy about revealing such private matters of the heart. And Graham did not like conflict with anyone, least of all an old friend.

Indeed, Graham prized loyalty in himself and in others—so much so that it is hard to know where fidelity ended and simple obtuseness began. Years later Graham seemed to excuse Nixon's misdeeds by attributing them to the influence of sleeping pills, "which just let a demon power come in." Given who Graham was, and given what he saw and wanted to see in an old friend, it is easy to see why he was so slow to see the truth.

The erosion of Graham's confidence in Nixon took time. The first break appeared in January of 1974. Graham told *Christianity Today* that the evidence that a criminal act had taken place was undeniable—but he insisted that no firm evidence implicated Nixon himself.

Then the revelation hit the news: in April the "smoking gun" Watergate tapes were released. They revealed Nixon's active involvement in the scandal and, maybe more to the point for Graham, Nixon's dirty mouth. At first Graham resisted reading the transcripts. But the following month he finally did. He admitted that he nearly vomited when he saw them—and the foul language.

Later the press ridiculed Graham for fixating on the trivial issue of bad words while overlooking the grave one of subversion of government. The criticism was partly fair. Without question Graham got his priorities wrong. At the same time, the press overlooked the role of a prescribed and proscribed vocabulary in the evangelical subculture.

As with most religious movements, partisans defined themselves in or out of the culture by a host of subtle behavioral cues, and vocabulary was one of them. Cussing euphemisms such as "darn" and "gosh" were undesirable but passable. Explicitly profane language was not. Lyndon Johnson had cussed routinely, and Graham knew it, but Johnson never pretended otherwise. Nixon did.

The simple truth is that the president rarely if ever played his religious—or, more precisely, irreligious—cards in front of the preacher. Nixon seldom swore in Graham's presence. This restraint led Graham to think that Nixon was, if not a forthright evangelical, at least a thoroughly upright, high-minded man. Moreover, Graham fancied himself a good judge of character. Nixon hammered that assumption. For a man who had built his ministry on interactions with other people, this was no small blow.

Though Americans' response toward Nixon's perfidy was unforgiving, their attitude toward Graham's foot-dragging ran the gamut. At one end stood Graham's sort-of-friend Norman Vincent Peale, who, as we have seen, privately excoriated him for abandoning Nixon in the president's hour of greatest need.

Christianity Today represented the middle. Its editors interpreted Graham's actions as the unfortunate but understandable response of a man who prided himself on loyalty, come what may. They showed what might be called restrained disappointment, attributing Graham's actions to well-intentioned naïveté.

At the other end stood the mainline Protestant and secular press, which found his unflagging support for the president, at least through

January 1974, utterly unfathomable. Some suggested that Graham was complicit by deliberately looking the other way. On campuses students led protest marches when Graham came to speak. When Graham spoke in the Duke University Chapel in 1973, for example, students protested outside. The dean of the chapel arranged for him to slip into the building through a side door.

*   *   *

Looking back on the Watergate episode later, in his 1997 memoir, *Just as I Am*, Graham moved in two directions at once. On one hand he emphasized the depth and longevity of his friendship with Nixon and the multiple efforts he had made to keep it alive in the half-dozen years after Watergate. He allowed that those efforts had gone unrequited. But Graham, ever the faithful friend, speculated that Nixon had avoided him because he wanted to protect Graham.

On the other hand, after 1974 Graham started to express regrets for his partisanship for Nixon. The experience, he said, "muffled those inner monitors that had warned me for years to stay out of partisan politics." Graham urged younger evangelists and pastors to avoid his mistakes.

This long, sorry story taught Graham priceless lessons about the dangers of political entanglements and, equally important, the dangers of letting personal friendship dim moral judgment. Speaking at Harvard in 1982, Graham said that government "will never be better than the men and women who have given their lives to it." He discerned that the integrity of government did not lie in its form but in the moral fiber of the people who ran it.

Did he have Nixon in mind? We do not know. What we do know is that the fallout from Nixon's misdeeds, and Graham's stubborn defense of—or unflagging loyalty to—the president, might have been the best thing that ever happened to the preacher. The experience opened his eyes to the dangers of dragging partisan politics into the pulpit. In subsequent decades Graham fell off the wagon several times. The lure was too great entirely to resist. But at least he saw the danger and tried, however imperfectly, to go another way.

SCENE 38

Ford, Carter, and Reagan

In August 1974, Gerald Ford succeeded Richard Nixon in the Oval Office. Ford was a cradle Episcopalian with evangelical leanings. His son Michael Ford was a student at Gordon-Conwell Theological Seminary (near Boston). Graham had helped found the seminary, which was nondenominational but decidedly evangelical, and for many years Graham served as chair of the school's board of trustees.

On the face of it, Graham and Ford should have forged a tight friendship. They held roughly similar theological views. And moderately conservative Republican political views, too. In 1976 Graham not only voted for Ford over Jimmy Carter but actually sent him what amounted to a condolence letter. Graham said that during the election he had prayed constantly for Ford and that he just could not "figure out why God did that to us." The two men evinced similar personalities too— irenic, smiling, able to laugh at themselves, and able to be as inclusive as their principles allowed. And they liked to play golf together.

Yet they never grew close. Though there is no evidence of a falling out, the chemistry just didn't ignite as it had with Nixon. Ford was reserved about his faith, while Graham wore it on his sleeve.

The 1976 election was significant for an event that did not happen. In early September Ford phoned Graham and asked if he (Ford) might greet the stadium crowd at Graham's crusade in Pontiac, Michigan, coming up in October—two weeks before the election. Graham declined. He said that if he allowed Ford to speak, he also would need to invite his election rival, Jimmy Carter.

Ford's request was not particularly out of line. As noted, Vice President Nixon had attended the New York crusade in 1957 and President Johnson the Houston crusade in 1965, and Graham had invited President Nixon to speak at the Knoxville crusade in 1971. Graham's decision not to let Ford speak marked a fulcrum. Before 1976 Graham had needed presidents more than they needed him. Afterward the reverse proved true.

The 1976 election marked a fulcrum in another way too. It was the first public evidence that Graham was beginning seriously to worry about the danger of partisanship in the pulpit. He had given lip service to this ideal in times past, but in the mid-1970s he started to take it to heart.

*　　　*　　　*

If the reserve that marked Graham's relationship with Ford occasioned surprise, the reserve of his relationship with Ford's Democratic successor, Jimmy Carter, occasioned even more. As with Ford, the two men were friendly but not close. There is little evidence of the kind of personal chemistry that sparked Graham's relationship with some other presidents.

Again, the reasons for the distance are not evident. Carter and Graham were very close in age. Both were Southerners, growing up on farms less than four hundred miles apart. Both were Southern Baptists, sharing an evangelical theology focused on personal repentance, heartfelt conversion, and faith in Christ. Both were active churchmen, Carter as a Sunday school teacher and Graham as a globe-circling preacher. Both were moderately ahead of the curve on civil rights (initially Graham more than Carter, later Carter more than Graham). And both enjoyed the lifelong support of strong, intelligent wives who played indispensable backstage roles in their husbands' careers.

Still, the differences are not entirely opaque either. Carter was a technician at heart. He trained as an engineer at the US Naval Academy and served as a submarine officer. He also proved to be a serious farmer, who enjoyed working with his hands, and would continue to do so throughout his own very long life. If Graham had any interests or abilities along any of those practical lines, little public evidence of it survives.

More important, by the time of Carter's election in 1976, his political instincts leaned away from Graham's—not dramatically, but discernibly. While Carter's outlook might be described as center-left, Graham's was center-right. They held roughly similar views on race, poverty, and war. Yet Carter supported the Equal Rights Amendment while Graham found the ERA unnecessary. Allowing for exceptional situations and persons, the mature Graham felt that on the whole men and women should seek honorably to fulfill the distinct yet complementary roles God had ordained for them.

Their views of abortion rights also ran center-left and center-right, respectively. Carter opposed abortion for his own family but supported the 1973 *Roe v. Wade* Supreme Court decision, which allowed legal abortion on demand. Graham never moved in that direction. To the end, Graham disapproved of abortion for any circumstance except rape, incest, or to protect the mother's health.

*   *   *

The election of 1980, which pitted Carter against California governor Ronald Reagan, brought to the surface a less savory episode of Graham's life. In it he revealed two traits only his most ardent supporters could defend: his inability to stay out of partisan politics, despite promises to the contrary, and his willingness to sail exceedingly close to the line separating honesty from duplicity in those matters.

First, the background details. Billy and Ruth Graham had visited Jimmy and Rosalynn Carter in the White House in May 1979. Afterward Billy dictated and Ruth handwrote a gracious thank-you letter. Four months later, in September 1979, Robert Maddox, Carter's religious liaison, sent a note to Carter describing a lovely meeting with Graham in Graham's home a few days before. "Dr. Graham assured me he has complete confidence in, admiration and love for the President. He supports the President wholeheartedly. He prays daily for the President."

But here the plot thickens. In October 1979, a short time after the Maddox note, Graham met with a cluster of conservative politicians and business moguls at the Dallas airport to settle on someone who could defeat Carter. A year later—September 1980—Graham sent a note to Reagan's campaign offering to do anything he could to advance Reagan's chances. But just eleven days later, Graham wrote Carter's liaison, Robert Maddox: "As you know, with the Lord's help I'm staying out of it."

Here we see Graham offering to help Reagan *and* almost simultaneously promising Carter that he would stay out of it. The contradiction is incontestable.

This episode replayed, with eerie precision, the one that had connected Nixon, Kennedy, and Graham twenty years earlier. We have seen how Graham promised Kennedy he would not bring Kennedy's Catholicism into play. But that is exactly what he did when he privately urged

Nixon to link himself with Graham in order to capture the Protestant vote. Graham evidently felt that private communications didn't count against his promise not to bring religion into the public discussion.

*   *   *

Exactly why Graham preferred Reagan over Carter is not entirely clear. Reagan represented the Hollywood entertainment industry. Granted, Graham rarely if ever denounced the industry itself, and he claimed many stars like Frank Sinatra, Roy Rogers, and Dale Evans as friends. But he certainly found aspects of the industry degrading to American morals. Reagan was divorced and remarried, a matrimonial state that Graham, like most evangelicals at that time, viewed with disapproval.

Yet the affinity between Reagan and Graham likely drew on deeper currents of Christian faith. Reagan had grown up in the Disciples of Christ tradition in Dixon, Illinois. Though this body was usually pegged among the most liberal of the mainline denominations, his influential mother, Nelle, was strongly evangelical. She taught Sunday school and led the missionary society. In his adolescence Reagan professed conversion, was baptized, and faithfully taught a Sunday school class until he headed off to Eureka College, a Disciples school.

On moving to Los Angeles, Reagan joined and played an active role in the Hollywood Disciples of Christ congregation. His religious biographer Paul Kengor allows that he was not scrupulous about church attendance, but he did maintain devotional practices throughout his life, especially in the earlier and later, or "bookend," years.

After Ronald married Nancy, the couple joined Bel Air Presbyterian in Los Angeles, served by Donn Moomaw. It is telling that Reagan and Moomaw became close lifelong friends. This strongly evangelical former UCLA football star declined to play professionally in the United States because he was not willing to play on Sundays.[1] He also helped found the evangelical parachurch organization Fellowship of Christian Athletes. Moomaw was, as we have seen, a colleague of Henrietta Mears and chum of Graham's. In short, Reagan, Moomaw, Mears, and Graham were all comrades of like mind.

Though Reagan rarely if ever talked about denominational specifics, he often referred to God's guidance in his own and in the nation's affairs, especially as he grew older. He regarded the struggle against Communism as much a religious encounter as it was political and military.

In the president's mind, God ordained the United States as a "shining City on a Hill"—a nation both privileged and obligated to herald a message of freedom under God to the rest of the world. The president liked to talk with Graham about theology, especially ideas about the second coming. Both men believed in it, but not, as commonly reported, as an event imminent enough to affect public policy decisions.

Beyond these religious affinities, there can be little doubt that Reagan's center-right and sometimes right-right politics appealed to Graham. They both affirmed muscular capitalism, suspicion of big government, bootstrap work ethics, and strong military defense. And both were comfortable hobnobbing with the rich and the famous.

On March 30, 1981, weeks after Reagan's inauguration, a deranged drifter named John Hinckley Jr. shot and severely wounded the president (and three others) as he exited the Washington Hilton. A half hour later one of Reagan's aides called Graham and asked him to come as quickly as possible to pray with the president and his family.

Graham immediately flew by private plane to the capital. The following day he met with Nancy. Given the protocol of silence about conversations with top leaders, we do not know what he said to Nancy, or even if he met with the president himself, but the symbolism was potent. We do know that Reagan phoned Graham from his hospital bed to discuss forgiving his would-be assassin.

With one exception (discussed later), there is little evidence that Graham and Reagan talked much about serious political issues, as he surely had done with Johnson and Nixon. Their wives, Nancy and Ruth, were friends with each other and with both men. When Nancy revealed that she had visited an astrologer, Graham certainly did not endorse her practice but remained typically nonjudgmental about her.

The relationship between the preacher and the president can be overanalyzed. It may be sufficient to say that an elusive personal alchemy played a role, as it had with Johnson and Nixon but not with Ford and Carter. Reagan was, Graham later wrote, "one of the most winsome men I have ever known."

Reagan returned the compliment. When Graham held a crusade in Paris in 1986, Reagan told French president François Mitterand that Graham was one of America's "most prestigious religious figures." Asking Mitterand to grant Graham an appointment, Reagan confided to the French president that he (Reagan) and the "world renowned" preacher had been "close friends for many years."

When the former president died in 2004, Nancy Reagan invited Graham to deliver the president's funeral homily. Graham was in his late eighties and not feeling up for the trip from North Carolina to California. But he made clear that he would have been pleased to do so if he had been physically able.

We have seen that Graham was not gifted to serve as a local pastor, and he knew it too. But time after time he also showed that he remained a pastor at heart.

PART 4

Senior Statesman

World Conferences

In time the story of Graham abroad may prove more historically important than the more familiar narrative of Graham at home. Indeed, Graham
biographer William Martin has said that the "most lasting part" of the
preacher's legacy may lie outside the United States. After Graham's death,
historian Melani McAlister, an expert on global evangelicalism, allowed
that other figures trained more missionaries, and reached more people
on television, and rivaled his preaching ministry, "But no one else did as
much to turn evangelicalism into an international movement."[1]

Evidence for Martin's and McAlister's judgment turns up in multiple
ways. Four quick examples suffice.

The first two are statistical. First, as noted in the introduction to this
book, Graham preached in person more than 70 countries outside the
United States and Canada, and live satellite feeds conveyed those preaching events to an additional 132 countries. Second, nearly half of the crusades Graham held took place outside the United States. By one journalist's count, the totals tallied 226 at home and 195 elsewhere.[2]

The second two are anecdotal. Historian Helen Jin Kim notes that the
very day after Graham's landmark Seoul crusade ended, he speculated
that "the gravitational center of world Christianity was shifting to Asia."
And finally, near the end of Graham's life one associate asked him what
he considered his single most significant accomplishment. Graham answered instantly: "The conferences"—by which he meant the meetings
he organized in Europe to foster world evangelization.

For many of the data presented in this scene and in the following one, I am deeply indebted to William Martin's superior treatment of Graham's global work in *Billy Graham:
American Pilgrim*, noted in the bibliographic essay.

The realization of a global evangelical movement with definable boundaries—as opposed to a fluid set of spiritual aspirations—emerges as one of his most notable achievements. This insurgence ranks alongside Roman Catholicism, mainline Protestantism, and charismatic Pentecostalism as one of the four major rivers crisscrossing the global Christian landscape in the twenty-first century.[3]

We have seen that Graham's relentlessly expansionist instincts manifested themselves early on. As far back as 1946, just three years out of college, he bravely set out to evangelize the British Isles and even parts of non-English-speaking Europe. At the time, probably most Americans—especially ones that had not served in the world wars—had never ridden in an airplane. Yet the young Graham seemed never to think twice about the mechanical, logistical, or cultural problems he might encounter in domestic or in international travel.[4]

Graham's ambition for the evangelization of the planet became particularly conspicuous during and after the 1960s. It took two main forms. One was the series of international conferences that he and the BGEA orchestrated and largely funded. The other was the succession of evangelistic crusades he held in cities around the world. This Scene focuses on the conferences, the next one on the crusades, and the following one on the significance of these international endeavors for appreciating both the limitations and extent of Graham's influence.

*   *   *

Three conferences stand out: World Congress on Evangelism in Berlin in 1966; International Congress on World Evangelization in Lausanne, Switzerland, in 1974; and International Conference(s) for Itinerant Evangelists in Amsterdam in 1983, 1986, and 2000.

When Graham organized the World Congress on Evangelism in Berlin in 1966, he was already an old hand at international gatherings of Christian leaders. He had served as a key player in the formation of the international Youth for Christ organization when it first met in Beatenberg, Switzerland, in 1946, just months after the end of World War II. Europe was still devastated and civilian travel extremely difficult.

Moreover, Graham attended the organizing meeting of the World Council of Churches (WCC) in Amsterdam as an observer in 1948, as well as the second meeting of the council in Evanston, Illinois, in 1954, and the third meeting in New Delhi in 1961. He would attend most subsequent meetings of the World Council too.

Leading figures at the Berlin congress in 1966 included *Christianity Today* editor Carl F. H. Henry; Park Street Church pastor Harold John Ockenga; and the redoubtable evangelical Anglican scholar/rector John Stott. Besides these men, twelve hundred theologians and evangelists, almost entirely from Western nations, gathered for several purposes. The primary one was to restore the evangelistic or conversion-centered aims of the historic Protestant missionary movement.

Graham immediately sought to stake out territory different from that of the WCC. He and the other delegates believed that the WCC had subordinated—if not totally abandoned—itself to a social gospel agenda. They had good reasons for this belief. The WCC had not only stated its social gospel aims clearly but also explicitly caricatured Graham and others like him as "traitors to Christ's cause." Whatever the reality on the ground, the Berlin group insisted that it did not aim to displace the WCC but to provide a balancing emphasis.

How did Graham and his colleagues at Berlin propose to implement this lost emphasis? First, they intended to keep front and center the conviction that the true biblical mandate for evangelism pivoted on the individual first, society second. Second, they wanted to show the relevance of this approach to the modern world. Far from being outdated, it addressed the world's problems where they started, in the sinful heart. Third, they wished to affirm the urgency of this vision. Though vague on the details, delegates affirmed the imminence of Christ's return.

One more point deserves notice. The delegates issued a statement on race. After affirming everyone's need for divine forgiveness and salvation, the statement continued, "We reject the notion that men are unequal because of the distinction of race and color. In the name of Scripture and of Jesus Christ we condemn racialism wherever it appears." Ethiopian emperor Haile Selassie's presence as a speaker intimated a new day coming.

Graham and friends tried to set denominational differences aside and establish common fellowship among like-minded Christian leaders everywhere. Though only 200 of the 1,200 delegates came from the United States, nearly all the delegates were well-educated white males, which made establishing consensus across language and culture divides easier.

*   *   *

Next up was Lausanne. In the summer of 1974, Graham organized and largely funded the International Congress on World Evangelization, which met for ten days in the eye-catching lake town of Lausanne, Switzerland. *Time* magazine described the event as "possibly the widest ranging meeting of Christians ever held." Historian Mark Noll placed it in the ballpark with Vatican II. Eventually known as the "Lausanne movement," or simply as "Lausanne," it proved to be one of the most long-lasting and far-reaching efforts of Graham's life.

Lausanne both resembled and differed from Berlin. Like Berlin, Lausanne drew evangelical leaders from around the world, but unlike Berlin, the demographic profile was strikingly different: 2,473 church figures from 150 countries and seven continents, with an additional 1,300 observers and several hundred journalists. Whites constituted only a minority. Though only one woman—Corrie ten Boom—served as a plenary speaker, women were conspicuous among the delegates.

We gain a sense of the drama of the occasion by viewing the opening meeting, in which the conference hall was festooned with banners in six languages that proclaimed: "Let the Earth Hear His Voice." We gain a sense, too, of the urgency of the occasion by noting a great population clock, hung at the front. By the end of the first evening, the world's population had grown by 163,569. By the end of the conference, that number had soared to 1,800,000.

Though Graham stayed in the background—another difference from Berlin—he did give the keynote address, which set the agenda. The marching order called evangelical Christians everywhere to reclaim the authority of the Bible, to bring individuals to Christ, to serve as a social witness, and to resist identifying the gospel with any particular culture. Given the new ethnic inclusiveness of the delegates, the word "world" gained enriched meaning.

Lausanne brought two fresh faces to the front, John Stott and Leighton Ford. Stott had gained global prominence as an evangelical clergyman in the Church of England. A lifelong bachelor, Stott was revered for his piety, learning, and abstemious lifestyle. Many called him a Billy Graham for intellectuals. Rector of All Souls Church in Langham Place, London, and author of more than fifty books, Stott was later designated by *Time* as one of the "100 Most Influential People."

Ford we met earlier. As Graham's Canadian brother-in-law and one of the three members of the Platform Team, he played a key organizational role at Lausanne. After the initial meeting in 1974, the executive committee appointed him chairman, a position he held until 1992, when he became honorary life chairman.

The Lausanne conferences proved notable for giving the social gospel a role in evangelism. This dimension was pioneered especially by Stott and Latin American evangelicals René Padilla and Samuel Escobar. Granted, social gospel ideals, summarized in what became *The Lausanne Covenant's* famous article 5, "Christian Social Responsibility," accounted for fewer than 10 percent of the words in the document. But they stood out, precisely because evangelicals, especially in the United States, had been reluctant to march in that direction at all. Ford, less bound by American conventions, threw his influence behind the new orientation too.

Here Graham weighed in. He never doubted the social import of true conversion to Christ—redeemed hearts proved themselves in redeemed hands—but he felt that this perspective should be emphasized in other organizations. In Graham's mind, one of the main reasons that evangelical visionaries had created the congress in the first place was to emphasize the part of the historic Christian message that the WCC had come to neglect. And so it was that Stott and Graham had to talk things through. In the end, Stott prevailed.

Lausanne expressed its goals in a short document titled *The Lausanne Covenant*. Graham later called it "a theological watershed for evangelicals for generations to come." He not only signed the *Covenant* but also agreed to be the first one to sign, with photographers on hand. Whether Graham signed because Stott had truly persuaded him or because he saw no point resisting may be debated. Either way, his endorsement gave the *Covenant* the heft it needed.

Lausanne's mandate took enduring form in just seven words: "a whole gospel for the whole world." Historian Darren Dochuk put it this way. "Lausanne . . . revealed evangelicalism's turn toward a different sensibility." The movement's list of accomplishments was long. Dochuk sums them up nicely. The Lausanne congress, he said, "defined common theological grounds on which they could act." It erased the distinction between "missionary-sending and missionary-receiving nations." Perhaps most important, Lausanne's pervasive spirit of humility stemmed from an attitude of "evangelical penitence" rather than "evangelical triumphalism."

In the late twentieth and early twenty-first century, socially engaged evangelicals worldwide would look back to the *Lausanne Covenant* as their Magna Carta. The movement powerfully influenced Rick Warren, one of the most influential pastor-theologians of the following generation. It also provided a platform—and megaphone—for Latino evangelical theologians, including, most notably, Padilla and Escobar.[5]

Stott, Graham, and other Lausanne leaders met again in 1975 in Mexico City, where they crafted a follow-up document called "Our Mandate from Lausanne '74." "Our Mandate" unequivocally affirmed the priority of individual evangelism, but it also insisted that Christian leaders must bear "a clearer, more balanced perspective on evangelism and social responsibility." The latter included aid development, attacking imperialism, confronting the population explosion, liberating the oppressed, and doing "God's work in the world."[6]

*　　　*　　　*

The year 1983 saw the birth of the third of Graham's major international conferences: the International Conference for Itinerant Evangelists in Amsterdam, with follow-up conferences in 1986 and 2000. Berlin had focused on forging a global theological platform; Lausanne, a global fellowship platform with a social gospel wedge. Amsterdam projected complementary but different aims.

Amsterdam pursued two additional goals. The first was to provide *practical* knowledge for carrying out evangelistic work. The kind of training Graham had in mind was seemingly routine but actually called for quite complex skills such as learning how to craft sermons, raise money, and negotiate travel logistics.

The second aim was to equip ordinary young men and women—not church leaders or professional missionaries—with tools for spreading the gospel back home. In the words of historian John Pollock—words Graham endorsed—these were the "foot soldiers" of the gospel, the ones "who pushed bicycles through jungle trails to proclaim Christ . . . or held missions in dense urban areas." The organizers designed the conferences for *itinerant* evangelists.

The scope and diversity of the Amsterdam conferences were breathtaking. Four thousand participants came to the 1983 meeting, 9,600 to the 1986 meeting, and 10,700 to the 2000 meeting. For every participant accepted, nine others had applied. Graham insisted that 70 percent of those accepted must come from the developing world, with preference given to folks under forty.

The diversity was breathtaking too. The first Amsterdam meeting saw 132 national flags and the proceedings simultaneously translated into nine languages. By the time of Amsterdam III, that number had swollen into 174 flags and fifteen languages. Spin-off conferences and schools ultimately trained tens of thousands.

The Lausanne and especially Amsterdam conferences began to crack the image—perpetuated by countless magazine covers featuring Graham's Nordic visage—of evangelicalism as a solid front of white male faces. Graham showed that he had moved into multiracial, multicultural, multi-linguistic awareness. He also showed that his heart, feet, and wallet were embedded in developing world concerns and aspirations.

One anecdote tells the larger Amsterdam conference story in a nut-shell. At the '86 conference Billy and Ruth entered the dining hall and sat next to an African participant. Graham's memory of the occasion offers a sense of what the Amsterdam conferences sought to achieve. It merits quoting a bit fulsomely.

> From his clothes, we suspected that he came from a poor coun-try and had very little. . . . "Where are you from?" I inquired. "I am from Botswana." . . . He said he traveled, often on foot, from village to village, preaching the Gospel of Christ to anyone who would listen. . . . "What is your background? Did you go to a Bible school or get any education to help you?" "Well, actually," he said, "I got my master's degree from Cambridge University." . . .
>
> I was immediately ashamed that I had stereotyped him as an uneducated man. I was also humbled, not only because he was far better educated than I was, but because . . . [any] man return-ing to his underdeveloped homeland of Botswana with a coveted Cambridge degree would have virtually unlimited opportunities for political power, social position, and economic advancement. And yet this man was completely content to follow Christ's calling for him as an evangelist.

Graham, like all great leaders, had faults aplenty, but he recognized parochialism in himself and tried to address it. He possessed a grand dream and the moxie, ambition, and resources to give it life.

SCENE 40

World Crusades

The energy that powered the international conferences also powered the mass crusades that unfolded on six continents and in more than seventy countries around the world over six decades. Apart from New York in 1957 (aggregate attendance: 2.4 million), Graham's four largest crusades unfolded outside North America: London, 1954 (2 million); Scotland, 1955 (2.6 million); Australia and New Zealand, 1959 (3.4 million); and Seoul, 1973 (3.2 million). As in the United States, some of Graham's ventures overseas failed, sometimes spectacularly. But on the whole, the record is one of remarkable success.

In 1956, just two years after "Harringay," Graham made his first visit to India. President Eisenhower and Secretary of State John Foster Dulles encouraged the trip. The preacher's motives were twofold: to spread the gospel of Christ and also the gospel of American democracy in the face of Soviet Communist expansion. Graham spoke to 100,000 over three days in Madras, to 75,000 in Kottayam—25,000 more than the city's population—and to 100,000 at Palamcottah.

Graham soon learned, however, that success abroad, like success at home, was a precarious business. Traditionally he excelled at making friendly contacts with the leaders of the countries he visited, but not this time, as an awkward visit with Prime Minister Jawaharlal Nehru showed. Among other problems, the prime minister had caught wind that Graham had disparaged Indian culture in his diary and letters home. Worse, a Graham fellow traveler had said that the country would be better off if Indians would "eat their cows instead of worshiping them." Graham apologized and vowed—with imperfect success—never again to criticize another culture or religion.

In 1960 Graham toured ten countries in eight weeks in Africa, with mixed results. He won the strongest response in Northern Rhodesia and Southern Rhodesia (now Zambia and Zimbabwe) and in Nigeria, with an aggregate attendance in those countries of 570,000. President William V. S. Tubman invited Graham to Liberia, where he received the nation's second-highest civilian honors, but five days of meetings saw only 13,000 attenders. Results in neighboring Ghana were disappointing too.

Muslims in Nigeria and the Sudan counterattacked Graham's criticisms of Islam, and in other countries partisans of native religions confronted Graham too. In these countries Graham broke his vow about not criticizing local culture—and paid a price. Graham traveled on to Jordan and then to Jerusalem. In Jerusalem he won permission to preach, but only to Christian gatherings, and authorities asked him not to mention Jesus in gatherings with Jews.[1]

Graham's visit to South America in 1962 offers a similar story of resistance and success. Before departing, Graham followed his pattern of checking in with the president, in this case the Catholic Kennedy. The president raised a red flag about evangelizing in countries already Christian. Kennedy proved right, for Graham encountered stiff resistance from Catholic leaders in Colombia and Paraguay as well as anti-American protests in Venezuela. Things went better in Brazil, Chile, and Argentina. The BGEA said relatively little about the five-week tour, suggesting that the results were less than stellar.

A return to India in 1972 attracted large crowds—100,000 over three days in Kohima—and better relations with the new prime minister, Indira Gandhi. A 1977 return engagement won similar support in Calcutta, Hyderabad, and Madras. When Graham died, Indian journalist Ashish Ittyerah Joseph—whose father served as one of Graham's translators—observed that "wherever he went, his crowd would be nothing less than hundred thousand people." Graham made a point to ensure that "all the denominations came together. He wouldn't come unless the whole city was unified."

*   *   *

Graham's journeys to Australia and New Zealand in his midcareer decades ranked among the most successful of his long career, at least if success is measured by the number of attenders and inquirers. In 1959 he spent four months Down Under, preaching in eight cities in Australia and three in New Zealand, with an overall attendance of more than three million with 150,000 inquirers. Appearing on national television—which had been introduced to Australia only two years before—he became something of a national celebrity. One Anglican bishop judged that Graham was the "biggest thing that ever happened in the church history of Australia."

Meetings in Sydney in 1968 and 1969 saw more varied results. The resistance likely owed less to disapproval of Graham himself than to disapproval of the American war in Vietnam. Even so, Graham's 1968 Sydney meeting posted 500,000 attenders over eight days. A follow-up crusade in Sydney eleven years later spanned three weeks with 491,000 visitors.[2]

In many ways the centerpiece of Graham's overseas crusades took place from May 30 to June 3, 1973, in South Korea. In those five days Graham preached to an aggregate audience of three million, with 72,000 registering decisions for Christ.

The concluding service was the largest of Graham's career. It took place on a mile-long former tarmac, turned into a parade ground, on an island in the harbor of Seoul. Aerial surveys showed 1,120,000 souls squashed together in the summer sun, undoubtedly forming one of the largest Christian gatherings in history.[3] The choir alone numbered 6,000. Since it was not feasible to ask inquirers to walk forward, Graham asked them simply to stand. Twelve thousand decision cards were turned in.

The magnitude of the moment was not lost on the preacher. Historian Helen Jin Kim reports that the day after the event, Graham ruminated, "I seriously doubt if my own ministry can ever be the same again."

Besides the numbers, perhaps the most remarkable feature of the occasion was the simplicity of Graham's words and the power of his understated yet charismatic presence to draw so many people into his direct hearing range. His sermon, "The Love of God," based on John 15:13, "Greater love has no one than this: to lay down one's life for one's friends," replayed a theme he had been talking about for three decades. Some local pastors and theologians found Graham's preaching thin. One suspects Graham would have agreed, and that is precisely the point: to communicate the gospel as effectively as possible, uncomplicated by theological abstractions.

An iconic photo of the scene, often reprinted, taken from behind, shows Graham speaking to a crowd that stretched as far off into the horizon as the eye could see. At the conclusion of the service, Martin reports, a helicopter lifted the preacher away. Looking back, Graham said, simply enough, "This is the work of God. There is no other explanation." But deep down he surely felt at least a tiny bit of personal accomplishment, too.

*　　　*　　　*

Results proved dramatic too in Brazil in 1974. Graham preached to a capacity crowd of 225,000 at the closing service of the Baptist World Alliance at Maracana Soccer Stadium in Rio de Janeiro. At the time, this was the largest crowd ever to attend an evangelistic service in the Western Hemisphere. Brazil's evangelical president arranged for the service to be televised, beaming it to a potential audience of more than 100,000,000 viewers.

The late 1970s and 1980s were marked by multiple forays into Eastern Europe, the Soviet Union, China, and North Korea. Starting small, with a low-profile visit to Hungary in 1977, Graham moved on to historically significant visits to Poland in 1978 and Moscow in 1982 and 1984. The later visit to Moscow seemed a reward for good behavior—in Soviet eyes—during his highly publicized and intensely controversial visit to Moscow two years earlier (as we will see later).

Though a calculated gamble, the trade-off paid handsome dividends. Graham won permission to hold crusades in four Soviet cities, including Moscow and Leningrad. In those sites he preached more than fifty times, almost certainly the first Westerner to do so. He stressed that religious people of whatever persuasion did not threaten civil order.

East Asia—overwhelmingly not Christian, let alone evangelical Protestant—presented special challenges. Graham held crusades in cities in Japan in 1956, 1967, 1980, and 1994, with mixed success. In 1988 he and Ruth fulfilled a lifelong dream of preaching in China. Ruth had grown up in China, as noted earlier, and this was a nostalgic trip back.[4] The China mission included five cities spanning seventeen days, along with a cordial hourlong visit with Chinese premier Li Ping.

Other Eastern and Western Europe visits in those years were equally climactic. His first visit to Hungary, back in 1977, had been tightly controlled and the crowds relatively light. In contrast, a return visit in 1989 unfolded with little state control and drew 100,000 attenders. The 27,000 inquiry cards turned in that day constituted the strongest numerical response of any single meeting in Graham's ministry. The event was even aired over state-owned television.

Graham's Soviet Union travels culminated in one of the peak events of his long career: an invitation to speak in Moscow in 1992, just three years after the fall of Communism. Expounding the gospel in the Indoor Olympic Stadium, Martin reports, he attracted more than 38,000 followers each of three nights, and then 50,000 the final night, with an overflow crowd of 20,000 outdoors. The invitation came with the support of 150 churches in the city and 3,000 elsewhere in the nation (now Russia). The wonder is not that his meetings attracted so many but that they took place at all in the Land of the Bear.

In 1992 and again in 1994, Graham (without Ruth) paid visits to the isolated nation of North Korea. The meetings came at the invitation of the Korean (Protestant) Christian Federation and the Korean Catholics Association, with government approval. In the course of the trip, Graham conferred at length with President Kim Il Sung, a visit that received extensive coverage in the state-run media. He gave the North Korean president, who had been reared with the Christian influence of his mother, a copy of *Peace with God*. Hardly a crusade of the usual sort, the North Korea visit found Graham preaching in the two churches in the capital city of Pyongyang—one Protestant and one Catholic.

A return visit in 1994 followed a similar pattern, which might be called diplomatic evangelism. Some American evangelicals sharply criticized Graham's apparent dalliance with the repressive North Korean regime. His effective response, entirely in character, was to say, "it never hurts to talk."[5]

Though Puerto Rico was of course a United States territory, it is nonetheless revealing that Graham's most sustained effort to proclaim the gospel to the entire world originated in a site strongly identified with Hispanic culture and the Spanish language. Broadcasting from San Juan in March 1995, Graham sought to reach one billion people—one-fifth of the earth's population—using thirty satellites to connect with 3,000 download sites in 185 countries in all twenty-nine time zones. Translated into 116 languages, his sermon constituted one of the great technological and linguistic feats in Christian history.

American Abroad

The story of the overseas conferences and crusades should be placed in a more personal context, for the personal story provides a foundation for the public one. Graham was intensely committed to his work—no one ever questioned that—but, like millions of Americans, he also enjoyed the adventure of life on the road. One associate dryly quipped, "Billy likes hotel rooms."

More precisely, Graham was a serious traveler, not just a tourist out to see the sights. Indeed, close associates said that he was remarkably oblivious to local attractions and natural scenery (except beaches and sunsets). Rather, he relished interactions with a wide range of individuals, running from heads of state to folk on the street.

From the mid-1930s Graham saw the gospel as a message for the whole world, and from the mid-1940s he saw himself as one of its messengers. The Mormon founder, Joseph Smith, once described himself as a "rough stone rolling." In Graham's case, the rough edges of Southern farm life soon wore off, but the rolling part never did.

Reporters overseas, like reporters at home, covered him wherever he went. Their work made him seem not only omnipresent but also connected to pretty much everything going on in the Christian world—and more. William Martin's account of Graham's visit to a leprosarium in Nigeria in 1960—based on a contemporary newspaper clipping—aptly caught the pathos of the moment. There, said one reviewer, the "oft-squeamish . . . preacher clasped the stumps that one woman had for hands and joined her in prayer." In such stories private acts quietly blended into public narratives played out on the world's stage.

Photographers kept their cameras trained on him too. Some of the most iconic pictures of Graham captured him in "real-life" situations in other countries. One of the most frequently reproduced (though unidentified) photos shows him sitting on the ground in khaki pants and open shirt—likely in Calcutta in 1977—surrounded by a gaggle of elementary-aged children. His and the children's heads are bowed, as he attempts—clearly with mixed success—to lead them in prayer.

Graham's travels also gave birth to a plethora of stories about his "real-life" courage, and those stories also enhanced his appeal both at home and abroad. A great lore of near-miss tales about his flying adventures—and misadventures—grew up over the years. After one especially turbulent flight—this time on Air France—a reporter asked if he had been frightened. Graham responded: "I would say tense." We can almost see the grin.

*　　　*　　　*

The international meetings followed largely the same pattern as those at home. Graham knew what worked, and he determined to keep it that way. He necessarily left myriad details to local organizing committees, but behind the scenes he quietly made sure that everything ran according to plan.

No field was too small to tend. Advance men and their families moved to the site months, sometimes a full year, ahead of the event. They launched the usual cycle of prayer meetings, training sessions, media connections, and mass advertising. Hoping always to minimize surprises, Graham took his own pulpit with him wherever he traveled and, insofar as feasible, also his own sound system and technicians.

The format of the meetings ran true to form, too. Testifiers, soloists, guest artists, massive choirs, a forceful sermon by Graham (or a stand-in if necessary), and a final invitation followed a tried-and-tested American-born script. In English-speaking settings abroad, as at home, Graham tried to preach with familiar words and short sentences. In non-English-speaking settings, he went out of his way to speak as simply as possible for easy translation. Graham's electric preaching style was the same, along with his characteristic wit and propensity toward overstatement. He invariably found the people exceptionally friendly and the natural scenery exceptionally beautiful.

Graham was so determined to maintain continuity that he also tried to use the same carefully screened interpreters whenever he entered non-English-speaking contexts. Billy Kim—a Bob Jones College graduate and South Korean national—became so much a fixture of Graham's Korean crusades that he earned a well-recognized voice in his own right.

*   *   *

Deep down Graham fervently believed that the gospel he preached was not distinctively—let alone uniquely—American but applied to everyone. Over and over he assured international audiences that he came not as a white middle-class American nor as an ambassador of the United States or its interests. Rather, he came as a proclaimer of a message that transcended all boundaries—nation, culture, ethnicity, race, and gender. After all, the Bible promised that Jesus Christ was the same yesterday, today, and forever. And everywhere.

And to a remarkable extent, he succeeded. When Graham died, Joseph Mar Thoma, a primate of the Syrian Church in India, said that in "different languages, different cultures and different races" he "preached and explain[ed] the human face of God."

Nonetheless, international audiences saw Graham as inescapably American, too. His Americanness showed up in multiple ways. For one thing, as historian Uta Balbier has shown, many observers, especially in Europe, thought he resembled a salesman "selling" Jesus the same way someone would sell soap or any other commodity. We have seen that Graham heard this criticism at home, too, but he reworked it into a compliment. If you have the best product in the world, he beamed, why not market it with all the tools you have?

What Graham likely did not see, however, was that selling Jesus—or soap—came with another attitude highly characteristic of Americans: quantification. This meant aggressive marketing, numerical tallies, and an underlying yet powerful conviction that enough was never enough.

Moreover, Graham's version of evangelicalism presented itself in a form that was as new as it was old. It had originated in England, Scotland, and the American colonies in the eighteenth century, but that form became increasingly American as it evolved in the nineteenth century—more individualistic, more formulaic, and more exportable. Graham added his own shaping force by making it more streamlined than ever.

Evangelicalism had never been much encumbered with liturgy, confessions, sacraments, priesthood, or nurture, but in his hands it became increasingly aerodynamic as sectarian distinctives such as predestination, baptism by immersion, speaking in tongues, and rapture of the saints quietly fell away.

Finally, in many instances Graham came as a representative of a political entity, the United States of America. Not primarily, of course, but inevitably. Historian Helen Jin Kim has tracked the process. When he got off the plane in Seoul in May of 1973, for example, he immediately laid his cards on the table. He came, he said, not as an ambassador of the American president, or American government, or American political interests. Rather, he came solely as an ambassador of Jesus Christ.

Even so, Kim shows, "Graham represented both God and America." Right off, he met with the US ambassador, Philip C. Habib, who briefed Graham and then hosted a dinner party. Next Graham visited South Korean president Park Jung Hee at the "Blue House." The president knew perfectly well that Graham might serve as a direct conduit between him and the most powerful nation and man in the world.

*   *   *

Yet if Graham remained inescapably American, why did he succeed so remarkably beyond American shores? Undoubtedly factors within each of the many countries he visited set the stage. It surely was not accidental that Graham proved most successful in countries that fell at roughly the same stage of economic, political, and technological development as the United States—the United Kingdom, Germany, Australia, New Zealand, and South Korea. In countries that were putatively ahead of the United States—notably Scandinavian nations—and putatively behind it—much of the developing world—he saw less success.

Analyzing the social configuration of each site Graham visited would be a huge task and one that mercifully falls outside the scope of this book. But this study does prompt us to ask what ingredients Graham brought to each situation that made him so culturally attractive and spiritually powerful.

Factors both internal and external to the message played a role. Internally, the message traveled very far very fast because there was so little wind resistance raised by encumbering doctrines and practices. Historian Seth Dowland exaggerates a point to make a point. Hearers learned that sin could be easily dealt with: "Deliverance was only a short prayer away."

More important, says Dowland, they learned that spiritual happiness in this life and spiritual joy in the life to come lay in a person's own hands. Everything depended on a decision, and the decision was theirs to make. Most important, they learned that something momentous really was at stake. The decision counted, for it meant closing some doors just as surely as it meant opening others.

Graham's international appeal also benefited from ingredients essentially independent of the message itself, and that was the second factor. His looks, style, sincerity, humility, and urgency, which propelled his success at home, propelled his success abroad, too. Then too Graham took the care to cultivate local churches abroad as he did at home. This included months of precrusade planning, advertising, prayer groups, counselor training, and connecting with area pastors.

And sometimes Graham gained by the status that his associations with American presidents and other high political leaders conferred. Not always, especially during the Nixon era, but more often than not. Local leaders gained too from Graham's almost invariable support for the government wherever he traveled.

Graham likely would have agreed with all these explanations—up to a point, anyway. He also would have insisted that explanations of that sort were but half the story. The other half lay in the power of the message itself. The gospel was timeless and universal because it addressed needs that also were timeless and universal.

When Graham died, Peggy Noonan, a columnist for the *Wall Street Journal*, drew on the words of the Reverend Charles Chaput, Catholic archbishop of Philadelphia, to capture Graham's contribution not only to Catholics but also to searching souls everywhere. "He had the ability to reach across all the fractures in Christianity and speak to the common believing heart," Chaput suggested. Comparing Graham to C. S. Lewis, Chaput continued: "In a sense, he spoke the same kind of 'mere' Christianity that Lewis did so well, but with an American accent."

Clearly, for many internationals, the accent overwhelmed the moment. But just as clearly, for many others, it conveyed not the limitations of the messenger but the force of the message.

SCENE 41

Sin of Total War

The SALT talks formed the backdrop for Billy Graham's changing thoughts on warfare. In 1972 the United States and the Soviet Union forged a Strategic Arms Limitation Agreement, commonly called SALT. Seven years later the two nations agreed to additional reductions, dubbed SALT II. Owing to the Soviet invasion of Afghanistan in September 1979, the United States Senate never ratified SALT II.

After SALT Graham had called for an agreement that he named SALT 10[1]—specifically "bilateral, verifiable eradication of all nuclear, biochemical and laser weapons used for mass destruction." Despite the Senate's refusal to endorse SALT II, Graham never backed away from his summons to the leaders of the two nations to embrace the essentials of his vision for a SALT 10.

This turn was particularly surprising, coming from Graham. We have seen that through the first half of his public ministry he had presented himself as the fiercest of hawks about the specter of Communism. But things changed.

In the late 1970s Graham started to talk publicly about the growing menace of war between the United States and the Soviet Union. And not just with nuclear weapons, either, but with all weapons of mass destruction. Again and again, in print and in media interviews, he called for mutual (and mutually assured) nuclear disarmament, as well as elimination of other "biochemical" arsenals of mass destruction. History lay in God's hands, for sure, but until God chose to bring history to an end, the stewardship of the earth continued to be humanity's responsibility.

Sometime in 1978—exactly when is not clear—unnamed "military experts from the Pentagon" visited Billy and Ruth in their home in Montreat. The experts detailed the global consequences of a nuclear war. Graham was horrified. He had always evinced a healthy respect for the judgment of top brass. Their status undoubtedly lent gravitas to the grimness of their message.

Graham also visited Poland in 1978. Arriving in October, he traveled to six cities, where he preached in Catholic, Baptist, Lutheran, and Reformed pulpits. In Poland Graham visited Nazi concentration camps at Treblinka, Auschwitz, and Birkenau. He said that the horrors that took place in those places were forever burned into his "heart and mind." In an extremely rare instance of Graham losing his composure in public, photographs show him leaving Auschwitz in tears.

The year 1979 saw major developments in Graham's pilgrimage. In March he used *CBS Evening News* as a platform for denouncing the nuclear arms race as "insanity, madness." Determined to speak forcefully about new measures to guarantee peace in a nuclear age, Graham said that he regretted the "hawkish sentiments of [his] youthful years." Having staked out a position on national television, he signaled that retreating in the face of opposition from the religious and political Right was not in the cards.

*　　　*　　　*

In the fall of 1979 Graham held crusades in Hungary. These preaching opportunities did not fall from the sky but resulted from arduous negotiations by Alexander Haratzi, a Hungarian physician who had immigrated to the United States after the failed Hungarian uprising in 1956. The daunting complexities of those negotiations introduced Graham to the extraordinary difficulties of working with Communist governments. But they also introduced him to cracks in the purportedly atheistic religious landscape of Eastern Europe and the Soviet Union.

Given Graham's increasingly vocal response to the catastrophe of nuclear war, the Russians saw a golden opportunity to try to exploit him. And so it was that in early 1982 he received an invitation from the patriarch of the Russian Orthodox Church to attend a conference in Moscow in May.

Though the event was billed as a commemoration of the 1,000th anniversary of the founding of the Orthodox Church in Russia, the church significantly called it the World Conference of Religious Workers for Saving the Sacred Gift of Life from Nuclear Catastrophe. Graham took the invitation with utmost seriousness. The stakes were high.

On one hand there were excellent reasons to say no. The most obvious, perhaps, was that by all accounts the event was a ruse, a platform for the

Soviet Union to trumpet its trustworthiness and the United States' duplicity. Graham knew perfectly well that the Soviets were touting peace talks at the same time that they were engaged in a massive buildup of their nuclear arsenal.

Moreover, Graham ran headlong into a solid wall of opposition at home. Resistance came from President Reagan (who later relented), Vice President Bush, and, especially, Arthur Hartman, the American ambassador to the Soviet Union. Some members of the BGEA's board of directors urged him not to go, and so did his wife, Ruth.

On the other hand, there were excellent reasons to say yes. To begin with, Richard Nixon and Henry Kissinger, two old government hands, now out of office but still highly respected for their grasp of world affairs, urged him to accept. Nixon in particular said that it was the chance of a lifetime. An unlikely pair of senators, Mark Hatfield and Jesse Helms, also urged him to go.

Graham ticked off additional reasons. Ever since he had visited Moscow as a tourist in 1959, he had vowed to himself that he would return someday as an evangelist. By April 1982 his motives for going back to Russia had grown more complex. Still mulling over the decision, he told students at Harvard that if he did not go to Russia to speak at the peace conference, the press would continue to portray him simply as an evangelist. They would pay no attention to his determination to help protect civilization from the flames of nuclear destruction.

Though Graham himself never put it quite this way, without doubt an old-fashioned sense of adventure also drew him. A chance to speak on the other side of the Iron Curtain, to call men and women to Christ and at the same time call them to pursue peace, meant that he would be doing what no other evangelist had ever done. And knowing that he would be speaking in the most powerful—and dangerous—restricted-access country on earth surely deepened the lure.

*   *   *

When Graham arrived at the Moscow airport on Friday, May 7, 1982, he immediately declared three reasons for the visit. The first was to learn about the Russian Orthodox Church, the second was to meet other Christians in the Soviet Union, and the third was to gain "practical insights" into how "this society and the society from which I come can find a way to help make this planet a safer and better place to live."

Graham went on to say that he hoped to find ways "multilaterally to reduce and eventually to ban nuclear weapons of all types." He then moved to a prophetic mode, unapologetically announcing that God will judge us "if we fail to take responsible action against the threat of nuclear catastrophe."

The conference started on Monday, May 10. At the outset Graham and the other American visitors—all wearing headphones for instant translation—were subjected to a stinging attack by Soviet and pro-Soviet delegates from the developing world on American militarism. Shortly into the proceedings, Graham conspicuously removed his headphones. Two other American speakers removed theirs too, so his gesture was not the only one the audience saw. But given his stature as one of the most famous preachers in the world, his actions counted.

The following day was Graham's turn to speak. Without mincing words, he strongly denounced the nuclear arms race. Everywhere he traveled, he said, he found that people lived in fear. They feared many perils, including starvation, disease, and environmental pollution. But above all, they feared that unless the superpowers changed their ways, nuclear war was inevitable. It would destroy civilization and even the planet itself.

Nations of the world, Graham continued, seemed to be relentlessly hurtling toward "the brink of chaos and even destruction." Time was short. Survivors might soon be "writing the obituary of much of humanity." In nuclear war, there were no winners, only a "complete catastrophe for all participants."

The preacher likened the two nations to two little boys playing with matches in a pool of gasoline. And the vast sums spent on armaments squandered precious resources that were better spent relieving world crises: "Everyday millions upon millions of people live on the knife-edge of survival because of starvation, poverty, and disease. . . . At the same time . . . the nations of the world are spending an estimated 600 billion dollars per year on weapons. If even one-tenth of that amount were diverted to long-range development programs . . . millions of lives could be saved each year."

All nations, large and small, including the United States and the Soviet Union, were at fault. Graham never asked either nation to disarm unilaterally. There were legitimate reasons to maintain national security, as well as local police and military forces. But he called for both to undertake a mutually assured divestment of all weapons. The stakes were staggering. The nations were dabbling with "a hidden holocaust of unimaginable proportions."

Though Graham recognized that working out the details would be hard—and he acknowledged that he was no expert on those matters—he argued that religious leaders could not shrink from their duty of offering guidance.[2] The ultimate goal? "SALT 10—the complete destruction by all nations of all atomic bombs, hydrogen bombs, biochemical weapons, laser weapons, and all other weapons of mass destruction."

On Sunday, May 9, the day before the conference began, Graham had preached at a Baptist church in Moscow in an early morning service, and later that morning at the (Orthodox) Patriarchal Cathedral. At the Baptist church he spoke mainly on John 5:1-14, which describes Jesus's healing of a man invalided for thirty-eight years. Along the way he tossed in a reference to Romans 13:1-7, which counsels Christians to obey the authorities. According to one sympathetic journalist's report, he clearly meant to say that becoming a Christian helped people become better workers and better citizens, along with many other marks of mature faith.

The reference occupied only a few seconds in a nearly one-hour sermon, but afterward it triggered fierce controversy.[3] Graham said he had preached the sermon five times before, and the Romans reference was simply part of the message. The sermon manuscript shows that the Romans reference was hand-scrawled into the typed outline. At this distance it is impossible to know if he added the Romans reference for the benefit of his Moscow audience or if it was part of the by-then standard presentation. Either way, he later admitted that he regretted saying it at all.

Graham made additional stops in Moscow. With reluctance, he also visited with a band of Siberian Pentecostals who had been holed up in the basement of the United States embassy for four years, demanding the right to emigrate. His reluctance grew from the Pentecostals' real or perceived aim to politicize the event. He also privately conferred with ranking party officials about the repression of Soviet Jews and lent support to their desire to emigrate to Israel.

Exhilarated by a week in the Soviet Union, Graham returned to London, where he received the 1982 Templeton Award, and then back home to the United States. Almost certainly he expected to receive praise for undertaking a hard trip for the sake of the gospel and world peace. But that is not the way things turned out.

Fallout at Home

Controversy enveloped Graham. Some commentators in the United States approved of Graham's efforts in the Soviet Union. The *Christian Century*, long a sharp critic of the evangelist, admired his courage for bucking the fashionable militarism of the time. The prominent evangelical journalist Edward E. Plowman, writing in the *Saturday Evening Post*, vigorously applauded Graham's determination to herald the gospel and the cause of disarmament in an unforgiving setting.

By 1982 *Christianity Today* had acquired a voice of its own and offered more measured approval. The fortnightly found Graham's willingness to shoulder a thankless task, in the face of grave opposition on the home front, commendable, and his words and actions while he was in Moscow, also commendable. Not free of complications and missteps, but on the whole, a job well done.

Yet the majority of prominent voices proved far less generous. Many evangelicals, both prominent and ordinary, especially in the United States and Great Britain, thought he had been duped. Lynn Buzzard, of the Christian Legal Society, for example, described Graham's statements in Moscow as "tragic" or at best "incredibly naïve."

Members of the secular press were even harsher. They targeted him repeatedly and without mercy. George F. Will, a conservative columnist, excoriated Graham as "America's most embarrassing export."[1] Calling the conference a "travesty," he pegged it as an exploitation of clergymen's "vanities and naïveté." Will hoped that men of the cloth—obviously including Graham—would "stop acting as though pious intentions are substitutes for intelligence, and excuses for irresponsibility." *Newsweek* called its coverage, "Billy Renders to Caesar." Colman McCarthy's blast in the *Washington Post* spoke for many others: "The Duping of Billy Graham."

What did Graham actually say and do in Moscow that caused such uproar? In the course of his visit, Graham did utter a number of things that he would regret. He said, for example, that he saw more people in church on a Saturday night in that city than on a Sunday morning in Charlotte. He observed that the Russians had treated him to caviar at every meal. Though both comments were tongue in cheek, elsewhere he indicated in all seriousness that the Soviet standard of living was better than Americans usually assumed. And he said that he personally saw little evidence of religious repression.

Graham's failure publicly to champion dissident Christian groups proved to be a weightier offense. He claimed that he did so privately. Even so, no one knew what he actually said or how vigorously he pressed the issue. The dissidents were irate, for a gesture of that sort would have given them badly needed legitimation and possibly some clout.

Conferring quietly about delicate issues was Graham's style. For years he had worked behind the scenes with Eastern bloc governments to try to persuade them to lift restrictions on Jews' right to emigrate and to teach their children Hebrew. But when he followed that pattern of quiet diplomacy in Moscow, he met fierce criticism in the press for allegedly failing to fight for the rights of religious minorities.

And Graham did not publicly support the Pentecostal band holed up in the embassy, either. He found them combative, not especially interested in a negotiated settlement with Soviet authorities, and fixed on persuading Graham to embrace their notions about the end times. Many evangelical and Pentecostal partisans at home and dissidents in the Soviet Union felt that he had left them twisting in the wind.

Graham tried to defend himself. He did not break his own rule and target his attackers by name. But he did offer some explanations. First off, he admitted that sometimes in the pressures of an intense five-and-one-half-day trip—immediately preceded by a grueling schedule of speaking engagements in New England—he had spoken incautiously. Sometimes the press took words out of context, or failed to see that he was joking, or overlooked his efforts behind the scenes, or ignored his desire just to be a good guest. Preaching the gospel in less-than-ideal circumstances was better than not preaching it at all. And he hoped that he would be invited back to proclaim the gospel in relatively free circumstances—which he eventually was.

Besides, in negotiations before the trip started, Graham said he had promised that he would not use the occasion to denounce the Soviet regime, which would have jeopardized his larger aims of evangelization and disarmament. The year before, the pope had stressed to Graham the usefulness of quiet diplomacy behind the scenes, a word Graham took to heart.

Defenders of Graham also observed that he was sixty-three, and that in Moscow he had subjected himself to more than five days of intense discussions, both religious and political. Only the most ardent critics could fail to empathize with Graham when he quoted a reporter who likened his job to the pope's: "'You stand naked before the press in every city.'" He faced this trial by fire all the time. "I'm not sheltered by a big denomination," he later added with an uncharacteristic trace of testiness.

*   *   *

Eventually the dark clouds blew over and then away. We have seen that on the way home from Moscow Graham stopped in London to receive the Templeton Prize for Progress in Religion. True to form, he immediately turned over the $200,000 prize—at that time the largest prize anywhere—to the BGEA to support Developing World evangelists.

Admirers soon forgot the ruckus, and critics would have been critics no matter what. Later on, some journalists retracted their disapproving comments and effectively apologized for them. The acclaimed CBS newscaster Dan Rather, for example, had been one of Graham's strongest critics. Nineteen years later, Rather said, simply, that he had been wrong and Graham had been right.

By almost any measure, Graham made a courageous decision even if one disagreed about the wisdom of how he handled things after he got to Moscow. He faced down a solid front of opposition from the most important people in his life. He gave flesh to the truism that it is easy to defy your enemies and hard to defy your friends. And given that his wife, Ruth, was nothing if not forceful, it is almost unimaginable that he would have defied her. But he did.

The long-term effects of Graham's efforts to demilitarize the world are easy to guess but hard to measure. He almost certainly emboldened the evangelical Left and progressive stalwarts like Jim Wallis. He may have helped draw the evangelical center and mainstream voices like *Christianity Today* into a more judicious assessment of global politics. He almost certainly stiffened the resolve of the evangelical Right—or fundamentalists—to avoid perceived compromises with international communism and terrorism.

The long-term effects of Graham's efforts on US-Soviet relations are even more elusive but still intriguing to consider. They seemed to exert little immediate influence on the president himself, for just nine months after Graham's return, Reagan gave one of the most pugnacious speeches of his career. In it, he assailed the Soviet Union as an "evil empire."

Yet five years later Reagan embarked on one of the most audacious changes in the history of American diplomacy: the concerted effort by the president and Soviet leader Mikhail Gorbachev to thaw the Cold War by drawing down both nations' nuclear arsenals. Soon, Reagan, standing at the Brandenburg Gate near the Berlin Wall, would demand: "Mr. Gorbachev, tear down this wall!"

Is it possible that Graham's work in the Soviet Union—first in 1982 and then far more successfully in his record-setting Moscow crusade in 1984—furthered Reagan's dream that the Cold War really could be stopped? The president never said that. But given Reagan's conviction that Communism posed a religious and ideological as well as a military and political threat, it seems reasonable to think that Graham may have played some small role.

SCENE 43

Parson and Pope

Graham distinguished himself as the first major Protestant evangelist who called for rapport with Catholics in general and the pope in particular. Four centuries of bitter—and sometimes lethal—hostility between Protestants and Catholics finally started to abate in the post–World War II decades.

Many streams contributed to the process. One was the improbable friendship—discussed earlier—that Graham and Boston archbishop Richard (later Cardinal) Cushing had formed with each other in 1950. The warmth flowed in both directions. Their common desire to foster spiritual renewal among Christians, whether Protestant or Catholic, transcended the collision of traditions one would expect from a Southern fundamentalist and a Northern prelate.

From beginning to end, Graham made it clear that deep theological differences between evangelical Protestants and Catholics remained, and they mattered, but he focused on the similarities. "Graham's theology was not boundless, but it was flexible," said historian Mandy McMichael. Graham affirmed that a shared faith in Christ's redeeming power was the fundamental ground of commonality. "His bullet point theology," McMichael continued, "provided space in which different Christian groups could fill in the blanks." If Graham had projected a detailed systematic theology along the lines of, say, Charles H. Hodge or Augustus H. Strong, there might have been much less room for discussion.

Beyond that, Graham took Catholic theology and theologians seriously. Once when a reporter asked what he'd do if the pope invited him to preach at St. Peter's, he responded simply and earnestly: "I would gladly and humbly accept . . . [and] study for about a year in preparing."

Equally important was the priority Graham placed on one-on-one relationships with Catholics. Over the years he would forge many working friendships with Catholic leaders, including Cardinals Richard Cushing and Francis Spellman, the enormously popular Catholic television personality Monsignor Fulton J. Sheen, Notre Dame president Theodore Hesburgh, and various members of the Kennedy family—especially matriarch Rose and son-in-law Sargent Shriver. In his sermons he sprinkled in examples from the life of Mother Teresa and dropped the names of Catholic luminaries such as John Cardinal Newman.

*   *   *

For sure, Graham's positive relationship with the Roman Catholic Church did not erase all suspicion toward Catholics that other evangelicals and fundamentalists harbored. Fundamentalists, especially, excoriated him for compromising the truth of the gospel even by cooperating with Catholics. Moreover, crusade counselors sometimes disregarded their training and urged inquirers of Catholic background to seek evangelical Protestant churches instead. And though the exact details of the fiasco with Norman Vincent Peale and the 1960 presidential election remain controverted, without question Graham had once associated himself with evangelical leaders' stout resistance to a Catholic in the White House.

The wariness ran both ways. Hesburgh may have been the most visible and influential Catholic leader in the nation. He considered Graham a personal friend but did not hide his distaste for Graham's political orientation. Hesburgh felt Graham said too little about the social demands of the gospel.

Many of the letters grassroots Catholics sent to Graham spoke of priests advising them not to go to his meetings. (One priest forbade his parishioner to attend a Graham service. She said, "I am going anyway." The priest said, "I am too.") Relations sometimes proved even worse overseas. After Graham preached in Villahermosa, Mexico, in 1981, for example, the local Catholic hierarchy declared him a "non-Christian."

But the late 1970s saw a notable warming between the two traditions with the emergence of ecumenical conferences designed to build bridges. Graham furthered this trend. In 1977 he held a five-day crusade on the campus of the University of Notre Dame. The following year Catholics in Poland opened their churches to him. Karol Cardinal Wojtyla of Kracow—soon Pope John Paul II—gave them thumbs-up. This 1978 visit may have been the first time Graham's eyes truly opened to the power of the church to resist Communism and fight for religious freedom and human rights. He also saw firsthand the power of the Catholic Solidarity movement, which was both religious and political, morally to renovate an entire society.

Graham reflected on his changing attitudes. "I am far more tolerant of other kinds of Christians than I once was," he allowed. "My contact with Catholic, Lutheran and other leaders—people far removed from my own Southern Baptist tradition—has helped me. . . . I've found that my beliefs are essentially the same as those of orthodox Roman Catholics. . . . We only differ on some matters of later church tradition."

In 1982, following the controversial trip to Moscow, Graham told a press conference in Vancouver that until then he had known little about the Russian Orthodox Church. But on this trip he discovered that the Orthodox believed everything he believed, "only more."

*   *   *

And so it was that Graham visited John Paul II at the Vatican three times, in 1981, 1990, and 1993. Granted, Graham solicited the invitations, the meetings were cordial but formal, and they lasted for only a short time, as most visits with the pontiff did. There is no indication that they dined together, let alone played golf or enjoyed some other recreational activity, as Graham was inclined to do with US presidents and other world leaders.

Even so, the affection was manifest and mutual. Both were extroverts and both desired to communicate, not grandstand. Graham reported that upon leaving the papal residence back in 1981, the pope had clasped his hands and proclaimed, "We are brothers."[1] Graham told the story not privately, as many evangelicals would have done, but to *Time* magazine, with an international readership in the millions.

When the pope died in 2005, Graham judged that the pontiff had been the "most influential force for morality and peace in the world in the past 100 years." He spoke on national television on *Larry King Live*, a microphone to the world.

The reasons for the special bond between Graham and John Paul II are not transparent, but we can guess. Graham said that they found camaraderie because both of them were always "on"—both always under scrutiny by the press, always visible to millions. The slightest slipup—a stubbed toe producing a public expletive—could have cost them dearly. They also shared an awareness that the looming threat of secularism meant that they had more—far more—in common than not. And clearly the two men simply liked each other.

More than one pundit said that John Paul II was a man for all seasons, and others said the same about Graham. Both had their critics and their enemies, but there are good reasons to believe that most Christians felt that their world was a better place for their presence—and their friendship.

Bush I, Clinton, and Bush II

Graham's relationship with George H. W. Bush resembled the one he had maintained with Lyndon Johnson. The analogy is instructive, for the dramatic differences of social background, personal wealth, formal education, and personal temperament between the two presidents say a lot about Graham's ability to befriend—and be befriended by—men of strikingly diverse profiles.

Bush biographer Jon Meacham reports that Graham publicly supported Bush for vice president in 1968 when Nixon competed against Governor Ronald Reagan for the Republican nomination for president. Graham also supported Senator Mark Hatfield for the same post, as we have seen. Graham clearly felt that both men could do the job.[1]

The two families—George and Barbara and Billy and Ruth—vacationed together at the Bush family compound in the coastal village of Kennebunkport, Maine. One widely viewed photo shows the president and the preacher out fishing on Bush's well-appointed motorboat.

Graham never said much about the religious interactions between Bush and himself, but friends acknowledged that they enjoyed mulling over theological questions. The village and the sea might well have offered a quiet venue for exchanges of that sort. At Bush's instigation, Graham preached more than once at St. Anne's Episcopal Church in Kennebunkport, where the family worshiped.

As tensions between the United States and Iraq rose in the fall of 1990, Bush contemplated war. On Christmas Eve, Graham phoned Bush to offer a word of encouragement. He cited James Russell Lowell's poem "The Present Crisis": "Once to every man and nation comes the moment to decide . . . and the choice goes by forever 'twixt that darkness and that light."

On January 16, 1991, the night before the president launched the bombing of Iraq, Bush asked Graham to join him and Barbara for dinner in the White House. At 9 p.m. Bush excused himself to report to the American people on national television his decision about the impending military action. Graham stayed with Barbara. When the president returned, Graham prayed that the fighting would be short, the casualties few, and the Lord's will be done.

The events of the following morning captured less press coverage. Graham journeyed with Bush to Fort Myer, Virginia, where Bush attended a memorial service in the chapel and then addressed military leaders about the battles ahead. He asked Graham to pray.

The preacher acknowledged that sometimes "we have to fight for peace." But he again prayed that the war would be brief and the casualties few. He hoped that the peace following the war would prove long-lasting. And again, he prayed that the United States would seek to follow God's will, not its own. There is no reason to think that Graham had Abraham Lincoln's Second Inaugural Address in mind, if indeed he knew much about it at all. But the inner logic was the same: let our actions fit God's will rather than the reverse.

Contemporary journalists and later historians evaluated this train of events in different ways. Was it Bush's exploitation—with Graham's consent—of Graham's clerical stature to legitimate the president's policies? Or was it simple pastoral care born of friendship? Another possibility, which seemed strangely absent from the coverage, was the likelihood that Graham judged the war a warranted expression of political and military force and he wanted to do his part. Or perhaps all of the above.

*   *   *

The 1992 presidential election pitted Bush against the Democratic governor of Arkansas, Bill Clinton. Though Graham almost certainly voted for Bush, he did not play his hand publicly. In this election, at least, he showed that he had learned a lesson from the Nixon debacle.

The relationship between Graham and Clinton was by then an old one. Actually, Graham entered Clinton's life long before they knew each other. Earlier we saw that a thirteen-year-old Clinton had visited Graham's integrated crusade in Little Rock in 1959. He came away impressed by Graham's bold stand, as Clinton saw it, for racial justice. When Clinton became governor of Arkansas years later, the two men forged a warm friendship. And once again, the friendship ran four ways, as both Ruth and Hillary bonded with each other and with their spouses.

After the presidential election, Graham made clear that he appreciated Clinton a great deal personally—not least, we can safely assume, for Clinton's forthright proclamation of his own firm Baptist faith. Their mutual fondness for Big Macs said something about both men's down-home roots and lack of pretense. "When he prays with you in the Oval Office or upstairs in the White House," Clinton later said, "you feel like he is praying for you, not the president." The affinities ran deep.

Still, the preacher allowed that he disagreed with Clinton "in some respects." This cryptic allusion almost certainly referred to Clinton's "don't ask, don't tell" policy about gays in the military. Graham's unwillingness to be more specific about his reservation offered a glimpse into how he typically handled questions that were partly moral and partly political. His commitments to traditional evangelical ideas about homosexuality prevented him from just looking the other way, as if it did not matter. At the same time, his instinctive inclusiveness—critics said evasiveness—prevented him from drawing lines in the sand if he could avoid it.

Graham's relationship with Clinton became a matter of public interest again in the late 1990s. How Graham handled it revealed aspects of his character that won both widespread approval and disapproval. It started when the press reported that the president had fallen into scandalous behavior with a young woman on the White House staff. Hillary Clinton sought pastoral advice from Graham. He never revealed the exact content of their conversations, but he almost certainly urged her to forgive Bill and keep the marriage intact.

Shortly afterward Graham said, on network television, that we should keep our priorities straight and focus on international crises rather than "some mistake the president may make or some failure in character, because none of us is perfect." This was Graham's pastoral side, which many people approved. But then Graham went on to say that he forgave Clinton. "Because I know the frailty of human nature and I know how hard it is—and especially a strong, vigorous young man like he is. . . . He has such a tremendous personality that I think the ladies just go wild over him."

A firestorm ensued. Pundits savaged him for presuming to forgive Clinton for a sin Clinton had not even acknowledged. Syndicated columnist Arianna Huffington snapped: "What is this? A kind of hormone excuse?" Hearing this from Billy Graham was "extremely disappointing." Clearly Graham had not considered the sexist—not to mention the theologically dubious—implications of his words.

*   *   *

The 2000 presidential election threw the Democratic vice president, Al Gore, into the ring against the Republican governor from Texas, George W. Bush. The vice president was a practicing Baptist. He had attended Vanderbilt Divinity School for a year, anticipating that he would enter the ministry. Though this plan did not work out, both Gore and Graham professed a long-standing personal friendship. Yet in Graham's mind Gore's candidacy was no match for Bush's. Graham's political instincts ran closer to Bush's, but there was more to it than that.

In the 1980s Bush had struggled with an alcohol problem. During a long walk with Graham on a Maine beach in the summer of 1985, Graham gently inquired about his faith. "Are you OK with God?" Graham asked. "No, but I'd like to be," Bush replied. Bush added that he tried to read the Bible to become a better person. Graham said in "his gentle loving way" that self-improvement was a good goal but not the point of the Bible. "The center of Christianity is not the self. It is Christ."

Graham soon mailed Bush a *Living Bible* with a reference to Philippians 1:6: "I am certain that God, who began a good work within you, will continue His work until it is finally finished." Another year and embarrassing experiences, lubricated by alcohol, would pass. But Bush later would say that the beach conversation with Graham marked the beginning of a long and difficult journey to recovery.

Graham's influence on other Bush family members showed up too. Once, when George W. was visiting the White House during his father's presidency, he fell into an earnest discussion with his mother, Barbara Bush, about whether people had to believe in Christ in order to go to heaven. George felt that the New Testament was clear: they did. Barbara countered that doing God's work by serving others counted too.[2]

Barbara decided to settle the matter by picking up the phone and calling Graham (a revealing turn in itself). When the first lady reached Graham, he allowed that George was technically correct, yet he had confidence that the Lord of all the earth would do the right thing. Which was to say, one should proclaim without compromise that Jesus Christ offered the only road to salvation but leave the final decisions to God.

Later we will see that Graham publicly preached the position he took with George W. all his life, but when journalists more or less privately pressed him on the matter, he backed away and offered the response he gave to Barbara. On this and other difficult questions, figuring out who the real Billy Graham was is not always easy.

*   *   *

One of the more grievous instances of Graham falling off the no-partisanship wagon took place in the 2000 election. Three days before the voting he enjoyed breakfast with Bush at a restaurant in Florida. By itself, the event was unexceptional. Breakfasting with a friend on the road should have raised no eyebrows. The problem was that Graham also posed with Bush for the benefit of photographers. Graham just could not see how his actions signaled a partisan choice. His real or perceived naïveté left some people incredulous.

Except for Graham's dramatic involvement in the aftermath of 9/11, he had little public involvement with Bush during his presidency. This was hardly surprising, for in those years Graham was growing frail and Ruth gravely ill. Yet it is tempting to speculate on what Graham might have said about the younger Bush's wars in Iraq and Afghanistan if they had taken place a decade earlier when he was stronger of mind and body.

Graham's track record intimates that he would have been torn. On one hand, loyalty to a president, and to a friend, and his lifelong willingness if not eagerness to support America's military ventures, however controversial, would have pulled him in one direction. On the other hand, his growing unease about the risks posed by nuclear war might have pulled him in another direction. We just do not know.

Why So Many Presidents?

At this point an overall assessment of the relationship between the preacher and all of the presidents is in order. Perhaps the most remarkable point is that those relationships existed at all. Did any other religious leader in American history ever come close to Graham's easy familiarity with nearly a dozen sitting presidents?

By all indications, Graham's relationship with presidents was unprecedented. Granted, scattered examples of close friendships between particular presidents and particular religious leaders turn up. Woodrow Wilson and John R. Mott, John F. Kennedy and Richard Cushing, for example, come to mind. Billy Sunday had dined with Presidents Theodore Roosevelt and Woodrow Wilson, and counted President Herbert Hoover as a friend, a tie strengthened by their common support for Prohibition. But that was a negligible record compared with Graham's. Indeed, could *any* other person of *any* position claim such proximity to so many presidents?

Admittedly, if the paucity of references to Graham in presidential biographies and autobiographies can be taken as an index of his importance, it is clear that the presidents were more important to Graham than he was to them. At least explicitly.

What presidents thought they gained in terms of public legitimation—and the poll numbers that legitimation conferred—can be guessed but not measured. Millions of people, including those who disliked Graham, acknowledged that he was a man of high moral principles in his personal life. So, if *Graham* thought that a president could be trusted, surely they could, too.

Then too there is little evidence that Graham actually changed any president's mind about anything. He may have persuaded—or helped persuade—Nixon to send arms to Israel in 1973. Yet Graham's efforts to win vice-presidential nominations for Hatfield and Bush in 1968 went nowhere. Without doubt, Graham legitimated plans that presidents already had in mind, as when Eisenhower asked "advice" about sending troops into Little Rock in 1958. But beyond that, the evidence runs thin.

Even so, Graham's personal relationship with the presidents seemed almost automatic. Journalists Nancy Gibbs and Michael Duffy quipped that he went with the White House like the drapes. He spent the final night of Johnson's presidency with the Johnson family in the White House and gave the prayer at the first inauguration of Richard M. Nixon the next day. And he similarly spent the final night of George H. W. Bush's presidency with the Bush family in the White House and gave the invocation at the first inauguration of Bill Clinton the next day.

Graham evidently felt not a trace of intimidation being with a president. He participated in nine presidential inaugurations, tying the record held by Chief Justice John Marshall in the early nineteenth century.[1] Indeed, Graham would have broken Marshall's record if his health had permitted him to accept George W. Bush's invitation to pray at his first inauguration in 2001.

So why did it happen for Graham?

The most obvious answer is also the one least acknowledged by him and by the BGEA: he strenuously sought it. Landing the initial audience with Truman, for example, required letters of request and leaning on political friends. He phoned presidents to let them know when he was "in town." He overnighted in the White House countless times, so often in fact that he once told another visitor which bed to avoid because of a lump in the mattress. Johnson urged him to consider the White House his hotel whenever he was in DC.

Graham sought those connections partly because he benefited from them. Not materially. He insisted that he asked a president for a favor only once, and that was for a postage reduction for BGEA bulk mail, which other magazines enjoyed. But a benefit of a more personal nature flowed to Graham: the pleasure of being near people who held great power. He did not like exercising power himself (outside his organization), but he certainly enjoyed sharing the spotlight with people who did.

Beyond this personal advantage lay another very powerful one. He was unapologetic about it. Hobnobbing with presidents, governors, and queens helped amplify the spread of the gospel. When people saw him playing golf with political power brokers, that lent credibility to his message. And it gave him leverage, especially with leaders outside the United States who knew that he had the ear of the American president, the most powerful person in the world.

It was also fun. The photos of such occasions leave no doubt that Graham simply enjoyed being with leaders in a variety of ways—dining, golfing, boating, schmoozing. Then too both Billy and Ruth held enduring friendships with several of the first ladies, especially Pat Nixon, Lady Bird Johnson, Nancy Reagan, and, above all, Barbara Bush. Clearly Graham—and often Ruth with him—was also a congenial guest just to have around. His wit, more evident in person than behind a pulpit, undoubtedly spiced up many evenings.

Though few if any journalists indicted Graham for manipulating high officials for personal financial gain, a great many indicated that his easy-going interaction with top officials came with a cost. That cost was the loss of prophetic judgment about the moral consequences of presidents' policies. Graham was sensitive to the charge—he strongly disliked it—but not sensitive enough to make any major changes in his actions until Nixon burned him, and even then, his changes were inconsistent. This feature of Graham's career has invited an enormous amount of scrutiny, usually unfavorable.

It is possible to overthink the relationships. In 2006, approaching his ninetieth birthday, Graham reflected on his connections with the presidents. "Their personal lives, some of them were difficult. But I loved them all, I admired them all. I knew that they had burdens beyond anything I could ever know or understand."

History will treat some presidents more charitably than others. But liked or disliked, all were men of strength, strong will, and public charisma. Graham shared all those traits too. It is easy to imagine a relationship built a foundation of real as well as perceived equality.

SCENE 45

Nation's Chaplain

The events that took place on December 7, 1941, and on September 11, 2001, stick in Americans' memories as the two most lethal attacks by foreign adversaries on the nation's soil. The September attack by terrorists on the World Trade Towers in New York, the Pentagon, and potentially the US Capitol in Washington, DC, did not trigger a world war as the Pearl Harbor attack did. But the magnitude of the tragedy, abetted by instant graphically colored communications technology, produced profound emotional shock to a nation that had come to see itself as invulnerable. A surge of patriotic grief followed.

The 9/11 attack fell on a Tuesday morning. Three days later, Friday, September 14, President George W. Bush hosted a memorial service at Washington's National Cathedral. In the absence of a state church, this Episcopal edifice had come to hold almost sacred significance for the nation. Besides the president, the speakers that day included the cathedral's pastor and its dean, a Muslim imam, a Jewish rabbi, a Catholic cardinal, a mainline Protestant pastor—and, of course, Billy Graham, giving the keynote address.

The choice of Graham was both natural and inevitable. Evangelical Protestants constituted about one-fourth of the country's Christian population. And among evangelicals, no other person came close to Graham in national recognition and stature. At age eighty-two, Graham brought respect earned by his venerability as well as his longevity in the public eye.

Beyond these factors, Graham had practice in this role. He had served a similar one six years before when the Alfred P. Murrah Federal Building in Oklahoma City had been bombed by two men aggrieved by the perceived tyranny of a swollen federal government. The dead numbered 168 and the injured 680. Four days after the bombing President Bill Clinton called on Graham to offer words of condolence to grieving families and a dumbfounded nation.

Graham's talk in the National Cathedral followed a tragedy only deepened by the extraordinary heroism of first responders, many of whom sacrificed their own lives to save others. "This event reminds us of the brevity of life and the uncertainty of life," Graham began. "We never know when we too will be called into eternity."

Unlike pundits on the right and the left, he did not try to give a theological explanation for the tragedy. The reason for it lay hidden in God's mystery. But he did assure listeners that God understood the pain. After all, God's Son had suffered the torment of death on a cross.

Graham then called on his hearers to make a choice, just as he had done in crusade meetings countless times before. Choose the grim knowledge that life holds no larger purpose, or choose the hope that God holds history in God's hands. That choice would not alleviate the pain, but it would give believers a way to find meaning in their loss.

About three-fourths of the way through, Graham made a rhetorical move that he had rarely made before—and one that his son Franklin Graham would stoutly refuse to follow. Graham set apart the Christians in his audience and addressed them specifically. "Here in this majestic National Cathedral," he said, "we see all around us the symbol of the cross. For the Christian, the cross tells us that God understands our sin and our suffering."

The point was not to draw an invidious distinction between Christians and non-Christians but the opposite: to honor the reality of religious pluralism in American life. The nation's pastor then spoke directly to Christians of the joys that Christian victims were now experiencing in heaven. If given the choice, they would not return to their former lives amongst the living.

Graham's effort to console the nation in general, and grieving loved ones in particular, was not entirely successful. The remark about heaven aroused anger among Graham's secular critics and undoubtedly some nonsecular ones too. An editor of the New Republic pounced: "It is not consoling, it is insulting. We are not a country of children." To them, Graham evaded the hard reality of inexplicable death. Still, most Americans, including the majority of them who were not evangelicals, surely appreciated the patriarch's efforts to place that morally incomprehensible event in a larger framework of meaning.

In the years following 9/11, fear of Islam in general, and of Islamist terrorism in particular, swept the nation. A few non-Muslim Americans sought to protect themselves by unleashing vigilante acts of their own against their Muslim American neighbors and Muslim mosques. Scholars and journalists debated whether the number of anti-Muslim incidents was surprisingly large, given American traditions of pluralism, or surprisingly small, given the magnitude of the provocation. Either way, Graham and his son Franklin Graham fell into that discussion.

The month after the attack Franklin took the offensive. Not mincing words, he told journalists that Islam was a "very evil and wicked religion." Muslims not only persecuted Christians living in preponderantly Muslim countries but also oppressed girls and women. He tried to make clear that his attack fell on the teachings of the Muslim religion, not on the individuals who inherited them.

Even so, Franklin stirred immediate and powerful responses. Many felt that he told the truth about Islamic religion in general and its threat to America in particular. They also felt that he showed great courage by not bowing to the forces of political correctness that embraced a "blame America first" ideology.

We have seen that in 2005 the *New York Times*'s religion writer Laurie Goodstein asked Billy Graham if he thought that Western civilization was hurtling toward a "clash of civilizations." No, he said. "The great divide is not between the West and Islam but between those who enjoy prosperity and those who suffer from poverty, hunger, and disease." Later that year the television talk show host Larry King asked Graham if he agreed with his son's view that Islam was "evil and wicked." His response exposed the torn heart of a father. "Well, he has [his] views and I have mine. And they are different sometimes."

At first glance the contrast between son and father was striking, but on second glance it may have been less stark than many people thought. In the 1970s Franklin helped establish Samaritan's Purse, which soon became one of the largest humanitarian relief organizations in the world. Samaritan's Purse distinguished itself for its immediate response to natural disasters as well as its longer-range efforts to combat disease, drought, and famine around the world.

Most remarkably, perhaps, Samaritan's Purse followed a strict policy of "no questions asked." When relief materials and personnel arrived on the scene, volunteers went straight to work, avoiding religious or political litmus tests for the aid they offered. That principle applied to Muslim-majority as well as Christian-majority nations.[1]

In October 2001 Billy Graham held a crusade in Fresno, California. According to an aide, when he arrived at the airport, he asked his hosts first to take him to the local mosque. He said that he wanted to do whatever he could to help heal wounds.

As it happened, the mosque was closed and no imam was present. The gesture bespoke both the potential and the limitation of Graham's vision of social reform. On one hand he revealed the expansiveness of his sympathies. On the other, he evidently seemed not to see how much a meeting with the imam might have accomplished if it had been prearranged and made public.

At the campaign meeting that night, Graham spoke from the heart. In a sermon titled "September 11 and the Love of God," he observed: "Much of the world is feeling the effects of terrorism and war right now, but there are other things [too] that are bothering us: disease, poverty, racism, hate, loneliness, [AIDS], unemployment, divorce, psychological problems, boredom, murder statistics—the world didn't stop sinning . . . after September 11."

To the end, Graham remained true to form. Pain was pain, yet the problem ran deeper. "Sin is what's wrong with the world and only Jesus Christ can solve it."[2]

Fractured Saint

If Graham's star soared in the fall of 2001, it plummeted six months later. On February 28, 2002, the National Archives released tapes of a private conversation among Graham, Nixon, and Nixon's chief of staff, H. R. Haldeman, that had taken place in the Oval Office on February 1, 1972, almost exactly thirty years earlier.

The first hour or so the men rambled about the events of the day, but then the bomb fell. Nixon started to blast Jews for controlling the media. Graham chimed in: "And they're the ones putting out the pornographic stuff and putting out everything." Shortly afterward he said: "This stranglehold has got to be broken or the country's going down the drain."[1]

The most damning part of Graham's comments came about fifteen minutes later. "I mean not all the Jews, but a lot of the Jews are great friends of mine. They swarm around me and are friendly to me because they know I am friendly to Israel (and so forth) but they don't know how I really feel about what they're doing to this country."

The conversation seemed to make no sense. Admittedly, many non-evangelicals had long suspected that evangelicals' nearly universal support for Israel masked underlying hostility to Jews at home. Even so, hardly anyone asserted that Graham had made an anti-Semitic remark in his entire life. He claimed close friendships with Israeli leaders such as Abba Eban, Menachem Begin, and Golda Meir, who appreciated his reliable support for Israel. In 1973 he had even invited Meir to address his crusade in Saint Louis (although, owing to a schedule conflict, she had to decline). He enjoyed warm relationships with Jewish friends such as Rabbi Marc Tanenbaum, the influential director of the Synagogue Council of America, and Rabbi Edgar Fogel Magnin, spiritual leader of a large synagogue on Wilshire Boulevard in Los Angeles.

Over the years Graham had received a host of awards from Jewish organizations for his role in promoting good Jewish-Christian relations, including the Torch of Liberty Plaque awarded by the Anti-Defamation League in 1969, the International Brotherhood Award from the National Conference of Christians and Jews in 1971, and the American Jewish Committee's first interreligious award. "Most of the progress of Protestant-Jewish relations over the past quarter century was due to Billy Graham," said Tanenbaum.

Graham allowed that he and Jews continued to differ on the identity of the Messiah, yet many Jewish leaders also made clear that they admired his pro-God, pro-America, promorality views. And though Graham had helped lead the Lausanne Consultation on Jewish Evangelism, he framed it as a message to be shared rather than one to be imposed. This distinction likely made more sense to Graham than it did to Jews. Regardless, he had quietly skirted messianic (Christian) Jews' efforts to bring their fellow believers into the fold, which nonmessianic Jews, observant and otherwise, found particularly offensive.

Perhaps the main reason people were stunned was that the Oval Office remarks seemed so far out of character. By the 1980s he was not only affirming the right of Muslims and other religious minorities to thrive in the American melting pot but also extolling the richness they brought to the nation's common life. In 1989 the editor of the Salvation Army's *War Cry* asked him about Islam in America. Graham replied that he had "great respect and tolerance" for his Muslim friends. "Because we are a pluralistic society," he said, "we are going to have to recognize that we are no longer just a Jewish and Christian society."

The comment was unusual but not unique for Graham. Barry A. Kosmin and Seymour P. Lachman's *One Nation under God: Religion in Contemporary American Society* (1993) analyzed a sweeping social scientific survey of American religious pluralism undertaken by the Graduate School of the City University of New York in 1990. "This study," Graham rhapsodized in a jacket blurb, "could make a major contribution to reversing this deplorable trend [toward intolerance] and renewing the spirit of genuine tolerance and respect for those of different traditions."

*   *   *

The reaction to the tapes was swift—and fierce. Graham himself was mortified. When he heard the tape, he initially made no response, believing it was a hoax. He told an aide, "I can't believe I talked like that. That is not my heart." But the tapes soon convinced him that the voice really was his. He issued an apology, in writing and orally, for "any offense caused by the remarks."

Graham said that his anti-Semitic statements that dark day, thirty years before, did not represent his true feelings then, or later, or now, and he deeply regretted them. His only explanation was that he had been rolling along with the president of the United States in the Oval Office, and he did not have the courage to stand up to him.

With the notable exception of Graham's high-profile daughter Anne Graham Lotz, who called her father's remarks "inexcusable and indefensible," the in-house reaction at the BGEA was defensive. Franklin Graham tried to spin the event by saying that his father was not talking about Jews in general but "a handful of elitists" who controlled the major outlets.[2] Franklin also said that many people had said things in private they would not want the public to hear. The revised second edition of Graham's memoir, *Just as I Am*, published in 2007 by the BGEA, did not mention the incident.[3]

Christianity Today echoed the senior Graham's contrition. Though it failed to quote the most offensive part of Graham's remarks—Jews "don't know how I really feel about what they're doing to this country"—it quoted enough of them to leave defenders with little ground to stand on. And it rehearsed the full range of outsiders' responses, including some of the most damning.

Then, speaking for itself, *Christianity Today* said that its founder's remarks were not merely offensive or politically incorrect but "a moral fault that called for repentance." Graham's repentance, the editor continued, "has set us a good example. The rest of us likewise need to examine ourselves for latent prejudices (of which we have plenty), and . . . resist them, repent of them, and find renewal and grace" with God.

The memorial edition of *Christianity Today*, issued immediately after Graham's death, carried an article on Graham and Jews by David Neff, a former senior editor. Neff placed the comment in the context of Graham's lifetime of cordial interactions with Jews but forthrightly acknowledged the details of the incident. He admitted that it would stand as an "indelible asterisk on Graham's legacy."

The secular press—along with Jewish media—broke into two camps. Many followed evangelicals who expressed deep sadness that Graham had incontestably tarnished his reputation yet showed willingness to take him at his word—that he was sorry and without excuse—and forgive him. After all, everyone erred.

Others offered other interpretations that put the story in a larger framework. Historian Elesha Coffman notes the reaction of Jewish television maven Norman Lear, producer of *All in the Family*. When he contemplated Jewish influence on the media, he said—presumably with a grin—"I would certainly hope so and believe so." And cultural historian Renata Adler thought it "silly" to try to draw big conclusions from small comments, which might or might not represent a settled prejudice.

The other camp was not inclined to forgive, let alone forget. The gashes inflicted by two millennia of Christian persecution of Jews in Europe, not to mention Christian complicity in the Nazi genocide of Jews, were raw. And memories of anti-Semitic attitudes and practices in America were raw too. Some heard his apology—for "any offense caused by the remarks"—as a classic nonapology.

The fact that Graham was one of the most famous Christians on the planet, who for decades had proclaimed his openness to Jews in public life and his affection for Jews in private life, only made things worse. The prominent atheist pundit Christopher Hitchens undoubtedly spoke for many when he said that Graham's words had proved what many had thought all along: that Graham was an "avid bigot as well as a cheap liar," "a gaping and mendacious anti-Jewish peasant."

In 2009, the tape of another conversation between Nixon and Graham about Jews emerged. This second conversation took place on February 21, 1973—just over a year after the first one—with Nixon phoning Graham at home one evening to talk about a number of things. One of them was the perceived overreaction of American Jews to evangelical efforts to win them to Christianity.

After a few minutes of conversation about this matter, Graham remarked that the Bible taught that there were two kinds of Jews. The first represented the "synagogue of Satan"—those "putting out the pornographic literature . . . [and] obscene films." Though Graham stopped short at that point, he evidently presumed that Nixon understood that the other kind of Jews did not do so.[4]

Some people felt that this second conversation gave clear evidence of Graham's continuing anti-Semitism, while others thought that it proved the opposite. Wherever individuals came down on this question, few seemed even to know about it, and it stirred little public controversy.

The larger significance of the second tape was not Graham's relationship with Jews at all but his relationship with Nixon. It showed that he was, as historian Steven Miller put it, part of the president's "kitchen cabinet." Or perhaps the largest significance was how it betokened Graham's perennial habit of going along with pretty much anything any president said.

*　　*　　*

But a redeeming moment of sorts did occur in June of 2002, three months after the initial Nixon/Haldeman conversation with Graham had surfaced. Graham had journeyed to Cincinnati for a long-scheduled crusade. The city boasted a large Jewish population and Hebrew Union College–Jewish Institute of Religion. During the crusade, Graham journeyed across town to apologize in person to a group of rabbis.

As Graham entered the room, one observer reported, the rabbis stood. Graham urged them to sit back down, saying he should be on his knees. Graham told the rabbis that the things he had said that day, thirty years back, were unforgivable. But he begged them to forgive him regardless. The rabbis applauded. The episode said as much about the rabbis' generosity of spirit as it did about Graham's willingness to shoulder responsibility, without excuses, for the things he had said long ago.

Still, only the most ardent admirer of Graham could say that this story ever saw a happy ending. It left most Jews—including his close friend Larry King, a self-described secular Jew—irreparably disappointed. The plain truth is that it inflicted a scar that eventually healed over but never disappeared.

Modern America

When the culture wars started pounding on Graham's front door in the late 1970s, he determined not to open it. He allowed that he agreed with some of the views of his friends Jerry Falwell and Pat Robertson, but he also said that they didn't talk enough about poverty and hunger. And even if they did, partisan politics did not belong in the pulpit.

Speaking in 1981 to *Parade* magazine—a venue with a wide popular readership—Graham said, "I don't wish to be identified with them. I'm for morality. But morality goes beyond sex to human freedom and social justice. We as clergy know so very little to speak out with such authority on the Panama Canal or the superiority of armaments. Evangelists can't be closely identified with any particular party or person."

Such words prompted political historian Kevin Kruse to say, at the time of Graham's demise, "we must reckon with both halves of his career—the quarter-century he spent working as a shrewd political insider, and the slightly longer span he spent atoning for it."

For sure, Graham had helped stake out the cultural and political space that the Christian Right increasingly claimed as its own. But he insisted that there was a difference between moral politics and partisan politics. Moral politics served the long-range interests of the nation as a whole and deserved a place in the pulpit. Partisan politics served the short-range interests of the Democratic Party or the Republican Party and did not merit a place in the pulpit. Individual Christians had a perfect right—indeed, obligation—to strive for partisan agendas, but only as private citizens.

Graham was not very clear about the boundaries, but he did offer examples. Discussions about racial injustice were moral, while discussions about the Panama Canal treaties were partisan. Apparently he assumed that the difference would be transparent to earnest, honest Christians when the time arose and they turned their minds to it.

*   *   *

In the 2008 electoral contest, Republican senator John McCain and Republican governor Sarah Palin, who were running for president and vice president, made a pilgrimage up the mountain in Montreat to visit the aging evangelist. More to the point, the candidates arranged for photographers to capture themselves sitting with Graham in his living room. Still more to the point, they made certain the press received those photos.

There is no way to know how much Graham's legitimating aura may have enhanced either candidate's appeal to voters in general or to evangelical ones in particular. Granted, come election day, McCain and Palin proved disproportionately successful among evangelical voters, but that outcome probably owed more to their politics and race than to their faith. McCain, reared Episcopal, regularly worshiped in a Baptist church. Even so, his firm but quiet religious identity did not register large on the public screen. Palin, in contrast, foregrounded her Pentecostal identity, yet talk of demon exorcisms in her home church in Alaska distanced her from the kind of temperate mainstream evangelicalism Graham represented.

In April 2010 President Barack Obama, who was vacationing in the Asheville area, also made the pilgrimage to see Graham. He was the first sitting president to visit the Montreat home. Since the visit fell halfway through the first term of his administration, long before the next election, it seems reasonable to assume that the purpose was less to court votes than simply to pay his respects. The two men talked for thirty-five minutes, and Graham gave him two Bibles, one for himself and one for the first lady. As their meeting drew to an end, Obama asked if he could pray for the evangelist—which he did.

Obama belonged to the United Church of Christ, one of the most theologically and politically liberal of the mainline Protestant denominations.[1] Even so, for many Americans, Obama's frequent and manifestly heartfelt expressions of Christian faith in general, and his public affirmation of Jesus Christ's death, resurrection, and fully divine/fully human nature in particular, looked very much like Graham's irenic, inclusive form of evangelicalism. And the two men also shared a commitment to personal morality and financial integrity—virtues not always abundant in Washington or among evangelical preachers.

Though Obama remained a suspicious figure in the eyes of many evangelicals, his brief visit with the patriarch may have given him a bigger boost in public esteem than McCain and Palin's photo op had given them.

*　　　*　　　*

In the summer before the election of 2012, North Carolinians fell into a bitterly contested battle over gay marriage. The controversy took the form of an amendment—commonly called "Amendment One"—to the state constitution prohibiting the state from recognizing marriages and civil unions among gay couples. Given Graham's status as the state's official unofficial "favorite son," his views mattered.

Here we need to pause the clock and consider Graham's thinking about the Bible's teaching about homosexuality. The story ran back to the 1960s, when his followers started seeking his advice about homosexual practice (not orientation). Their questions were not abstract theological ones but problems of daily life. "Should we let our gay adult son bring his partner home?" "Should we let them share a bedroom?"

The BGEA's boilerplate answer was No! They should urge their son to seek God's forgiveness and then help in overcoming this sinful practice. It should be stressed that Graham never veered from that position, even as the wider culture and many evangelicals slowly evolved toward more-accepting views.

That being said, in the 1990s, if not before, Graham made clear that the question ranked low—actually, very low—on his list of priorities. He insisted that gay men and lesbians were welcome in his meetings, that they should not be targeted as if their sin was any worse than other sins millions of evangelical Christians committed every day without remorse. Christians needed to get their house in order on divorce and nonmarried sex too. Why did the church focus on homosexual behavior seemingly to the exclusion of everything else? And above all, love should come first.

The weekend before the election, the BGEA ran full-page op-ed advertisements in fourteen North Carolina newspapers strongly supporting Amendment One. Many readers believed that the ads accurately represented Graham's true feelings about gay people. When Graham died, for example, the *Advocate*, an LGBT-interest bimonthly, headlined its story: "What the Obits Aren't Saying: Evangelist Billy Graham Was a Homophobe."

Yet others doubted the ads' authenticity and attributed them to Graham's son Franklin. "The voice is Jacob's voice, but the hands are the hands of Esau," they reasoned—not least because the accompanying large photo of Graham seemed to depict a man younger than his actual age of ninety-three.

Reports of Graham's frailty, isolation, and impaired eyesight and hearing left many wondering if Graham was even capable of entering into this discussion. Finally and most important, doubters also felt that the spirit of the ads was simply inconsistent with the irenic position Graham had taken for decades.

As it happened, in May 2012 North Carolina primary voters decisively approved Amendment One, but that did not quiet the controversy. It continued to rage on bumper stickers, in churches, and at family dinner tables across the state. The furor finally subsided in October when a federal court ruled the amendment unconstitutional.

*   *   *

Graham's role in the 2012 election, which pitted Obama against the Republican challenger Mitt Romney, is extremely hard to pin down. Shortly before the election, the BGEA, led by Franklin Graham, splashed another large photo of Graham, accompanied by a short essay, in newspapers around the nation. The essay touted profamily, prodefense, and pro-America values. It did not explicitly tell voters which candidate better fit those values but left no doubt that Romney was their man.

Any honest person should know, the ad intimated, that the senior Graham too considered Romney the man to choose. Indeed, Romney had visited Graham in his home three weeks before the election, the same day that he held a rally in Asheville.

Graham never played his hand about the election, at least in public. Yet we can be reasonably certain that he would have voted for Romney, not because he thought that Romney's personal life differed from Obama's— both were impeccably upright—but because of the general coalescence of Romney's moderately conservative economic, social, and political views with his own.

What we do know is this. The fact that Romney was Mormon would have posed no problem. Historically evangelicals had deplored Mormons as polytheists and closet polygamists. But never Graham. Mormons such as the hotel mogul J. W. Marriott and Mitt's father, Michigan governor George Romney, ranked among his "closest friends" (of which there were many). And over the years Graham had gone out of his way to avoid targeting Mormons as potential converts. His actions implied that he considered Mormons theologically off base but certainly not far enough to cast their faith in Christ in doubt, let alone undermine personal friendships.

*　　　　*　　　　*

Graham's ninety-fifth birthday celebration in Asheville featured guests Donald Trump, Sarah Palin, Fox News owner Rupert Murdoch, Fox News commentator Greta Van Susteren, and the conservative Republican governor of North Carolina, Pat McCrory. No Democrat took the microphone that evening. Franklin was the only member of the Graham family who spoke.[2]

In the bitterly contested 2016 election, which fell on the very day of Graham's ninety-eighth birthday, neither Franklin Graham nor the BGEA suggested that the patriarch supported either the Democrat Hillary Clinton or the Republican Donald Trump (although Franklin Graham strongly supported the Republican nominee). Which is to say, by then no one pretended that age had not taken its toll.

What a younger and more intellectually vigorous Graham would have thought about the overt politicization of evangelicalism, powered by his son Franklin and other high-profile evangelical and fundamentalist leaders, is impossible to know for sure. But based on his track record in the 1980s and 1990s, when he went out of his way to distance himself from Christian Right sentiments, we can surely guess.

The Reverend Doctor Graham

As the years passed, the preacher's followers asked him countless questions. Though the data are hard to pin down with precision, the volume of questions seemed steadily to increase as Graham matured and his stature grew.

The queries touched on many topics, ranging from the cosmic to the trivial. Yet almost all had two points in common. First, the writers invested him with authority because his views mattered. And second, they had faith that Graham would tell them the truth. Even though you are Baptist, one allowed, we "know we will receive an honest answer."

Probably the largest number of questions were straightforward ones about theology. These were not the kind of queries that seminary professors debated in seminar rooms but the kind that ordinary people worried about.

Two theological puzzles seemed to trouble Graham's followers more than any others. The first was very specific. Have I committed the unpardonable sin? Questioners were uncertain about exactly what it was. "I need to know if I've lost my salvation and have I committed the sin that cannot be forgiven as I feel no peace?" wrote a woman in the Northwest. Others wondered too. Was the unpardonable sin making fun of speaking in tongues? Cursing the Holy Spirit? Relapsing back into drugs and alcohol?

The second, more general, and far more common theological question was about assurance of salvation. How can I be sure of my standing with God? How can I know—really *know*—that I am saved? Bottom line: Am I going to heaven?

The temptation to backslide, the persistence of lust, and the propensity to get priorities all mixed up forced many souls back to the drawing board. Stranded there, they implored Graham to ease their minds.

Questions about the unpardonable sin and assurance of salvation predominated, but the topics questioners touched on ranged far beyond those two. Uncertainties about the future turned up often. Hardly anyone queried him about immediate events in the real-life world. No one asked, for example, about the future of the stock market or who was going to win the presidential election. Rather, they concentrated on the landscape of the life to come. Is there a chance to repent after death? Does suicide forfeit salvation?

Questions about the Bible's description of the past turned up almost as often as questions about the Bible's description of the future. When the Bible said Methuselah died at 969 years, did that really mean 969 of our years? Another zealot asked Graham a question so starkly logical Graham had to be taken aback. "If Jesus turned five loaves and two fishes into enough to feed 5,000, who fed them afterward?"

Evangelical exclusivism troubled many souls as well. Would Elizabeth Taylor, a Jew, make it to heaven? For many questioners there was, obviously, a subtext: how to fulfill the evangelical mandate to witness about their faith without embarrassing themselves or the friends they were trying to witness to. One asked, what should I say to my neighbor, who is a Mormon? And another, what should I say to a Catholic friend at work who insists that her doctrines are right and mine are wrong?

Many believed that Graham could help them untangle the knot of God's apparent unfairness. "If God is no respecter of persons," one asked, "how come some people are so smart and can achieve anything and others are afflicted and don't have enough mind to earn a decent living?" Another heard that Graham's trusted lieutenant Dawson Trotman had drowned at the untimely age of fifty while rescuing a girl from drowning in Schroon Lake, New York. "Could not God protect him?"

Closer to home, a woman with a "very disattractive case of pigment" on her face wondered what sins she had committed to cause it. "I can't see why God would put such a terrible curse on me when . . . millions of people . . . have committed the worse sins . . . and yet they are defected in no way." The list went on. For these people Graham became, as the historian Heather Vacek put it, "a public vehicle for private pain."

Some writers asked searching questions, not easy to answer. "Do you believe everything literally that is stated in the New Testament or do you believe that a great deal of it is parables?" Some, by any reasonable measure of things, were touching. "My husband was called home after 30 years of happy marriage. Can he see me now? It would make me so happy if I knew he could." And some were brutally honest—and heartrending. "What happens if I can't forgive Jesus for letting my darling wife die of cancer?"

Questions about behavior turned up almost as often as questions about belief. The rules for marriage were especially troubling. Can a Christian marry an atheist? How about people of different races? And what about marrying someone you do not love? People needed advice for handling dilemmas within the family, too. What should I say to my daughter who has taken up with a Zen cult? Cutting close to the quick, another asked, "is it a sin to hate someone of your own kin? I mean—really hate them?"

God's rules for sex created puzzles aplenty. In principle, fornication and adultery were off the table, of course, but in real life things got more complicated. One woman wrote that her marriage had been dead for years, but now she was madly in love with a married man and she loved him more and more every day. What to do? Another soul wrote that her husband was "completely irresponsible" about fathering more children than they could afford. So was birth control okay?

Mapping the faithful use of money was not easy, either. Was it acceptable to give Christmas gifts when missions needed money so badly? Did taking out insurance belie trust in God?

The faithful use of money blended into the faithful use of the workplace. A military policeman sought guidance about the morality of getting rough on lawbreakers. Another wondered if a Christian could be an "air hostess." Another asked about the ethics of how to handle unemployment. "I am over 50, out of a job," wrote one earnest soul. "No one will hire anyone over 45. Is it a sin to say I am 45?"

Many of the questioners wondered about matters strikingly mundane, as well. Was it okay to get saved at home rather than in a church? A Midwestern woman admitted that her life, like her house, was always cluttered. How could she learn to keep things neat? A woman from the South, who lived in a duplex, grumbled about the neighbor's kids banging on the cabinets all day. "Am I the only person in the world who loves quietness?" And then, sometimes, it was hard not to read between the lines. "Will people who go to nudist camps go to hell?"

Concerns equally mundane but of greater moral gravitas came Graham's way too. One man wondered what he should—or even could—do about a friend who beat his five-year-old son "mercilessly." The grown son of an Midwest woman was gay. He insisted that God had made him that way. The woman's husband would not permit the son's partner in the house. "What should we do?"

Some of Graham's followers occasionally—not often but occasionally—sought his opinion about matters of broad moral import in society. "I oppose capital punishment because maybe those people could be saved. What do you think?" And: "What do you really think about integration? Most politicians and celebrities talk about it being good but don't want to sit next to a black person at church or at a show. Or let their white daughter be escorted by a black boy." Is that right?

Questions about borderline situations filled Graham's mailbox. The theological meaning of suicide troubled many. "You say a man who commits suicide while insane [is] not responsible. But what about a Christian who is either normal or is mentally and emotionally disturbed, but not to the point of psychosis (insanity)?" For another: Is it okay to go to a dance? Not a "dive" but a high school prom?

A woman living in the Midwest admitted that she did not always know the difference between God's word and her own views. She undoubtedly spoke not just for a few but for millions when she sighed to Graham: "Wouldn't it be nice if God would send an 'Air-Mail' with all the 'Do's' listed on one side and all the 'Don'ts' listed on the other?"

Eccentrics—there really is no other word for them—sent their share, too. A West Coast man remembered that the previous fall he had dreamed that "the weight of people on the earth would soon throw the earth off balance and in a few years it will collide with the planet Saturn and that will be the end of the world. So what you said in your column was mistaken." Not exactly a question, but at least he was giving Graham a chance to defend himself.

School students viewed Graham as a useful educational resource too. One asked, "Mr. Graham, please explain the Mayflower Compact to me." Another requested help on a paper about Graham's home state of North Carolina. Please send "pictures, brochures, or factual information," he wrote. The report was due in a month, so time counted. The student promised Billy he would let him know how the grade turned out.

But not all missives were so serious. Undoubtedly they were for the writers, but for Graham and his assistants, one suspects, they were more likely to bring a smile. "In heaven, will we be married? If so, will I be married to the same woman?" And again: "My wife and I . . . have been married, and peacefully, for many years. . . . My problem is, I just can't imagine spending an eternity with my wife. One hundred thousand years or so, yes. But eternity—well I just don't see how I can stand it." For some questioners, the evangelical rubber hit the road before the wedding. "Isn't it natural to have sex thoughts when looking for a woman to marry?"

Did writers think that Graham himself would answer their letters? Many clearly did. One teenager thought her pastor was too busy to answer her questions, so she decided to address them to Graham instead. One woman unfurled a litany of the many forms of abuse she had experienced in her short life. She thanked Graham for "reading this letter," then asked that he *personally* write her back. Many asked him to phone. They routinely gave him the number to use and the times they would be available. A few explicitly asked him to read and respond himself, not turn the task over to assistants or even to Ruth or Cliff or Bev. Not a few said they hoped to hear back soon; the problem was urgent.

Yet the great majority of letters did not raise the question of who would read them at all. Either they did not think of it or, more likely, it did not matter. The point was just to write him, someone they respected or even loved.

Those who asked Graham to pray for them had something concrete to gain, for they were confident that Graham had God's ear. Some undoubtedly were genuinely seeking help while others undoubtedly found writing itself a means of purging themselves of guilt, whether or not they changed their ways. They wrote to him because they sensed in some hard-to-describe way that he knew them, too. One spoke for many: "We have never met, but you know me." Not only did Graham let them into his life, but also and maybe more important, they let him into theirs.

This sampling of the questions Graham received contains significant omissions, too. First of all, almost no one asked specific questions about current events such as elections or economic trends. A tiny number wondered about racial integration, but only a tiny number. A few spoke of needing a job, or a better job, but no one mentioned needing a hand to get by. If any of the writers were destitute, they did not say so. If any suffered discrimination or marginalization because of their racial or social location, they did not say so.

If the letters were largely—not entirely but largely—silent about "real-life" issues, they were also surprisingly silent about many theological claims that roiled church officials. We have seen that a few critics challenged Graham's stated views on one or another doctrine, but all things considered, not many. Hardly anyone asked Graham about the theological warrant for creeds or sacraments or miracles or any number of issues leaders wrangled about.

What did the omission of these two great streams of concerns that millions of Americans did worry and think about—the first one "this worldly" and the second "otherworldly"—tell us about the people who actually wrote Graham? Does it say that those concerns simply fell outside the daily lives of most of Graham's constituents? Or does it mean that these issues were real enough, but not pressing enough, to warrant the time it took to sit down, write a letter, find a stamp, and hike to a mailbox?

The bigger question is this. Did folks write Graham to learn his opinion about this world and the world to come? Or was it to share their lives by sharing their words?

Second Chances

Graham's frequent preaching about the imminent end of history fostered not dread about grim days ahead but hope for a second chance for individuals and for societies. It would be risky to say that he changed the global spiritual landscape as Pope John Paul II did, and even riskier to say that he changed the American political landscape as Martin Luther King did. But he did leave a mark.

From the very beginning to the very end of his career, Graham preached about the end times in general and the second coming in particular. The BGEA sermon index contains thirty-seven entries under "Second Coming" alone. Two of his best-selling books were *World Aflame* (1965) and *Approaching Hoofbeats: The Four Horsemen of the Apocalypse* (1983). The latter was reissued with revisions in 1992, 2010, and in 2011 as *Storm Warning*. All focused on the end times and the second coming.

Yet the verb "focused" requires comment. More often than not Graham wrote and preached about those topics in a surprisingly general way. He was not much interested in the arcane and fiercely contested speculations about how the world would end. We have seen that he personally believed in the rapture of the saints, the antichrist, the great tribulation, Armageddon, the millennium, and the final judgment. But he did not preach about them often or with fine-combed precision. And even if he had, the letters that people sent him leave little doubt that those details were not the part of his message that caught their attention and stirred their hearts.

Rather they were listening for the grand narrative of how Christian faith offered hope for themselves and for the nation (and for a tiny few, the family of nations). This hope found its footing in the biblical promise of a glorious consummation of history just around the corner. A time was coming, Graham preached, when "God shall wipe away all tears from their eyes; and there shall be no more death, neither sorrow, nor crying, neither shall there be any more pain: for the former things are passed away."[1]

No wonder that message landed on receptive ears. Over the years, we have seen, millions of letters flowed into Graham's Minneapolis office. They described lives twisted by sin, marriages on the rocks, kids gone astray, bodies broken down, and emotions in disarray. Yet no matter how badly you have messed up your life, Graham responded—directly and in sermons and in "My Answer" columns—Christ offers forgiveness and a new start.

But in Graham's hands the gospel's promise foreshadowed more than a means for coping with earth's trials today and blessed fellowship with the Lord tomorrow. That was too passive. Rather, he issued marching orders. Living in the shadow of the second coming meant not lying back, waiting, but moving out, doing God's work with hands strengthened by God's Spirit.

One of the most influential sermons Graham preached, "The King Is Coming," formed the closing address of the Lausanne Conference in 1974. It pulsed with anticipation. It touched on the life to come, for sure, but it also constituted feet-on-the-ground marching orders about life right here.

"In view of the world in which we live, and the return of the King, what kind of persons should you and I be?" Graham opened. The message called for zealousness, dedication, and hard work. Expect danger, loneliness, burdens, a sense of urgency. Embrace the necessity of boldness and discipline and be willing to live more simply. "Are we willing to deny self and take up the cross[?] . . . Are you willing? Am I willing? The King is coming!"

If the personal is the political, as the saying goes, for Graham the individual was the social, too. Graham called Christians to raise their vision from their own personal destiny, however rewarding that might be, to view the great political and cultural crises of the age. He saw those crises as signs of the approaching finale of history. The 1992 edition of *Storm Warning* bore the revealing tagline "With the Collapse of Communism the Nuclear Threat Has Diminished but Ominous Shadows of Deceptive Evil Loom on the Horizon." A 2010 revised edition bore another and even more revealing tagline: "Whether Global Recession, Terrorist Threats, or Devastating Natural Disasters, These Ominous Shadows Must Bring Us Back to the Gospel."[2]

By Graham's reckoning, then, the world faced a future of grim judgment but also glorious hope. The judgment was deserved, but the hope was real.

This ideal of a new day dawning ran back to the very beginning of the American story, and Graham drew on it, both implicitly and from time to time explicitly. Puritans imagined themselves a "City on a Hill." Revolutionary firebrand Thomas Paine declared, "We have it in our power to begin the world over again." Nineteenth-century Holiness believers proclaimed a *second* moment of grace. The Statue of Liberty offered Europe's huddled masses a new opportunity to "breathe free." And the resonances of political movements and programs of diverse origins and identities—Progressive Party; New Deal; Square Deal; New Frontier; Compassionate Conservatism; Yes, We Can; Stronger Together; and Make America Great Again—uniformly prefigured or paralleled Graham's abiding sense that Americans wanted to hear a message of the possibility for renewal, for themselves and for the nation and (often) for the family of nations.

*   *   *

Graham's evolution on the subject of race shows how he applied Christian teachings about hope for a second chance to entire societies as well as to hurting individuals.

The year 1973 marked a milestone. In March Graham preached in Durban, South Africa, to a crowd of forty-five thousand in the first major mixed-race meeting in the nation's history. This was not the first time he had staked out his position in Africa. In his sweep through nine countries of the continent in 1960, he had repeatedly proclaimed that Jesus was not a white European, and he refused to preach in Johannesburg because they would not meet his demand for integrated seating.

In Durban, however, Graham declared God's love for all people, "the black world, the white world, the yellow world, the rich world, the poor world." Using some of the most ringing words of his career, Graham declared: "Jesus was . . . not a white man. He was not a black man. He . . . probably had a brown skin very much like some of the Indian people here today. Christianity is not a white man's religion, and don't let anybody ever tell you that it's white or black. Christ belongs to *all* people." A video of the event shows Graham denouncing white racialism—the idea that Jesus was white—with electric force.

Graham's use—or nonuse—of the incendiary word "apartheid" in Durban became an issue in itself. In a televised press conference just before he spoke, he did use the word and judged that the system of apartheid simply could not work. In his public sermons, however, he did not use it, which profoundly disappointed those who wanted him to press for greater change. When Graham died, the (white) South African Methodist theologian Peter Storey judged that his "messages, so winsome and personal, were also sanitised of any engagement with the social and political realities of his world." Yet Graham had left no doubt about where he stood. After the Saturday night meeting in Durban, the Sunday paper headline boomed: "Apartheid Doomed."

One week later Graham addressed sixty thousand in Johannesburg at the first major mixed-race event in the city's history. Among other topics, Graham spoke about the tragedy of racial injustice. "There is coming a day when the dream that Martin Luther King gave in Washington will come true, when all prejudice will be gone and men will have love for each other, but until that time we are called upon to do the best we can dealing with fallen human nature."[3]

Graham kept moving. Back home, in 1974 he endorsed most parts of the landmark Chicago Declaration of Evangelical Social Concern, which condemned fellow evangelicals' "exploitation of racism at home and abroad . . . by perpetuating the personal attitudes and institutional structures that have divided the body of Christ along color lines."[4]

In 1982 he would say, in the Patriarchal Cathedral in Moscow, that he had undergone three major conversions in his life: to Christ, to racial justice, and to nuclear disarmament. If pressed, Graham undoubtedly would have given priority to his conversion to Christ. But for a "purebred fundamentalist" the rest of that autobiographical story struck home.

A bright Sunday afternoon in the fall of 1991 showed the new Graham at work. Standing before a quarter-million people spread out on the grass in New York City's Central Park, he preached to the largest gathering of his career in the United States—and the second largest in the park's records. Mayor David Dinkins said it may have been the "most multicultural revival" in the city's history. Surveying the crowd, one veteran reporter judged that minorities constituted fully half. The *New York Times* gave the event front-page coverage.

Writing for the Baptist World Alliance at the end of the decade, near the closing of his career, Graham argued, "Racism may be the most serious and devastating social problem facing our world today. . . . [It] is a deadly poison . . . resulting always in a bitter harvest of hatred, strife and injustice." For a man who grew up in the South in the 1920s, those words formed a forceful affirmation of the gospel's promise for fundamental social change from top to bottom.

It is important not to exaggerate Graham's progress in these matters. He never marched in the streets or went to jail or fought off snarling police dogs (a set of choices he ultimately said he regretted). But by defying his friends, and integrating his crusades, and taking fierce criticism for it, he staked out his position, in his own way. Critics then and now felt his choice of witness was not nearly good enough. Supporters felt that it amply reflected his sense of what he was equipped by personality and circumstances to do.

*   *   *

The scene of Graham's final major crusade—seventy thousand folding chairs set up on the lawn at Corona Park, in Flushing Meadows, New York, in the summer of 2005—symbolized how Graham tried to build hope for millions, not only in the life to come but also in the here and now. Not only for relations between whites and blacks but also for an increasingly multiracial and multicultural society.

The event was sponsored by 1,400 churches and drew coverage from seven hundred journalists from around the world. No wonder. By then Graham's fame in the American evangelical world was unparalleled. Thirty-five million people—one in six adults—had heard him preach in person or via live video feed. Over three nights the aggregate crowd totaled 242,000 souls. Fittingly, Flushing Meadows was one of the most ethnically mixed sections of New York City, where more than one hundred languages were spoken within one zip code. The crusade's counselors represented more than twenty language groups, including Arabic, Armenian, Korean, Portuguese, Punjabi, Russian, Tamil, and Mandarin.

Former president Bill Clinton, New York City mayor Michael Bloomberg, and New York senators Hillary Rodham Clinton and Charles Schumer starred as the platform guests the second evening. "New Yorkers share an appreciation for faith," said Bloomberg. "After all, our city was built by people who came here to worship God freely."

Bill Clinton remembered that Graham's stance on integration at his 1959 Little Rock crusade had made a powerful impression on him. "He had nothing to gain by it," Clinton would say. We have seen that Clinton had publicly told that story several times before. By then nearly a half century had slipped by, but the impression stuck. "This man I love . . . is about the

only person I have ever known who has never failed to live his faith."
Veteran *Time* journalist Michael Duffy remembered another journalist
whispering, "I just don't get it." Duffy's response: "You're not the first."

The theological vision that Graham projected in the final three sermons of his public ministry at Flushing Meadows in 2005 told the tale.
The old themes were certainly there. The story started with humans' sin
and ended with God's forgiveness.

What was different was the tone and the balance. In the beginning—
back in Los Angeles in 1949—talk of damnation was prominent. And so
were references to the threat of Communism abroad and the menace of
immorality at home. Christ's imminent return portended judgment.

But over time the tonality and proportions changed. As early as 1964
Graham confirmed this evolution in his thinking and spirit. Now, he said,
"I stress a great deal the love of God from the Cross saying to the whole
world, 'I love you, I love you, I will forgive you.'" By the time Graham
reached the end of his crusade ministry, the notion of Christ's imminent
return mainly—not exclusively but mainly—had come to mean not a
threat of damnation but a pledge of hope for a second chance.

The choice of texts that Graham used for his sermons changed—
rather dramatically—over the years. Historians Daved Anthony Schmidt
and Allison Brown have documented that in the 1950s he drew on Old
Testament passages 33.50 percent of the time, in the 1960s 29.06 percent,
in the 1970s 25.00 percent, in the 1980s 21.59 percent, in the 1990s 17.05
percent, and in the first decade of the new century 9.62 percent.

The mature Graham's expanding vision grew from an underlying conviction that the gospel offered people and peoples everywhere a chance to
renew their societies as well as their lives. The idea was at once profound
and simple. In Christ, in the gospel, wayfarers might find fresh water in
dry wells. This was the legacy of a builder of hope.

Seasoned Soldier

The steady shift of emphasis from Old to New Testament preaching texts signaled other changes, especially in the later years of his career.

Those differences showed up especially clearly in Graham's beliefs about the Bible, new birth, and human origins and destiny; in the content, style, and delivery of his preaching; in the demographic profile of his followers; in the music of the crusade meetings; and in his moderating influence on the broader evangelical culture.

First, however, we should note the beliefs and practices that showed little change. He continued to uphold the Bible, without a hint of qualification, as the final authority for Christians; faith in Christ's redeeming death and resurrection as the sole means of salvation; the centrality of a new birth experience; the necessity of works of compassion, justice, and missions; heaven as the believer's final reward; and hell as the unbeliever's final penalty.

Practices remained largely the same, too. Unlike his near predecessors Billy Sunday and Aimee Semple McPherson, Graham continued to attract big crowds to the very end of his active ministry. Indeed, his career seemed continually to soar, as he posted some of the largest attendance figures in the meetings at the very end.

The trademark media broadcasts of *Hour of Decision* on the radio and television persisted, albeit somewhat less frequently and not always with original content. The principal publications—*Decision* and the "My Answer" columns—rolled off the press as before, with little visible change

---

This Scene is adapted with permission from "Billy Graham and American Culture: Legacies," in *Great Awakenings: Historical Perspectives for Today*, ed. David Horn (Peabody, MA: Hendrickson, 2017), 86–99, and from "The Remarkable Mr. Graham," *Christianity Today*, November 7, 2016, http://www.christianitytoday.com/ct/2016/november -web-only/remarkable-billy-graham.html.

in content or format, and World Wide Pictures continued to turn out a feature-length film every year, as before.

The signature practice, the crusade meetings, continued apace at home and abroad too, with the same meticulous preparation, counselor training, and follow-up visits. The actual services witnessed little variation, with rousing choirs and unending lineups of celebrity guest artists and notable figures sharing testimonies of lives reclaimed.

A dynamic sermon from Graham (whenever possible), and an invitation to commit one's life to Christ in a publicly visible way, continued to mark virtually every service. Graham's sermons followed the same established patterns too: a litany of international, national, social, and personal crises, for which Christ offered the sole final answer.

*   *   *

That being said, a lot did shift with time. We should begin where Graham himself began when reporters asked him how he had changed: with matters of belief. Some of Graham's beliefs evolved, sometimes considerably.

Graham's view of the Bible, evangelical Protestants' final source of authority, logically came first. As noted far back in this book, he had never explicitly argued for the Bible's factual inerrancy or called for a strict literalism in its interpretation, but much of his earliest preaching either presupposed it or allowed people to hear it if they wanted to.

Very soon, however, Graham came to rely on a pragmatic test: the Bible was true primarily because it worked. Scripture was authoritative not because it was historically or scientifically accurate in every detail, but because it did what it promised to do: infallibly bring people to faith in Christ. As it happened, we have seen, Graham did believe in the Bible's factual accuracy, at least if it was translated correctly and interpreted reasonably, but that was not the main point. The main point was that the Bible earned its authority because it worked.

The differences between this early post-Templeton posture and the mature Graham were twofold. First, as his career soared and he grew more confident of himself, he also grew more willing explicitly to articulate his views about the Bible—always a flashpoint among evangelicals—when journalists asked him about it.

Second, and more telling, Graham refused to wade into the fight over biblical inerrancy that engulfed his Southern Baptist Convention and split

252

it into conservatives and "moderates" in the 1980s. "Sincere Christians," he told *Newsweek* in 2006, "can disagree about the details of Scripture and theology—absolutely. . . . I am not a literalist in the sense that not every single jot and tittle is from the Lord. . . . There is a little difference in my thinking through the years."

Privately he allowed that his sympathies lay with the old guard, but he also insisted that the controversy could be settled if both sides really wanted to do so. And he wished they would.

The mature Graham saw the new birth experience in fresh ways too. In the early days he had called for something like a "ready-set-go" conversion experience. Stand up, walk to the front, sign a decision card, join a church, and then witness to your neighbor.

But over time Graham came to see—or at least came more often to acknowledge—that people could show their commitment in other ways. He allowed that many people, including his wife, never experienced a single moment of decision. They just grew up as children of the covenant and never saw themselves otherwise.[1] And he knew too that many inquirers were coming back to Christ after their first love had grown cold.

Graham's notion of the spiritual and moral results that should result from the new birth also evolved. His primary emphasis *always* fell on the absolute necessity of individual conversion. This point merits stress. But we have seen that he also came to see the need for *intentionally* working for social reform, sometimes through legislation.

As for human origins, Graham refused to get bogged down in fights between theistic evolutionists and so-called scientific creationists. He allowed that he was comfortable with the conventional biblical account involving a literal Adam, a literal Eve, and a literal garden. But he immediately moved on to stress that the facticity of that narrative was beside the point. The point that counted was that an active personal God stood behind it all. Naturalist premises, which automatically ruled out any kind of supernatural intervention, were incompatible with an evangelical understanding of Christian faith.

Graham's thinking about humans' final destiny evolved too. Heaven no longer emerged in literal terms of saints strolling streets of gold. Rather, it became a time of enjoying the presence of the Lord, luxuriating in the company of family and dear friends and even beloved pets, and turning one's celestial hands to productive work. Graham remained vague about the exact content of those activities but left no doubt that his own sedulous work ethic would find new uses.

Graham's understanding of hell also shifted with time. He never denied it, but he did redefine it. In the early days, Graham portrayed hell in lurid terms of fire, brimstone, and everlasting torment. But he soon felt that this evangelical chestnut simply was not biblical. Hell was separation from God's love. And what could be worse?

More controversially, the older Graham refused to speculate about the ultimate fate of Jews and other non-Christians. To reporters who asked, he invariably said, in one way or another, "All that is up to God, and I have no desire to play God." In 1978, for example, he told *Newsweek*, "I used to believe that pagans in far countries were lost if they did not have the gospel of Christ preached to them. I no longer believe that."

With qualifications, that is. Shortly after the *Newsweek* interview, almost certainly under pressure from the BGEA, Graham nipped and tucked the statement to bring it more into line with evangelical orthodoxy. Yet in later decades he repeated the 1978 statement, in one way or another, again and again. "Those are decisions only the Lord will make. . . . I don't want to speculate about all that. I believe the love of God is absolute. . . . I think [God] loves everybody regardless of what label they have." That was Graham in 2006.

Such comments ram us into a brick wall of paradox. On one hand, from beginning to end Graham affirmed without qualification, especially in his preaching, that a person's eternal destiny depended on a person's overt commitment to Christ. On the other hand, at least from the late 1970s on, he affirmed in personal settings that it was simply not up to the evangelist, or anyone else for that matter, to declare exactly how God will fulfill God's purposes.

A paradox, to be sure. Proclaim the hard truth that the Bible taught that there was only one way to heaven. But don't presume to know God's mind.

Part of the historical problem of figuring out exactly where Graham stood on momentous questions of this sort is that he was a doer, not a thinker. He reacted to questions as they arose. Preaching in a public setting, he toed the evangelical line. His head prevailed. Sharing in one-on-one settings, he backed off. His heart prevailed.

This flexibility fit into a growing disinclination to try to explain the deeper mysteries of God's ways with humans. It might be called something like principled silence. Graham did not use those words, but that is what they came to: a studied refusal to speak on God's behalf when common sense and common grace challenged easy formulas.

Consider, for example, Graham's principled silence at the National Cathedral on September 14, 2001, when he forthrightly argued that the reason for the tragedy of 9/11 was locked away in God's providence. And again about four years later when he visited the devastation wreaked by Hurricane Katrina in New Orleans. While allowing that the devil might have had some role, he did not want to assert it. "I don't know. But God has allowed it, and there is a purpose that we won't know maybe for years to come."

*   *   *

The broad content of Graham's preaching registered both the continuities and changes in Graham's doctrinal beliefs, and the style of his preaching reflected a similar duality. Straightforward proclamation it was, shorn of irony, and subtle allusion remained the order of the day—or night.

At the same time, the style became more measured, less apocalyptic. He grew less prone to paint history in stark contrasts of good and evil, less inclined to say that the world teetered on the brink of the greatest revival, or greatest disaster, it had ever known. Exaggerations and factual inaccuracies faded as he grew more inclined to talk about enduring problems of human life on this planet.

And he grew more comfortable bringing up the gray areas, the dilemmas, that Christians faced as they tried to figure out exactly what the Bible taught and exactly how to live their lives as faithful Christians in a turbulent world.

If the content and style of Graham's preaching evolved, so did the manner of delivery. It moved from the swashbuckling bombast of the earliest days to the thoughtful directness and precisely timed pauses of the middle decades to the grandfatherly pace of the mature years. He freely acknowledged that the energy to chop and pace and blaze had diminished with the years. Time taught Graham the beauty of brevity. The trademark forty minutes drifted down to twenty or fewer. A matured message evoked a matured approach.

*   *   *

The demographic profile of Graham's followers, at least in the United States, similarly stayed the same in some respects and changed, sometimes dramatically, in others. As noted, women predominated from beginning to end, roughly 60 percent. Social class remained similar too: the stable working class (manual laborers) through the lower middle class (service workers). Region and rural/urban representation changed little. Decade after decade a plurality hailed from small towns in the South and Midwest. Despite wide variations, throughout Graham's ministry the typical letter writer was a white female, with a high school education, employed in a service position, living in a small town in the South or Midwest, and worshiping in a Baptist church.

But some features did see transformations with time. The percentage of African Americans and Hispanics steadily grew from something like nil in the beginning to a conspicuous number, often commensurate with minority presence in the surrounding area. Crusade photos show continual increase in the number of attenders with special needs, especially the deaf, complemented by counselors with sign-language skills. Denominational representation shifted from a clear majority of Baptists and Methodists to a mix of Baptists, mainstream evangelicals of various stripes, Pentecostals, and, surprisingly, Catholics.

And above all, observers saw in the attenders at a Graham crusade a steady lowering of the median age. He claimed that adolescents and twenty-somethings dominated. This was an exaggeration—the wish evidently fathered the thought—but he certainly got the general trend right. The age of the inquirer recorded or intimated on the cards alone showed a definite trend toward youth.

More revealing perhaps was the shift in the musical styles that drew crowds. Gospel gems favored by the middle-aged crowds of years past gave way to the strikingly upbeat sounds of newer music. Traditional hymns and toe-tapping gospel favorites were complemented by music that especially appealed to younger people.

Actually Graham's attention to youth was not new. The legendary Explo '72, orchestrated by Bill Bright and Campus Crusade for Christ at the Cotton Bowl in Dallas in 1972, featured performances from the likes of Johnny Cash, Kris Kristofferson, Andraé Crouch, and the "Elvis" of Christian rock, Larry Norman. Graham preached six times to crowds topping one hundred thousand.

In the following decades, a growing portion of services, especially on youth nights, featured newer artists—Jars of Clay, dc Talk, Michael Smith, and Amy Grant—and the rock and the praise-and-worship music those artists had pioneered. He called rock bands his "interpreters to reach this generation." He astutely surmised that they functioned very much like his language interpreters in foreign countries.[2]

Though Graham clearly preferred the ponderous favorites of Shea's generation, Barrows—who made the final decisions on all music choices— knew what the market demanded. Graham admitted that he did not like young persons' music very much, but he liked *them*.

* * *

Finally we come to the question of the mature Graham's impact on evangelical culture, again, especially in the United States. Without doubt, when someone lives far beyond his active years, it is inevitable that his work will be associated with people, institutions, and movements he did not create and might not even endorse. Yet Graham's contribution, forged and refined in the fires of those final years, took forms that are likely to endure.

The change that probably generated the most attention from the media was Graham's steadily growing willingness to work with Christians of (almost) all stripes, as long as they did not ask him to alter his own message. The Flushing Meadows event in 2005 brought together eighty-two different denominations, prompting one newspaper to deadpan that they were groups "not known for working together."

Newsweek's senior editor Jon Meacham captured precisely the delicate balance Graham projected in those years: "Graham represents American Christianity at its best: faithful to the Gospel but tolerant of others, dedicated to Jesus but committed to openness and freedom of conscience."[3]

Graham's ability to serve as a badge of credibility for evangelicals in the broader culture was another deposit in the bank account of his legacy. He was not extreme by anyone's standards. He drew evangelicals out of the margins and taught them how to take a seat at the table of conversation in the public square. And how to do it with good manners, too.

Credibility grew from a finely tuned—perhaps more instinctive than designed—sense of where to draw the line and where not to. Liberals viewed Graham as a rock-ribbed fundamentalist impervious to the breezes of modernity, while fundamentalists viewed him as a weather vane twisting in the wind. In some ways both were right and both were wrong.

The genius of Graham's ministry was his deftness at being both at once. He steadily reduced the size of the core of nonnegotiables that had to be defended at all costs while he steadily expanded the zone of the peripheries, which were worth talking about and maybe rethinking or even giving up. The mature Graham understood that the church did not have to have an opinion on everything, and neither did he.

Differently put, Graham did not introduce but he did reinforce the notion of scale within the evangelical world. Pick your battles. Don't fight for keeps on every issue. Christ did not come to save people from dancing or cigarettes but to share a life-transforming message of God's grace.

And finally, by the concluding years Graham had effectively defined the center of the evangelical river. Other leaders positioned themselves by their proximity to him. Though his place in the center was partly a product of how other evangelicals saw him, Graham self-consciously sought that position. He intended to synthesize evangelical impulses and pockets of believers scattered across the landscape into a coherent movement that would weather the storms of change and serve as a beacon of stability.

Graham acutely grasped the importance of the changes he projected. "During most of my life I have been on a pilgrimage in many areas," he had told an audience at the John F. Kennedy School of Government at Harvard in 1982. "I have come to see in deeper ways some of the implications of my faith and message."

A decade later, at age eighty-three, he enlarged on the line. His pilgrimage meant "constantly learning, changing, growing, and maturing . . . not the least of which is in the area of human rights and racial and ethnic understanding." Viewed whole, then, the mature Graham had grown more tolerant of differing theological positions, more skeptical of political partisanship, and more assertive in his calls for social justice at home and abroad.

"Mrs. Billy Graham"

The public image of Ruth Bell Graham was integral to Billy's too. We have seen how the media loved to feature her—"pretty in pink"—hovering over her large brood of children, faithfully running the show while her husband spent eight months a year on the road. Though the portrait was sentimental, the woman at the center was anything but. Ruth exemplified the proverbial Southern steel magnolia.

As we have seen, Billy and Ruth lived to the end of their long lives in a rambling log house, which local craftsmen had built according to her specifications, a half century earlier, atop a mountain just outside Montreat. Ruth had borne the main responsibility for rearing their five children, overseeing a zoo of (mostly large) family pets; written fourteen books of essays and poetry; and played an important role in the authorship of both editions of Billy's signature theology book, *Peace with God*.

Clear-minded she was. In the preface of *Peace with God*, first published in 1953, Billy acknowledged—almost certainly too briefly—that his "loyal and faithful" wife had "read and reread" the text. In 1966 he forthrightly acknowledged her coauthorship: "Ruth and I wrote that book."

The preface of the second edition, published in 1984, was more explicit about Ruth's substantial contribution. In that second edition Ruth quietly sanded down some of the hard edges of the first edition by placing more emphasis on God's astounding grace. "She wanted to open the Christian message up to a new generation of readers in the 1980s," said Ruth's biographer Anne Wills, "by emphasizing the importance of a personal relationship of humans to God and Jesus, rather than emphasizing religious institutions or the abstract phenomenon of 'religion' itself."

Strong-minded too. Beyond her work on *Peace with God*, and her authored books, Ruth spoke at countless meetings, sometimes on Billy's behalf and sometimes on her own. Deeply but never ostentatiously pious, she remained a lifelong Southern Presbyterian, unimpressed with Billy's Southern Baptist theology. She liked to tell their children that "there comes a time to stop submitting and start outwitting." Ruth famously refused to sign the clause of the *Lausanne Covenant* that called signatories to embrace a *simple* lifestyle. Simpler, she could go with, but for a mother of five, and wife of the world's most prominent preacher, with a constant stream of guests to entertain, simple seemed too much to promise.

If anyone ever doubted the acuteness of Ruth's thinking, her lightning wit put that illusion to bed very quickly. Stories proliferate. Once, when asked if she had ever considered divorcing her usually-gone husband, she shot back, with a twinkle, "No, I've never thought of divorce in all these 35 years of marriage, but . . . I did think of murder a few times."[1] Ruth's car once plunged seventy feet down a hill near their house and hit a tree. Emerging unhurt, she dusted herself off and directed the family to nail a stop sign to the tree. At the end of her life, though suffering greatly, her wit remained in control. A sign fixed above the portal of her bedroom door read "Nobody Knows the Trouble I've Been."

Ruth is well described as a force of nature. In press accounts she consistently emerged as an exceptional woman, attractive, stylishly dressed, and remarkably nonjudgmental. Her close lifelong friendship with her Montreat neighbor Patricia Cornwell, a nonconformist and one of America's most prominent murder mystery writers; her (unsuccessful) advocacy for clemency for condemned murderer Margie Velma Barfield; and her efforts to befriend convicted preacher-swindler Jim Bakker when no one else would left little doubt that Ruth was a woman of strong convictions and deep Christian faith, conservative by nature and upbringing but unconstrained by the conventions and platitudes of Southern evangelical piety.

Ruth's spunk was on full display in Charlotte, Mecklenburg County, North Carolina, in May of 1975. Ruth's friend and biographer Patricia Cornwell told the tale.

In Cornwell's narration, President Ford was in town giving a speech celebrating Mecklenburg Independence Day. Ruth was seated on the front row, next to the aisle. During the talk, Daniel Pollock, a twenty-eight-year-old barefoot, shirtless protestor, and a member of the antiwar Red Hornet Mayday Tribe, slipped through the guards. He raced to the front, heralding a placard that said, on one side, "EAT THE RICH" and on the other, "DON'T TREAD ON ME."

Ruth's hand shot out, snatched the placard, and smacked it on the ground. When the protestor kneeled at her chair, asking for the sign back,

Ruth patted him on his shoulders. Police whisked him away. The next day former president Richard Nixon phoned Ruth to congratulate her for standing tall.

And Pollock filed charges for assault.

When Ruth received a summons to appear in court in August, Cornwell goes on, Ruth declared beforehand that she would rather go to jail than pay the $50 fine. Well-wishers offered to pay it for her. Pollock had a perfect right to protest, she told the press, but not during the president's talk. It was disrespectful to obstruct others' right to hear the president.

In court, the case was quickly dismissed for lack of evidence since Pollock admitted that Ruth had only patted him. Nixon phoned again, and so did Ford two weeks later. On leaving the courtroom, Ruth tried to give Pollock a leather-bound *Living Bible*. Pollock refused to take it. The press was on hand everywhere. Cornwell's account leaves little doubt that Ruth won both the legal battle and the publicity war.

Ruth was the brains behind the Cove, a retreat and conference center, opened in 1993, on a 1,200-acre preserve near Asheville. Tucked far back into the Blue Ridge forests, the Cove's picturesque accommodations, manicured lawns, and quiet seclusion bore the imprint of Ruth's hand.

Ruth's story formed a significant part of Billy's story, as her many fans, both in person and in the letters posted to Billy, made clear. And from time to time her place in that story received formal recognition: in 1996 she received, with Billy, the Congressional Gold Medal in the US Capitol Rotunda in Washington, DC.

"An odd kind of cross to bear" was how the mature Ruth described being "Mrs. Billy Graham." On one hand, she unhesitatingly embraced her role as a supportive wife and mother. The "Mrs." part of her identity was for real. On the other hand, she stood tall not by accepting secular feminism but by challenging it.

More conservative than Billy in politics, she opposed his peace trip to Moscow, supported capital punishment (with significant exceptions), personally confronted at least one anti–Vietnam War protestor, and preferred Fox News over Billy's favorite, CNN. Even today, organization veterans around Montreat and around Boone, North Carolina (Samaritan's Purse headquarters), like to quip that Franklin is Ruth's son.

Ruth shared Billy's calling. She taught him that the Southern Presbyterian mainline offered theological ballast for the emerging evangelical movement that Graham had done so much to shape. And she broadened his perspective. Growing up in China in the 1920s and 1930s, she had witnessed poverty and suffering unlike anything Billy had seen. Their shared callings—hers mostly at home, his mostly on the road—came with a price. "We live for a time secure," she wrote, "beloved and loving, sure it cannot last for long then—the goodbyes come again—and again—like a small death, the closing of a door."

After years of acute suffering, Ruth was taken off life support, at her request, on June 14, 2007, four days after her eighty-seventh birthday. Though the details are murky, Franklin may have managed to override his mother's wishes to be buried at the Cove. Rather she was entombed in a memorial garden a short walk from the Billy Graham Library in Charlotte. A road sign she liked graces her tombstone: "End of construction. Thank you for your patience."

In the high-profile world of television and prosperity evangelists, marred by Elmer Gantry antics, Graham's devotion and fidelity to Ruth remained beyond question. We have seen that the press liked to portray their marriage as syrupy sweet, yet Billy and Ruth themselves never did. "I haven't got tired of him," Ruth said, grinning, when someone asked about Billy. "[But] it's been a job sometimes." Both freely acknowledged that they had experienced their fair share of ups and downs. "If two people always agree," Ruth quipped, "one of them is useless."

Ruth's public profile never rivaled Billy's, but his is unimaginable without hers.

SCENE 51

Gentle Patriarch

The sun set slowly on Graham's storied career, more like a long Indian summer than a sudden nightfall. And with good reason.

Far into his seventies and even beyond, Graham cut a dashing profile. He well fit the American media ideal of the "seasoned yet still virile male": tall, lean, blue-eyed, with flowing silver hair and a million-dollar smile. One journalist said that "he looks like the aging athlete." A baritone voice, as steady and sonorous as ever, along with a distinctive Southern accent, rounded out the image.

A *Time* magazine cover showed the same square jaw along with a physique decked out in a white turtleneck sweater and sporty black blazer. The caption simply read, "A Christian in Winter: Billy Graham at 75."

For many people Graham seemed both invincible and timeless. Though prone to sniffles and accidents, he maintained a work and travel schedule that required amazing stamina, year after year. He had shouldered at least one hundred outdoor crusade meetings, some in driving rain, some in bitter cold, and some in broiling heat. "Thousands Ignore Coliseum Heat for Message of 'Wonderful Man'" ran a headline in the *Toronto Globe and Mail* in 1955.

But time eventually took its toll. As noted, Graham designated his son Franklin CEO of the BGEA in 2000 and president in 2001. Aging dropped the volume and slowed the pace of his sermons. By the end they had come to sound more like fireside chats. He readily admitted that he now favored less demanding indoor auditoriums.

In 1989, when Graham was seventy-one, he was diagnosed with Parkinson's disease (later rediagnosed as hydrocephalus). Six years later he collapsed while speaking in Toronto, but soon he climbed out of a hospital bed to preach to a SkyDome record crowd of 73,500 on the final night of the crusade.

Charlotte Observer journalist Ken Garfield rightly said that Graham was given the "gift of being an icon one moment and human the next." The mature Graham perfected the fine art of poking fun at himself, even when it came to mounting infirmities. "You know what happens when you get Parkinson's? Your handwriting gets illegible and your sermons longer," he quipped.

Journalists repeatedly asked him when he planned to step down. He said he would not retire until the Lord released him—and the Lord had not done that yet. "How do you retire from a calling?" he asked. Elsewhere he joked that when people asked if this or that meeting was his last one, many asked it "hopefully." Yet declining health finally forced his hand. Though nothing like an official announcement or retirement party ever took place, the 2005 crusade proved to be the final major one he endeavored on his own.

*   *   *

The Billy Graham Library in Graham's hometown of Charlotte was dedicated on May 31, 2007. The ceremony stood as an enduring tribute. All three of the living former presidents of the United States attended, George H. W. Bush, Jimmy Carter, and Bill Clinton. It is worth noting that two of the three presidents were Democrats, and the one Republican was noted more for his centrist positions than for his partisanship.

Their words glowed with praise. Bush described Graham as "America's pastor." Carter said that before, during, and after his presidency he had found Graham a trusted friend whom he admired as few others. In a sense, Clinton said the most. Quietly observing that Graham had been "the most influential person" in his spiritual life, the former president reminisced about Graham's consistent kindness, especially in private, when no one was looking.

The Billy Graham Library officially opened to the public one week later, on June 5, 2007. Located near a handsome four-lane boulevard named, fittingly enough, Billy Graham Parkway, the 40,000-square-foot building, situated on twenty acres of prime suburban real estate, featured exhibits stretching across Graham's entire life.

Granted, the library wasn't much of a library—it housed only a bookstore showcasing BGEA publications—and the exhibits unabashedly portrayed Graham at his very best, in every situation. The library's outer architecture resembled an old-fashioned (upscale) barn, and the inner architecture matched the Southern rural motif throughout, down to the sinks in the restrooms, fitted out to look like big milk basins. By 2018 the library had hosted more than one million visitors.

Even the most skeptical visitors should have been impressed by the large collection of poster-sized photos of Graham interacting with luminaries from all walks of life, including Bono, Martin Luther King Jr., Muhammad Ali, Queen Elizabeth, and Bob Hope. If visiting evangelicals came hungry for status, vicarious or otherwise, they found their needs amply met in the lineup.

*   *   *

As Graham entered his nineties, failing hearing and eyesight and the dramatic erosion of physical strength made clear to everyone (and almost certainly to Graham himself) that he would never preach a final sermon he once dreamed about delivering once again in London.

In a late book, symptomatically named *Nearing Home: Life, Faith, and Finishing Well*, published in 2011,[1] the nonagenarian Graham acknowledged that he suffered infirmities. "Old age is not for sissies," he sighed. One admirer wrote that Graham's ability to "accept illness and aging with peace" offered solace to others facing the pains and fears of their own sunset years.

When my wife, Katherine, and I visited Graham one final time in his home in 2011, he struggled with considerable difficulty to get up from his easy chair and shake Katherine's hand. "I have always been prepared to die," he said, very softly, "but I haven't been prepared to grow old." Shortly afterward the family decided that he would receive visitors no more.

Shea and Barrows, Graham's two closest associates—and friends—had worked by Graham's side for more than a half century. Shea lived the final two decades of his life a few miles down the road from Graham in Montreat. He died in 2013 at age 104.

Later that year Graham's family arranged a ninety-fifth birthday celebration in the venerable Grove Park Inn in Asheville. Near the end of the evening Graham, sitting in a wheelchair, asked for a handheld microphone. He gestured toward Barrows, also sitting in a wheelchair, a few feet away. Graham whispered a thank you to Barrows "for everything." Those were the only words Graham uttered, and, as it turned out, the final words he would ever utter in a public setting. Barrows died in 2016 at age 93.

We have seen that Graham was not a profound thinker or eloquent preacher, but he dealt with serious things in serious ways. As the physical signs of slowing down became more manifest in the later decades of his life, he began to ruminate on the passing of time. Once, in his midsixties, a teenager asked what most surprised him in his "old age." He answered without hesitation: "the brevity of life." Elsewhere he said that what most surprised him about his extended ministry was "how quickly it passed."

His long march had taught important lessons. "I urge each of you to invest your lives, not just spend them," he told a group of young people. "Each of us is given the exact same [number] of seconds, minutes, and hours per day as anyone else. The difference is how we redeem [them]. . . . You cannot count your days, but you can make your days count." Graham understood, said historian Leonard Sweet, that a good life was not the same as a "good time."

Graham noted that many people tried to avoid the inescapable reality of death by playing word games—by changing the title of a cemetery to a memorial park, for example. But he left them no loopholes. First, he said, "accept the fact that you will die." Second, "make arrangements." Third, "make provision for those you are leaving behind." And finally, "make an appointment with God." Graham was not an introspective man, but he was not a superficial one either.

Until the final decades of his ministry, Graham seemed not to dwell very much on the subject of his own death. For one thing, he always had been consistently outwardly focused. If there was an introspective bone in his body, no one, or at least no one outside the inner circle, ever saw it. That outward orientation fostered a perennially sunny disposition, especially in public. "I don't have many sad days," he once told Larry King. He admitted that after the excitement of a crusade had subsided, and he went back to the quiet of his secluded mountain home, he felt some down times. But they never lasted long.

But in his closing years Graham did finally turn to the subject of his own death. He saw his demise as a door to a new life in heaven. "I'm looking forward to it, I really am," he said as he approached his ninetieth birthday. "I'll be happy the day the Lord says, Come on. I've got something better planned."

Graham admitted that he did not look forward to the dying process itself. He had seen "some of the terrible things that happen to people that are dying. I don't want that."

But beyond the event itself stood heaven as a place of glorious fellowship with the Lord, with saints, and with loved ones. In heaven, Graham promised, there would be invigorating work to do. "Think of a place where there will be no sorrow and no parting, no pain, no sickness, no death, no quarrels, no misunderstandings, no sin and no cares.' He even speculated about golf courses and beloved pets—whatever it took to make folks happy.

*   *   *

Graham spent his final half-dozen years quietly at home. Except for nurses and a brood of children, grandchildren, great-grandchildren, and other family members regularly stopping by to see him, he chose to live, if not exactly alone, at least far out of public view. Though he had spent a lifetime interacting with countless people of all ranks and vocations and life situations, at the end he preferred the solitude.

The end came quietly. A nurse sitting by Graham's bedside early one morning noted that the evangelist—eight months shy of his 100th birthday—had simply stopped breathing. Nine days later he was laid to rest beside Ruth.

Back in 2006, seven inmates at the Louisiana State Penitentiary at Angola, the nation's largest maximum-security facility, had handcrafted Graham's pine plywood box in the prison's workshop, just as they had crafted Ruth's box earlier. Lined only with a mattress pad, it cost $215. They nailed a wooden cross to the top, and three of them burned their names into the side. The main carpenter, the late Richard "Grasshopper" Liggett, serving a life sentence for murder, said that of everything that had ever happened in his life, "the most profound" was the opportunity to build Billy Graham's coffin.

At one point Graham had wanted his stone to bear just one word, "Preacher." The family expanded his request. Under an inscribed cross they wrote the following.

BILLY GRAHAM

NOVEMBER 7, 1918 FEBRUARY 21, 2018

PREACHER OF THE GOSPEL

OF THE LORD JESUS CHRIST

JOHN 14:6[2]

What Manner of Man?

In the twilight of Graham's long life, observers found themselves asking, in William Martin's apt words, "What manner of man was he?" That was not a question about specific successes or specific failures that one might tally up on some kind of balance sheet. Rather, it was a question about character, about the abiding dispositions that governed his life.

A complex man he was, not only presenting different faces in different situations but also constantly mixing virtues and flaws, not in equal measure, certainly, but in a conspicuous way. The story recounted in this book reveals a real man, with real strengths, real weaknesses, and real complexities.

We begin with weaknesses, partly because they were, by any reasonable measure, fewer in number and easier to sketch. Graham was not the varnished mannequin that emerges on the BGEA websites and in authorized accounts. Some weaknesses he outgrew as he matured, some he struggled with all his life, and some he seemed not to see in himself at all.

To begin with, Graham was a prodigious name-dropper. Even his closest friends and admirers admitted this trait. Name-dropping was a form of credentialing. Sometimes his very identity seemed to lie in the people he knew. Some defenders tried to explain the trait—or explain it away—as a sign of his insecurity about growing up on a farm, or not coming from old money, or not attending a prestige college, or not going on to seminary.

But it is hard to make this line of explanation stick when Graham rubbed shoulders with many of the richest, most powerful, most elite people in the world and received adulation as no other preacher in America since George Whitefield in the eighteenth century. The explanation for Graham's name-dropping is, in short, stubbornly elusive. Sometimes it is more persuasive to accept a fault simply for what it was, a fault.

Beyond name-dropping, Graham loved to bask in the limelight of his friendships with the rich and the powerful. For a good thirty or forty years, his photo routinely appeared in leading newspapers and magazines with leaders of government and, to a lesser extent, leaders in the business and entertainment worlds. There was never a hint of personal impropriety in any of these spreads, but there also was never a hint that he felt the slightest reluctance to share the glory of their fame.

Then, too, plenty of times Graham enjoyed his own renown. Historian Michael Hamilton limned the paradox precisely: "He was a genuinely humble person who spent his long life drawing public attention to himself." He even saw the paradox in himself. "Pride is an insidious thing," he once mused. "I've never quite known whether I was proud or humble."

Then too Graham liked to see his name front and center. In the 1954 London crusade, for example, anxious about attendance, he told one of the organizers, "I do not see my picture up enough." For sure, when the BGEA was organized in 1950, Graham protested that he did not want it named after him. But he gave in when Ruth and others said his name would help draw people in. Perhaps so. Yet that reasoning did not persuade even Franklin Graham—who was no wallflower—to change the name of Samaritan's Purse to his name when he inherited the organization from World Vision in 1970.[1]

Closely related to basking in the limelight was Graham's readiness to speak beyond his knowledge. We have seen that reporters routinely asked his views about things great and small—-and he routinely told them. Biographer Marshall Frady rightly notes Graham's habit of "ceaseless extemporaneous free-form punditry" on topics as varied as the culture of the Congo, the Common Market, and the utility of bomb shelters.

Part of the problem lay with journalists, who constantly plied him with questions about topics they surely knew he knew little or nothing about. But they wanted to sell papers, and Graham obliged them. In later years he admitted this fault and chastised himself for it.

Then, too, Graham was oblivious to others' *deeper* views. Here we must be careful. By numerous accounts he was a wonderful listener in person, patiently hearing out students' questions in Q & A sessions on campuses, or paying close attention to the trials of life that seatmates on planes shared with him. He also proved eager to ask people, especially older men, questions about subjects he wanted to learn about, such as the history of evangelism in a particular country.

That being said, he rarely asked people about their *worldviews*, especially if they differed from his. There is little evidence of Graham interrogating Buddhists about the rewards of their faith, or secularists about the reasons for their position, or those who left evangelical Christianity about why they had chosen to go another way. When it came to religious conversations, Graham was almost always on the giving, not the receiving, end.

*   *   *

But Graham's strengths far outweighed his weaknesses. If he had more admirers than critics, there were good reasons for it.

Start with the demonstrable achievements. By any reasonable measure of such things, and certainly by Graham's own professed values, the most notable was the three million decisions for Christ registered in his crusades, as well as the countless souls who found hope for new life in other venues of his ministry. Setting attendance records, schmoozing with presidents, and topping approval polls were all nice. But Graham insisted, repeatedly and without qualification, that they meant little next to the one thing that truly mattered.

On the social and political front, Graham's record was mixed. On women's equality he was behind the curve, on race and poverty he was moderately ahead of his evangelical peers. On nuclear disarmament he was far ahead. Ecumenism with believers outside the circle of card-carrying evangelicals was another area in which he was far ahead.

And then there's charisma. To some extent this trait was less a strength than a natural expression of the genes he inherited and the favorable circumstances he enjoyed. Yet Graham chose to use his charisma, however naturally derived, less for personal gain—after all, he could have gone into enormously lucrative careers elsewhere—than to further his evangelistic work.

A potpourri of comments from folks in various walks of life, each eminent, makes this point in different ways. The famed country singer Barbara Mandrell said that when Johnny Cash and Billy Graham walked into a building, you could sense their presence. One businessman once offered Graham one hundred dollars a minute for the privilege of just talking with him. Samuel S. Hill, sometimes dubbed the dean of historians of Southern religion, remarked that he would not walk across the street to hear Graham preach—but he would walk a mile in the snow to be able to chat with him in person. Such data are of course anecdotal, but as soon as one starts to research Graham's story, they accumulate.

Personal probity was one of his most celebrated strengths. Though the press exaggerated the number of evangelists who fell into moral sin, the number was always great enough to keep the fires of suspicion burning brightly. Graham looked strong in contrast, not least because his commitments persisted without wavering across the seven decades of his public ministry.

The four guidelines of the "Modesto Manifesto"—integrity, chastity, truthfulness, and cooperation—became so strongly associated with Graham's ministry that they actually acquired another label: the Graham Rules.

By 2017 these rules had grown so strict that a fictional Netflix episode prompted one American journalist to call and quiz me about them. In the scene, Elizabeth II, the Queen of England, invited Graham to Windsor Palace to talk about the theology of forgiveness. Graham seated himself on a couch in front of her in a cavernous state room, no one else in sight. Had he violated his own principle about not being alone with a woman? The point is that Graham's personal probity had become so set in the public mind that it exceeded even the commonsense boundaries he envisioned.

Another enduring trait was Graham's ability to serve as something like a public moral gyroscope for six decades. He spoke with authority across the years. The burning issues of the day paraded past him, one after another, and then disappeared. Yet his voice remained, somehow seeming to transcend them all. In the words of *Christianity Today* editor Ted Olsen, "It's one thing to be quick with a quote, as many were. But it's something more to command the moral respect that inspired enthusiasm for the second half of the twentieth century."

Graham knew the danger of hitching his wagon to the star of partisan and culture-war shibboleths instead of focusing on truths that remained firm generation after generation. Knowing the danger was not the same as always avoiding it, but he tried and, to a remarkable extent, succeeded, especially in his later years.

Hard work—plain old-fashioned hard work—marks the list too. Of course, Graham had plenty of help all along the way from employees, associates, and, above all, his multitalented wife, Ruth. And he understood the importance of rest times, with regular visits to the golf course and vacations on sunny beaches. Even so, he could not have mounted thousands of public speaking engagements, authored or authorized uncounted printed words, and orchestrated a far-flung global evangelistic empire for more than six decades without intense and sustained labor. But viewed whole, it is clear that these were times of *re*-creation rather than mere leisure.

Another trait was personal humility. A gaggle of similar—not identical but similar—words denoting closely related concepts crop up too. Observers repeatedly spoke of his sincerity, authenticity, earnestness, and guilelessness. Described however, virtually all journalists and historians who encountered Graham talked about this trait. Even hostile ones who could find little good to say about the man almost always remarked on the striking and undeniable humility he displayed when they interviewed him.

Yet here we must proceed carefully. For one thing, Graham was not by any means a perfect example of humility. Some of the traits noted earlier— overstatement, name-dropping, basking in the limelight, and obliviousness to others' worldviews—leave little doubt that Graham occasionally veered off the humility highway. Sometimes the Lord had to hit him with a two-by-four to get his attention, one associate deadpanned, but invariably the Lord soon succeeded.

More important, humility should not be confused with meekness. Graham's adroit use of self-deprecating humor would not have worked unless it came with clear awareness of his achievements. His description of his formal education offered case in point. Though he had never gone to seminary, he told a graduating class at Gordon Conwell Seminary in 1982, he had, along the way, "picked up a thing or two." A video of the event reveals a wry grin.

So where did Graham's humility really lie? I think we see it in four places: his willingness to face up to his mistakes, his habit of self-forgetfulness, his feelings of gratitude for the gifts he had received, and his unflagging obedience to his calling.

Blunders scarred Graham's record, and he knew it and apologized for them. When he died, eulogists repeatedly remarked on Graham's willingness to discuss his missteps and regrets. Most conspicuously, he opened his memoir with his disastrous visit with President Truman fifty years earlier.

In his mature years he repeatedly apologized in person and in print for falling into the perils of political partisanship, for spending too much time away from his family, for not spending enough time reading and studying, for accepting too many invitations to speak, for declining to speak against the Vietnam War, for failing to address racism more forcefully, for slandering Jews in the media, and for allowing himself to be suckered by Nixon. He even apologized to himself for watching too much television.

The apologies for mistakes and failures were not just general expressions of remorse but often took a very specific focus. In 1993, for example, he preached that AIDS might be a judgment from God. Two weeks later he publicly retracted the statement, attributed it to exhaustion, and then pleaded: "I am very sorry for what I said." There were no crocodile tears, Jimmy Swaggart style, just a straight-up acknowledgment of wrong roads taken.

Self-forgetfulness followed. Again and again we see him keeping himself in the background, giving credit to others, especially to his associates. He showed little inclination to exercise power outside the BGEA. He formed no denomination such as Aimee McPherson's International Church of the Foursquare Gospel, or college such as Oral Roberts University, or media empire such as Pat Robertson's Christian Broadcast Network, or philanthropy such as Franklin Graham's Samaritan's Purse, or megachurch such as T. D. Jakes's Potter's House Church and Ministries.

Observers repeatedly noted Graham's ability to discipline the temptations of ego. "Graham could not have done what he did without ego," one of his closest associates remarked, but he "knew how to put a governor on it." Aides remembered his demand that they critique his sermons—and the tart response they got if they tried to avoid it.

Ever haunted by a fear of failing—himself, the church, and especially God—he fervently hoped never to stumble or take credit from the Lord for what the Lord alone had done. Associates uniformly spoke of the words he uttered repeatedly: "I am just a spectator watching what God is doing."

The British journalist David Frost once asked Graham if he had questions he hoped to ask God when he got to heaven. "Yes, thousands," he responded. "Some things in my life I would be embarrassed if anyone else saw. I would like God to edit the film."

Gratitude flowed as well. From beginning to end Graham showed awareness of unmerited grace infusing his life. When people asked him, as they often did, why so much attention had fallen on him, he invariably responded the same way: "I have no idea." The first thing he planned to ask the Lord when he got to heaven, he said, was why the Lord had chosen him, a very ordinary farm boy from North Carolina, to preach the gospel to millions around the world.

And of course, gratefulness to Ruth, too, not only for standing by him for more than six decades of marriage but also for helping prepare his talks, for honestly critiquing his sermons, for keeping him away from politics (with mixed success), for taking the lion's share of responsibility for rearing their five children.

One Soul at a Time relates a few—a tiny few—of the instances where Graham deflected praise from himself to others and especially to the God who merited it. To some extent it was a posture, of course. Evangelicals schooled themselves to think and speak that way. Yet those deflections happened so often in so many settings that only the most hardened skeptic could dismiss them as a mere affectation.

At the time of Graham's death, the *Washington Post* op-ed columnist Michael Gerson—who was not uncritical of the preacher—offered words that captured the heart of Graham's enduring spirit. "For Graham faith was not the instrument to some other end; it was the prize itself. He had no ulterior motives. No trace of cynicism. He was consumed by grace, and spoke in gratitude." Gerson got it right. Graham did not always speak with the same voice, but few doubted that the dominant one, the one that surely will linger in history, was the voice of gratitude.

And finally, obedience to his calling. Ironically, it is not clear exactly when Graham concluded that a general calling to Christian service— which he experienced as a very young man on that fabled moonlit night on a golf course in Florida—morphed into a specific calling to be an evangelist. But soon enough, probably early on in his Youth for Christ days, Graham grew certain that God had summoned him for that line of work and no other. His life was not his own to do with as he pleased.

Graham's obedience to his calling rode on the rails of confidence in his ability to do the job that God had given him. This is a subtle but critically important point. He *never* minimized, let alone disparaged, his accomplishments, which would have minimized the magnitude of the work that God had accomplished through him. And it would have been a lie. He knew perfectly well who he was and the power he wielded.

Graham exemplified the words of the Olympic track star Eric Liddell: "I believe God made me for a purpose, but he also made me fast. And when I run I feel His pleasure." He left little doubt that he too felt pleasure in obeying God's calling. Graham's biographer David Aikman captured his determined obedience to his calling with brilliant succinctness. His great achievement, said Aikman, was not how he handled adversity but rather how he handled success.[2]

An honest portrait of Graham's character—the manner of man he was—requires willingness to paint a multihued portrait. He evoked strong feelings both ways. Why did so many people care so much about him? Why did this rather ordinary farm boy from the South become a lightning rod for venomous criticism from thousands as well as an icon for breathless praise from millions? The story recounted in this short biography offers clues to both questions, but definitive answers it does not.

That elusiveness is part of the mystery of the man. If Graham himself were able to weigh in, he likely would make a self-deprecating quip about too much about too little. Not an outright denial, for sure, but a call to remember from whence it all came. By all externally visible evidence, Graham diligently sought never to forget that God, not Billy Graham, was the one true source of his success. He walked the talk.

They Called Him Billy

Billy Graham offered children a safe space for pouring out their fears and hopes. They provide a clear window into the sensibilities of heartland America—and other parts of the world, we can be sure.

Adult letters normally addressed him as Dr. Graham, or Mr. Graham, or Rev. Graham, but children's letters typically addressed him with his full name, Billy Graham, or very often just Billy. The kids who wrote were commonly from seven to eleven years old, but a few ran as young as five. In their innocence, their letters said a great deal about the role he played in their lives.[1]

When Billy appeared on television in their living rooms, he became part of the family. They listened because he seemed to be talking directly to them, almost by name. Many made clear that they expected him not only to write back but also to write back himself, not turn the job over to an assistant (who didn't know them as Billy did). Many also made clear that time counted. They needed a response sooner rather than later.

Children, like adults, trusted Graham to tell them the truth. Lest there be any doubt, Shirley emphatically assured Billy: "I believe every word you say!" So too Hilton needed clarification on one especially gnarly point. "You said on your show that to love the world is a sin. I love animals and the animal world, is that a sin?"

Children's letters left no doubt that adults were not the only ones who pondered theological questions. In their own unformed—not unin-formed but unformed—way, young folk thought seriously about things that mattered. They wrestled with questions of beginnings and endings about themselves and about the entire world too. "I love God because if he didn't make the world we wouldn't be here," Helen matter-of-factly explained.

Other theological questions arose too. Children wanted Billy to know that they agreed with him that good and evil existed. "I believe in God and the devil," said Sam, without elaboration. No one used the word "episte-mology"—the science of knowing—but children discerned the problem nonetheless. Alice cut to the heart of the issue. "I know that if the lord was not real how could we move. I know the Lord is real for I can feel him in my blood."

Putting theology to work through prayer was important, too. Chil-dren shared their feelings readily. Jane assured Graham, "I prayed one time and Jesus did just what I prayed." We do not know exactly what Jane prayed for, but do we do know what Arlene prayed for. "One night I had the stomache. I prayed to God. In fifteen minutes it was gone."

Children likely understood more about sin than their parents real-ized. Adults had synonyms for sin and its manifestations. Children did not. "I like what you said about the Devil," Martha observed. "I have done a lot of wrongs." Not a few letter writers were very specific about their sins. Lois was a bit older than most. "[My life] was routen. I use to talk with boys that sware and say bad words and lie. I did things I shouldn't."

Kids also knew from personal experience that the Christian pilgrim-age could be a hard one. "When I was nine I thought I knew the Lord personally but when I was eleven I found out different, I feel so bad. . . . I've got to admit I'm not a Christian," was how Ezra told his own story.

But if sin abounded, grace did too. For some, the moment of salvation was remarkably specific. "I gave my life to God . . . March 15 1972," Helen said. After Sarah got saved, she exulted, "I felt like jumping up and down." Whatever the difficulties, the Christian life made everything worthwhile. Another young soul seemed barely able to contain her joy. "I love everyone but I love Jesus more."

Granted, even for children backsliding loomed as a very real and very grim possibility. Sandra, eleven, allowed that she had discovered God's love when she was five and learned "the plan of salvation when [she] was six." Nonetheless, in the next three years, she had drifted. Yet grace abounded, and so did joy. It was important for Graham to know.

Children understood that they, like Graham, were obliged to share the good news with their friends. But they also knew that it was hard to do. "Pray for me," Jake pled. "I am still scared to witness." And some places were harder than others. Young David invited Graham to hold a crusade in his hometown of Philadelphia. The reason was compelling: "Who needs it better than Philadelphia?" Yet difficulty was no excuse. The good news was meant for everyone. "God loves white and red and black and brown," one earnest young soul shared.

Pets held a warm spot in their hearts, and they wanted Billy to know about them. Children instinctively framed their pets' lives in theological terms. One young man happily reported, "I think my dog just turned Christian." Pets' sickness was a problem, too, and kids thought Billy might be able to help. One young lady shared that she had prayed for her fish, without success, then scratched the fish on the head, still without success. "What do I do?" The question was urgent. "Write me back." Children, like adults, worried about their beloved pets' afterlife. Andrea said it as simply and clearly as language permitted. "I hope my cat went to heaven."

And then there was money. Graham himself never said a lot about money, but one way or another children heard about it enough to feel a tug on their hearts—and piggy banks. They freely sent to Graham the financial rewards they received for doing chores, or for getting a good report card, or for just growing up. "Here is the money I got from my teeth," said one.

Coming up with money to give was, however, easier said than done. Not a few kids put the burden back on Graham. "You know anybody who want a bunny or a kitten?" The writer would take $1.50. Another youngster did not let his empty piggy bank deter him. He allowed that he "would like to send money but have none to send—PS using mother's money."

For some Graham served as a model of aspiration. They wanted to be like him. A few turned that aspiration into a clearly defined vocational goal. "When I grow up," John wrote, "I am going to be a Babtist preacher. . . . Almost every day I crave to preach in front of one million people. . . . I might be another Billy Graham." Other letters were so straightforward in their flattery that they elicit a smile. "Are you sure you are 53 . . . you only look like you are 30 years old."

Children believed Graham was probably God's best friend. Little Shirley wondered, "How is God doing?" Not everyone thought in such heavenly terms, however. Charles's mother wrote on his behalf. When he grew up, he told her, he wanted to be president. "President for what?" she asked. "President for Jesus."

And so it is not surprising that invitations to Graham to visit their house or church or school popped up remarkably often. "Maybe you can come to our church sometime," ran a typical invitation. Not a few kids made the invitation town-specific. "When you come to Atlanta feel free to sleep at our house," said Nicholas. "Come to Boise," another urged. Or event-specific. Lydia wondered if he would be the minister for her wedding. Children's cultural location revealed itself in the invitations. No one invited him for lunch or dinner, but many invited him for supper. "I like to watch you on t.v. come to my house for supper if you can."

Graham reminded children that no matter what, God loved them. One way God loved them was by patching up family relationships. After your services, wrote Maurice—who identified himself with precision as exactly twelve and three-fourths years old—"my dad has changed." At the end of one service, Maurice's dad looked at him and then at his sister and brother and then said, "I love you all. So thank you Billy Graham."

And so it is not surprising that a great many of the letters were actually thank-you notes. "You made me a Christerian yesterday," said Jennifer. "Jesus is lucky to have a man like you," Scott assured Graham. Children's gratitude ran deep. "I pray that God will keep you alive for a hundred years, so you can keep up the good word for him." Kate put the point as precisely as possible: "Don't die until there's someone to take your place."

The closings that children used to end their letters spoke volumes about their feelings for Graham. "Your buddy." "So long." "Praise you." "God bless you." "Your unknown friend." "A Grate fan of yours." "That's all I have to say." Closings frequently involved love—"Much love"—"I love you"—"With all my love." But by far the most frequent one consisted of just one word. "Love."

Omar asked "Mr. Gram" to send a book so he could read it to his baby brother. He then signed off, "Tell Mr. Jesus hi."

If Billy Graham's lifetime of witness was on the mark, at 7:46 a.m., Wednesday morning, February 21, 2018, he fulfilled Omar's request.

Appendix on Letters

No one knows exactly how many letters streamed into the Minneapolis office of the BGEA, since the organization did not keep track. But between 1950, when the BGEA was formed, and 2005, when Graham retired, the number easily soared into the millions. Office veterans remember that in the peak years they arrived each morning in trucks. Every letter received a personal answer, drafted by assistants who used boilerplate paragraphs preapproved by Billy and Ruth. The response letters told the writers that they came from assistants because Graham could not possibly read all of them himself, but the substance of the responses carried his endorsement.

For reasons of space and confidentiality, the BGEA destroyed nearly all the letters, but several thousand, mostly posted in the late 1940s, early 1950s, early 1960s, and throughout the 1980s, somehow survived. No one knows why—possibly a clerical error. Whatever the reason, they offer a priceless resource, rarely consulted by researchers in a systematic way.

The letters do add several features to the profile of Graham's followers that are not readily available elsewhere. Missives with racially or ethnically distinctive names (such as Jamal or Natalia), or names with education-related tags (such as MD or PhD), or with rural route return addresses, or with return addresses in tony parts of big cities (such as Evanston, Illinois) or college towns (such as Chapel Hill, North Carolina) never amounted to more than a trickle.

Though the messages arrived on every imaginable size, shape, and color of paper, with and without letterhead, the majority were standard

---

The first three paragraphs of the appendix are adapted from my "Introduction: 'He Brought the Storm Down,'" in *American Pilgrim: Billy Graham, Religion, Politics, and Culture*, ed. Andrew Finstuen, Anne Blue Wills, and Grant Wacker (New York: Oxford University Press, 2017), 1–2.

8½" x 11" or 5" x 6" sheets and simply white. And though many were typed, the majority were carefully handwritten, suggesting the seriousness of purpose behind them. Many contained enclosures, such as a photo, or an uplifting poem, or a "My Answer" column snipped out of a local newspaper, or a material object (always removed and tagged by archivists). One letter even contained a wedding ring, which the sender wanted Graham to keep until the sender's marriage was restored.

A word about how I researched and used the letters may be helpful. My wife, Katherine Wacker, and I read about five hundred, housed in the Billy Graham Center Archives at Wheaton College. We selected them in random but systematic ways (such as reading the "A" folder in one collection box, the "B" folder in another collection box, and so forth). We took careful notes on about two hundred. Owing to the difficulty of deciphering the handwriting, the process proved unexpectedly time-consuming, which limited the number that we could read in the time available. That being said, after working through the first hundred or so, we found that they began to repeat themselves, so that studying a thousand or even all of them probably would not change the story very much. We also read about two hundred children's letters. We sampled those too in a random but systematic way.

In accord with the Billy Graham Center Archives' rules, I have shrouded the writers' identity by using no actual names. But in order to provide at least a hint of the authors' social location, I have typically included two demographic markers: gender, stage of life, or region of residence. In a few instances, the actual name is not gender-specific (for example, Pat or Tracy). Since we know from other evidence that women outnumbered men at Graham's meetings, I have used a female pronoun when a pronoun is needed. Otherwise, all the markers are authentic, which is to say, nothing is made up.

Four additional points are worth noting. First, all the quoted material is accurate, except for spelling and punctuation, which we have corrected. It is often hard to decipher handwriting and interpret abbreviations with confidence. Second, we have tried to find typical thoughts and sentiments, not the most picturesque ones. Third, we have emphasized original letters rather than the ones the BGEA published in the "My Answer" columns. The latter were filtered by other hands, so it is hard to know what the originals actually said. Even so, once in a while I have used a letter published in "My Answer" if it voiced a common concern in an especially clear way. Finally, in a very few instances I have drawn on comments that inquirers (or converts) made to counselors or researchers. I regarded these unedited comments as functionally equivalent to a letter.

The letters from children are housed at the BGEA headquarters in Charlotte. The files contain about one thousand, organized in folders according to the age of the writers. They came in countless forms, everything from brief notes scrawled on scraps of paper to carefully typed (presumably by parents) 8½" x 11" sheets of white office paper. Most contained drawings and very often photographs of themselves. The letters are a priceless resource; to the best of my knowledge, no other historian has read them. My wife, Katherine, helped with the research for this project too. We masked children's identities by shuffling their actual names and ages among those that commonly appeared among the two hundred or so letters we read.

Appendix of World Preaching Events

Selected List and Chronology of Countries or Distinct Cultural Regions Outside the United States and Canada in Which Billy Graham Held Preaching Events

This list represents most but not necessarily all of the countries outside the United States and Canada in which Graham held preaching events. It is not definitive for several reasons. Some countries have changed identities through division or amalgamation; some distinct cultural regions might—or might not—count as "countries," depending on the criteria used; preaching events varied in length from extended crusades to single-night services; and Graham sometimes spoke in conjunction with associates. Although the BGEA sometimes (though not always) counted live video feeds as preaching events, the lists below are restricted to face-to-face meetings. Other lists compiled by other scholars and by different arms of the BGEA have come up with somewhat different tallies. Still, the two lists below, organized chronologically and alphabetically, offer a compelling overall picture of the magnitude and longevity of Graham's overseas ministries.[1]

Newly Visited Countries by Decade and Year

1940s

1946: England, Scotland, Northern Ireland, Ireland, Sweden, Denmark, Netherlands, Belgium, France, Wales
1947: Switzerland

1950s

1952: Japan, South Korea
1954: West Germany, Finland
1955: Norway
1956: India, Thailand, Hong Kong, Philippines

1958: Barbados, Costa Rica, Guatemala, Jamaica, Panama, Puerto Rico, Trinidad, Mexico

1959: Fiji, Australia, New Zealand, USSR (Russia)

1960s

1960: Nigeria, Ruanda-Urundi (Burundi), Ghana, Kenya, Southern Rhodesia (Zimbabwe), Northern Rhodesia (Zambia), Tanganyika (Tanzania), Ethiopia, Egypt, Jordan, Liberia, Brazil, Israel

1962: Argentina, Venezuela, Colombia, Ecuador, Peru, Chile, Paraguay, Uruguay

1966: South Vietnam

1967: Yugoslavia (Croatia)

1968: Singapore

1969: Austria

1970s

1970: Portugal

1971: Italy

1972: Iran

1973: South Africa

1975: Taiwan

1977: Hungary

1978: Poland

1980s

1981: Vatican City

1982: Czechoslovakia (Czech Republic), German Democratic Republic (Germany), Bahamas

1984: USSR (Estonia), Romania

1987: China

1988: USSR (Ukraine), Nicaragua

1990s

1992: North Korea

List of Countries with the Years Billy Graham Visited

Argentina: 1962, 1991

Australia: 1959, 1968, 1969, 1979, 1980, 1984, 1996

Austria: 1969
Bahamas: 1982
Barbados: 1958
Belgium: 1946, 1974, 1975
Brazil: 1960, 1962, 1974, 1979
Chile: 1962
China: 1987, 1988, 1992, 1994
Colombia: 1962
Costa Rica: 1958, 1994
Czechoslovakia: 1982
Denmark: 1946, 1954, 1955, 1965
Ecuador: 1962
Egypt: 1960, 1975
England: 1946, 1947, 1948, 1952, 1954, 1955, 1959, 1961, 1964, 1966, 1967, 1969, 1970, 1971, 1973, 1975, 1976, 1979, 1980, 1981, 1982, 1983, 1984, 1985, 1988, 1989, 1991
Ethiopia: 1960
Fiji: 1959
Finland: 1954, 1984, 1987
France: 1946, 1952, 1954, 1955, 1963, 1970, 1986
Germany (West): 1954, 1955, 1960, 1963, 1966, 1969, 1970, 1976, 1990, 1992, 1993
Germany (East, GDR): 1982
Ghana: 1960
Guatemala: 1958, 1976
Hong Kong (China): 1956, 1975, 1988, 1990, 1994
Hungary: 1977, 1981, 1985, 1989
India: 1956, 1972, 1977, 1980, 1991, 1994, 1995, 1998
Iran: 1972
Ireland: 1946, 1947, 1972
Israel: 1960, 1969, 1975, 1995
Italy: 1971
Jamaica: 1958, 1978
Japan: 1952, 1956, 1967, 1968, 1970, 1975, 1978, 1980, 1994
Jordan: 1960
Kenya: 1960, 1976
Liberia: 1960, 1972
Mexico: 1958, 1975, 1979, 1981
Netherlands: 1946, 1948, 1954, 1955, 1971, 1982, 1983, 1986

New Zealand: 1959, 1969
Nicaragua: 1988
Nigeria: 1960
Northern Ireland: 1946, 1947, 1961, 1972
Northern Rhodesia (Zambia): 1960
North Korea: 1992, 1994
Norway: 1955, 1978
Panama: 1958
Paraguay: 1962
Peru: 1962
Philippines: 1956, 1977
Poland: 1978, 1981
Portugal: 1970
Puerto Rico: 1958, 1967, 1995
Romania: 1984, 1985
Ruanda-Urundi (Burundi): 1960
Singapore: 1968, 1978
Scotland: 1946, 1947, 1954, 1955, 1961, 1976, 1977, 1991
South Africa: 1973
Southern Rhodesia (Zimbabwe): 1960
South Korea: 1952, 1956, 1973, 1984
Sweden: 1946, 1954, 1955, 1963, 1974, 1975, 1977, 1978, 1987
Switzerland: 1947, 1948, 1955, 1960, 1968, 1974
Taiwan: 1975
Tanganyika (Tanzania): 1960
Thailand: 1956, 1980
Trinidad: 1958
Uruguay: 1962, 1998
USSR (Estonia): 1984
USSR (Russia): 1959, 1982, 1984, 1987, 1988, 1991, 1992, 1997, 1998
USSR (Ukraine): 1988
Vatican City: 1981, 1990, 1993
Venezuela: 1962
Vietnam: 1966, 1968
Wales: 1946
Yugoslavia (Croatia): 1967

Notes

PREFACE

1. Readers seeking documentation for *One Soul at a Time* can readily find it in *America's Pastor* or in the articles that I have published about Graham, which are listed at the end of the "Further Reading" section of this book.

2. The Billy Graham Evangelistic Association (BGEA) used admission tickets, turnstile counts, aerial photographs, and police and journalists' assessments to estimate attendance at meetings, yet ambiguities remained. On one hand there was no way to index repeat attenders. On the other hand, some meetings were one-off affairs in which no one even tried to "count the house." Calculating the number of countries Graham visited is equally fraught. It is not clear how the BGEA tabulated instances in which Graham spoke as part of a group, or how it enumerated occasions when he did not formally preach but spoke more or less spontaneously. Finally and perhaps most important, Graham's ministry stretched over six decades and involved hundreds of local organizing committees around the globe. That their data-gathering practices varied seems beyond doubt. As it happens, my tabulation of the number of countries Graham preached in outside the United States and Canada is more than seventy. See the Appendix on World Preaching Events for my working criteria and other details.

3. The BGEA states that 3.2 million people "responded to the invitation" at Billy Graham crusades. This figure is likely firmer than the others since it is drawn from actual decision cards turned in.

INTRODUCTION

1. Pope John Paul II may have celebrated Mass before larger groups, but he did not preach, as Graham did.

2. The final on-air broadcast evidently ended in 2014 and the final online version, in 2016.

3. A dry-run version of *Hour of Decision*, mostly taped in a studio, ran from 1951 to 1954.

4. Following historian Elesha Coffman, in this book I use "mainstream" to refer to the center-right theological impulse that informed the fluid evangelical tradition in post–World War II America. Things get tricky in the Old South, where the historic,

established Baptist, Presbyterian, and Methodist denominations were often socially and culturally "mainline" but theologically "mainstream," especially in urban areas.

5. By 2018 the circulation had dropped to 425,000—still a hefty number in the crowded field of popular religious publications.

6. The exact details of the authorship of the books that bore Graham's name are ambiguous. It is hard to know where his hand stopped and where other hands started, especially in the later ones. When he died, the memorial edition of *Christianity Today* stated that "with the help of his staff, Graham himself published 24 books."

7. Some sources claim that *Peace with God* was published in 1952 (not 1953), that it sold more than five million copies, and that it was translated into fifty languages. These disparities may arise from the difference between printing and release dates and from different ways of calculating formats (print, digital, excerpted, and miniaturized).

8. This statement requires qualification. We shall see that Truman can hardly be considered a friend. Graham's one—albeit very congenial—personal discussion with Obama lasted only thirty-five minutes. Trump sat near Graham at Graham's ninety-fifth birthday celebration at the Grove Park Inn in Asheville, North Carolina, but Trump was not president at the time, and there is no evidence of extended conversation between them. As a practical matter, then, Graham knew ten presidents as friends, and four—Johnson, Nixon, Reagan, and Bush I, as well as their first ladies—Lady Bird, Pat, Nancy, and Barbara—as close personal friends.

9. Admittedly, some American religious historians might rank itinerant evangelist George Whitefield or even hymn writer Charles Wesley—luminaries of the early eighteenth century on both sides of the Atlantic—over Graham. All judgments of this sort depend of course on the criteria one chooses to emphasize.

SCENE 1

1. Now Bob Jones University, located in Greenville, South Carolina.

SCENE 2

1. Now an evangelical interdenominational school named Trinity College of Florida, located in Trinity, Florida, near Tampa.

2. The building's distinctive Middle Eastern architectural style likely gave rise to the bogus rumor, which persisted for years, that Graham was a closet Mason.

3. Anne Blue Wills's biography of Ruth, forthcoming in the Library of Religious Biography series from Eerdmans, has deeply informed my comments about Ruth, here and elsewhere in this book.

4. Billy and Ruth later acquired seventy-five acres of contiguous property.

SCENE 3

1. That year Memorial Day fell on Tuesday, May 30.

2. Stories about Graham's exact words vary, but all versions make the same point.

3. Graham's first citywide meeting took place in Grand Rapids, Michigan, in September 1947. Though this event is often dubbed his first fully fledged American event—and in some ways it was—it actually unfolded under YFC auspices, not his own.

NOTES

SCENE 4

1. They visited Scandinavian countries, as well as Belgium, Luxembourg, Holland, and France.

SCENE 5

1. Occasionally Graham slipped up and did speak of converts. Once, describing the main character in his movie *Mr. Texas*, he even said that the plot was about a cowboy going astray "until I save him." But those mistakes were rare.

SCENE 7

1. Zamperini recently has become famous again as the hero of Laura Hillenbrand's blockbuster book (and later movie) *Unbroken: A World War II Story of Survival, Resilience, and Redemption*.

SCENE 8

1. Finstuen suggests that invitations to more mainline or radical religious figures such as Reinhold Niebuhr, Martin Luther King Jr., and Malcolm X probably came from student groups too.

SCENE 9

1. After 9/11, the BGEA changed "crusades" to "festivals" and, later, to "celebrations."

SCENE 10

1. The acronym BGEA soon became so common in the evangelical world that it rolled off the tongue just as IBM did for International Business Machines. Insiders typically elided the *E* and called it simply *B-G-A*.

2. Like many other radio and television programs in those days, the word "hour" actually meant thirty minutes.

3. Fulton J. Sheen saw a succession of title changes according to the phase of his career: Father, Bishop, Archbishop, and Monsignor. Since he appears several times in this story, for economy I will use Monsignor throughout.

4. BGEA data on the history of World Wide Pictures are not entirely consistent, but the discrepancies are not great enough to invalidate the larger picture. In 2018 the BGEA claimed that in their showings, more than two million viewers had recorded decisions for Christ.

SCENE 11

1. A more personal influence likely played a role too. As noted, Communists had forced Graham's parents-in-law, Nelson and Virginia Bell, to leave their missionary hospital post in China in 1941. Nelson's ardently anti-Communist views (which he held till his death in 1973) may have influenced Ruth Bell Graham too, along with her own alarming experience with Communism in China in her youth.

Notes

SCENE 12

1. Connally began his political career about 1956 as a Democrat, switching to the Republican Party in 1973.

2. Since then, every president has attended, and every meeting has included the American head of state.

SCENE 13

1. When I first visited Graham in 2007, I asked where he pulled down the ropes. Without hesitation he responded, "Chattanooga." The promptness and the firmness of his response must be taken seriously. I must acknowledge that Miller researched the incident carefully and made a good case for Chattanooga. Then too contemporaneous newspaper accounts that I have not seen may shed more light on the question.

2. Graham implies that his friend was a fellow student at the college, but college yearbooks from those years suggest that no African Americans were enrolled at that time (although they were, both earlier and later). More likely his friend was enrolled in a military training unit housed on campus.

3. Graham held a crusade in St. Louis, April 16 to May 16, 1953, but I have found no evidence from that event that sheds light on his views and practices regarding racial equality.

4. Even here, the evidence is not entirely consistent, but I judge that on balance it supports this reading.

5. In other cultures, Graham sometimes felt that he had to look the other way in order to proceed with any meeting at all. In his crusade in Kottayam in India in 1955, for example, he chose not to comment when women were relegated to separate and unfavorable seating in the back. He conceded that the situation rankled his sense of justice, but he saw no practical alternative. He received sharp criticism for having allowed racially segregated meetings at home (before 1953) but largely escaped criticism for ethnically or gender-segregated meetings abroad.

6. Frady evaluated Graham's later actions regarding race much less favorably.

SCENE 14

1. This and the following seven paragraphs describing *Peace with God* are reprinted from my *America's Pastor: Billy Graham and the Shaping of a Nation* (Cambridge, MA: Belknap Press of Harvard University Press, 2014), 33-34. I am grateful to Harvard University Press for granting permission to reuse them here.

SCENE 15

1. Graham believed that a state leader's death freed him from the vow of confidentiality.

SCENE 16

1. By the mid-1970s Graham would take a more centrist and eventually center-left stand on questions of economic justice. But by then Pew, who died in 1971, was out of the picture.

2. Historian Elesha Coffman uses "mainline" to mean members of the theological center-left socially acculturated denominations, typically including Congregationalists, Disciples of Christ, Episcopalians, Lutherans, (Northern) Methodists, (Northern) Baptists, (Northern) Presbyterians, all mostly white, and members of the African Methodist Episcopal Church and the National Baptist Convention, both mostly black. In contrast I use "mainstream" to refer to the center-right theological impulse that informed the fluid evangelical movement in post–World War II America, both white and black. As noted, in the Old South, Baptist, Presbyterian, and Methodist denominations were often socially and culturally mainline but theologically mainstream.

3. Though theologians, both mainline and mainstream, sometimes spoke about the end of history as "last things" or as "eschatology," Graham preferred the more vernacular terms "end times" or "second coming." Occasionally he also spoke about the rapture. This notion argued that before Christ returned to earth in the second coming, he would rapture his saints (or truly converted Christians) to heaven. They would remain in heaven with Christ for a period of years, usually seven, while non-Christians on earth suffered through a period of great tribulation preceding Christ's visible second coming. We will return to the social and cultural import of these concepts for Graham later on.

4. From the beginning until the 1970s, the *Christian Century* was issued every week. In the 1970s the editors started reducing the number of issues during the summer and at other times. Since 2002 the editors have published it every two weeks.

5. Graham's entrepreneurial efforts in the 1950s, 1960s, and 1970s ranged far beyond print. Some of the more important endeavors that he helped launch include Campus Crusade for Christ, Compassion International, Fellowship of Christian Athletes, Fuller Theological Seminary, Gordon-Conwell Theological Seminary, the Navigators, *The Living Bible*, National Association of Evangelicals, Samaritan's Purse, World Vision, Youth for Christ, and Young Life.

6. Graham privately believed in the rapture and some other details of a dense theological subsystem called dispensationalism, which meant that God had divided history into discrete eras called dispensations. Dispensationalism did not appear in *Christianity Today* and rarely in his preaching. Later we will see that he did preach a great deal about the Lord's second coming but in a general way with surprisingly few specifics.

7. By 2018 *Christianity Today*'s print and digital reader base dwarfed the *Christian Century*'s. That said, without question the *Christian Century*'s influence in Protestant and even Catholic pulpits vastly exceeded its reader base. It continued to be the flagship periodical of the mainline.

SCENE 17

1. In 1968 this body changed its name to its current one, the Council of Churches of the City of New York.

2. In *One Soul at a Time*, all biblical quotations are from the King James Version unless otherwise noted.

3. Though the data are not entirely clear, the BGEA evidently continued live broadcasts over ABC through 1958, and in the mid-1960s started buying airtime over local affiliates, including NBC and CBS, for both the radio and television versions of *Hour of Decision*.

4. The statistical records for the New York crusade topped all his meetings in the United States and stood among the top four of all of them around the world. The attendance figures likely saw some bloating, since there was no way to control for repeat attenders. But of course, this problem compromised the statistics for all of Graham's four-hundred-plus crusades, as well as those for other evangelists.

SCENE 18

1. "For God so loved the world, that he gave his only begotten Son, that whosoever believeth in him should not perish, but have eternal life."

2. Graham often used the New International Version in his writings and *The Living Bible* for personal devotions.

SCENE 19

1. In the pulpit, that is. Ironically Graham's responses to reporters' questions in press conferences were littered with qualifications, especially "I think." Whether those locutions represented humility or evasiveness or just habit was open to debate.

SCENE 20

1. Whether Graham required a literal majority or just a conspicuous number of local pastors is not clear. Graham looked for the involvement of representative local laypersons too, although the exact formula evidently varied from site to site.

2. Graham preached at the same site in 1983 to one million, with ten million more watching a simultaneous telecast.

SCENE 21

1. My treatment of Shea, Barrows, and the crusade music in the following several paragraphs, and elsewhere in this book, is deeply informed by Edith Blumhofer's forthcoming volume on that topic, published by Eerdmans.

2. Canadians played a conspicuous role in Graham's ministry. As noted, they included soloist Bev Shea, preacher Leighton Ford, and pianist Tedd Smith, as well as associate evangelists Joe Blinco and John Wesley White.

3. Until the late 1950s, counselor training was supervised by a cousin organization, the Navigators.

4. Until the 1970s, captains may or may not have taken race into consideration when assigning counselors to potential inquirers, but given the mores of the time, especially in the South, it seems likely that they did. Veterans report that after the 1970s, however, race played no role.

5. Lotz was never ordained, and her ministry, AnGeL Ministries, remained independent of any formal denomination.

6. Southern Baptists did not ordain women until 1964, and even then, only sporadically. In 2000 they proscribed women's ordination entirely. Graham's natal denomination, the Associate Reformed Presbyterian Church, did not ordain women at the time (and in 2018 still did not).

SCENE 22

1. This post-9/11 pulpit was also enlarged with a built-in seat to allow the aging evangelist to sit as needed.

SCENE 24

1. The now-common phrase "man in the arena" originated with President Teddy Roosevelt's famous talk, "Citizenship in a Republic," which came to be known as the "Man in the Arena" speech.

SCENE 25

1. See the appendix for more detail on these letters and how I used them.

SCENE 27

1. Commonly attributed to Senator Adlai Stevenson, or theologian Reinhold Niebuhr, or Bishop Fulton J. Sheen, or "Anon," or others.

2. "Being confident of this very thing, that he which hath begun a good work in you will perform it until the day of Jesus Christ."

SCENE 30

1. For years Bell shouldered the task of writing truculent response letters to folks who challenged Graham's theology. Confrontation was not Graham's style, but stopping his father-in-law from speaking confrontationally on his behalf was not his style either.

SCENE 31

1. Even here, however, Graham's thinking was not entirely consistent. Griffith notes that in 1960 Graham joined the unsuccessful crusade for clemency for Caryl Chessman, sentenced to die for a series of assaults and kidnappings in 1948, on the grounds that Chessman had reformed.

2. Hill moved to Los Angeles in 1961, but, according to Dochuk, he traveled back to Houston throughout the late decade "to monitor social developments."

SCENE 32

1. Graham's sole reservation may have pertained to the wording on gender equality. I will discuss this later.

2. Over time Graham's definition of the most troubling social consequences of the sinful heart shifted. In the 1950s it was poverty, illiteracy, Communism, and juvenile delinquency; in the 1960s racism, overpopulation, and sexual license; in the 1970s boredom and self-absorption; in the 1980s AIDS, abortion, environmental pollution, and nuclear war.

SCENE 33

1. The story had an afterstory, minor in itself, but bearing ramifications for understanding Graham's place in American religious life. The day after the protest, an-

other, smaller, protest unfolded. In the course of it, one of the designated counselors approached a young man and engaged him in conversation about his standing with God. One can imagine the visual contrast the two must have cast. As the minutes passed, the young man stepped forward and signed a decision card. We know nothing more, which is the usual ending of such stories. One suspects, however, that neither one changed their politics but embraced a kind of understanding that transcended politics.

2. I owe many of the details in the following paragraphs about the Honor America Day to historian Kevin Kruse (see "Further Reading").

SCENE 34

1. Later we will see that he urged Nixon also to consider George H. W. Bush, who was not antiwar but not hawkish either.

2. In fairness, Graham sometimes acknowledged that he did talk about larger political issues with presidents, but not specific policies or strategies.

SCENE 35

1. Graham spoke at Harvard at least four times between 1962 and 1999. On the basis of the clothing styles, I am assuming that the photo I am describing depicts the 1962 visit.

SCENE 36

1. In 2000, Graham's son Franklin was named CEO of the BGEA, and in 2001 president.

2. Two qualifications should be mentioned. First, the fixed-salary arrangement did not apply to Shea, who worked on an independent contract basis. Unlike the other members of the Platform and Backstage Teams, Shea had no duties beyond the contractual ones. Second, Graham accepted payment for his newspaper columns and royalties for some of his books, which he designated for the education of his children and grandchildren. As far as I know, he never disclosed exact amounts or how they were calculated. At the time of his death, Graham's most recently published stated salary was $82,190, plus approved benefits, including home health-care expenses.

3. Almost all were men. One important exception was Mary C. Crowley, founder of Home Interiors & Gifts, Inc., and the first woman to serve on the BGEA Board of Directors. It may be relevant that Crowley was the sister-in-law of Mary Kay Ash, founder of Mary Kay cosmetics. Both organizations relied on direct marketing—bootstrap entrepreneurialism entirely consonant with Graham's own business and spiritual instincts.

4. In 1977 business manager George W. Wilson put the average figure at ten to twelve dollars per letter.

5. In 1977 the *Charlotte Observer* found that the BGEA had failed fully to disclose the funding arrangements of a BGEA-related organization in Dallas. No charges were ever filed since no one in the BGEA personally profited and the arrangements evidently grew from misunderstanding of tax regulations for nonprofits—and perhaps carelessness. Contrite, Graham quickly sought to rectify the mistake. In 1979 he played a key

role in founding the Evangelical Council for Financial Accountability (ECFA) to help prevent repeat mistakes of this sort by his organization and others.

SCENE 38

1. Moomaw did work in Canada, where the professional league didn't play on Sundays.

SCENE 39

1. If *One Soul at a Time* gives disproportionate attention to Graham's career in North America, that focus reflects my own interests and training as a US historian, not the global scope of Graham's vision and influence. When Graham died, I immediately received requests for interviews from Voice of America and commercial and public radio outlets in Canada, Scotland, England, Australia, Germany, and Saudi Arabia.

2. These figures are rough because, as noted, it is hard to pin down the definition of a "country." Moreover, the records do not always distinguish crusades from brief preaching events or simple public appearances. But the pattern is clear enough. By the tabulation in the Appendix on World Preaching Events, more than seventy "countries" is credible too.

3. Many historians would add the Eastern Orthodox and the Latter-day Saint traditions to this picture, though the Orthodox and LDS rivers are considerably smaller than the other four.

4. Ruth undoubtedly helped expand her husband's horizons. Like many missionary kids, Ruth seems to have accepted long-distance travel as a normal part of life. She had grown up in China, attended boarding school in Korea, was educated in Illinois, and made her permanent home in western North Carolina.

5. The original congress reprised itself as Lausanne II in Manila 1989 and as Lausanne III in Cape Town 2010. Significantly, Lausanne III would boast four thousand leaders from 198 countries.

6. Graham drew this list from a letter from a partisan. He hedged slightly, saying that he affirmed "most of it." It is hard to imagine what part he could not affirm. It seems likely that this was more a matter of Graham's perennial style—always leaving himself some wiggle room—rather than a substantive disagreement.

SCENE 40

1. Graham's successful return trip to Africa in 1973 is discussed later in this book.

2. Secularism Down Under continued to pose challenges. Associate evangelist Leighton Ford, speaking at Victoria University in Wellington in 1987, was targeted with rotten eggs and tomatoes. The school newspaper accused him of being antigay, anti-woman, and anti-intellectual—without showing any substantive acquaintance with the actual content of his preaching or writing. Still, as often happened, the crusade continued, and audiences grew.

3. As noted, outdoor masses conducted by Pope John Paul II may have been larger in number, but they were not one-person preaching events, as Graham's was.

4. It was not Ruth's first time back, however. She had visited China with her siblings in 1980. Perhaps the larger significance is that global travel was unexceptional for both Billy and Ruth.

5. These visits laid the foundation for Franklin Graham's later visits to North Korea and for Samaritan's Purse's opportunity to establish a sustained ministry of humanitarian aid.

SCENE 41

1. Graham used the Arabic not Roman numeral for ten. He did not explain why.

2. Graham outlined concrete steps. First was repentance, not only by individuals but also by nations and peoples. Second was a "moratorium on hostile rhetoric." Third was a commitment to learn to listen, really listen, to each other, despite differences of ideology. Fourth, they were to find ways to come to know one another personally through "educational exchanges, trade relations, tourist travel." And fifth, they should respect the rights of religious believers, as already guaranteed by the United Nations Declaration of Universal Human Rights.

3. Graham's handwritten note to himself on the sermon outline read: "Kept the law. Kept the laws of Rome. Never led a demonstration against Rome." Another handwritten note compared the invalid's suffering to "People Hurting In Inner City."

SCENE 42

1. Will's actual words were "But handcuffs are not America's most embarrassing export." Will clearly meant that Graham filled that role. The sentence appeared in a 1982 *Washington Post* article tellingly titled "Let Us Pray for a Little Skepticism."

SCENE 43

1. Stories about the pope's exact gesture vary. By one account he linked his right index finger with Graham's, by another he embraced Graham in something like a papal bear hug.

SCENE 44

1. Graham's endorsements of Bush and Hatfield fell at different points in the election process: Bush before Nixon won the nomination, Hatfield after.

2. Bush told slightly different versions of this story elsewhere, but the main point was always the same.

INTERLUDE

1. Marshall administered the oath of office to six presidents in nine ceremonies. Graham offered the inaugural prayer for Johnson, Nixon, Reagan, Bush I, and Bush II and, as noted, for both Clinton inaugurations. In addition, he participated in additional inaugural events for Johnson, Nixon, and Reagan.

SCENE 45

1. Samaritan's Purse also won distinction for its Operation Christmas Child program. Between 1993 and 2019, it collected and delivered 168 million shoebox gifts, containing toys, school supplies, and personal care items, to children in more than 160 countries and territories. Even so, controversy dogged the organization. Critics charged that it left a heavy footprint by making clear, in a variety of ways, that it hoped to bring its beneficiaries to Christ. They also charged that its witness was compromised by its inevitable association with Franklin Graham's culture-war politics.

2. The Fresno crusade ran from October 11 to 14, 2001, with an aggregate attendance of two hundred thousand, and fifteen thousand decision cards turned in. Though Graham's words did not compete with the publicity of his remarks the previous month at the National Cathedral, they still received a wide hearing.

SCENE 46

1. Haldeman's brief notes on the meeting, published back in 1994 in *The Haldeman Diaries: Inside the Nixon White House*, had intimated the anti-Semitic thrust of the conversation. Graham immediately denied that he had made unfavorable comments about "the Jewish people" to the president, then or ever.

2. When Graham died in 2018, Franklin dug in deeper. He insisted that his father was talking about "the immorality and cursing being perpetuated by Hollywood and the press," especially through television in American homes. Some of the perpetuators "happened to be Jewish," but Jews were not the focus of his comments.

3. HarperCollins published the first edition in 1997. It may—or may not—be significant that the second edition, issued after the tapes' release in 2002, was published by the BGEA. On one hand, the decision not to mention the tapes may have been Graham's own. On the other hand, he was nearly ninety at the time, and the book was published by insiders. One suspects—or at least hopes—that a younger man, with more influence in the organization, would have addressed his mistake in print as candidly and honorably as he did in person. Even so, none of the museum exhibits of Graham's life at the Billy Graham Center at Wheaton College, or the Billy Graham Library in Charlotte, or the North Carolina State Museum of History in Raleigh, or the Museum of the Bible in DC have mentioned it either.

4. Revelation 3:9: "Behold, I will make them of the synagogue of Satan, which say they are Jews, and are not, but do lie; behold, I will make them to come and worship before thy feet, and to know that I have loved thee." A short section of the 1972 conversation, not released until after Graham's death, shows that he had discussed the meaning of the "synagogue of Satan" passage with the president at that time as well as in 1973. I owe this insight to the historian Mike Hertenstein.

SCENE 47

1. In 2008 Obama withdrew his membership from Trinity United Church of Christ in Chicago, purportedly owing to controversy surrounding charged political remarks by the church's pastor, the Reverend Jeremiah Wright. To the best of my

knowledge, Obama had not rejoined a local congregation at the time of his visit with Graham.

2. Graham's old friend Bill Clinton had been invited but at the last minute backed out. At the party, no one mentioned the Clinton invitation.

SCENE 48

1. Revelation 21:4.

2. When the book was reissued in 2011, Franklin Graham was listed as the co-author. That Franklin coauthored or at least helped author previous editions seems highly likely.

3. Evidently no full transcript or audio or video recording of Graham's Johannesburg sermon exists.

4. Graham did not say why he embraced most but not all parts of the declaration, but another person close to him said he held reservations about some of the language on gender equality.

SCENE 49

1. Having grown up in the Associate Reformed Presbyterian Church, and having lived most of his adult life in the Southern Presbyterian enclave of Montreat, North Carolina, Graham undoubtedly knew, early on, that Ruth's pattern was not all that rare among Presbyterians and other more confessional traditions.

2. Johnny Cash and the Gaithers were staples. As far as I can tell, the rock star Bono never actually performed in a Graham meeting, but he publicly supported Graham's ministry.

3. As an aside, it is worth repeating here a point noted before: over the years Graham built personal friendships with Mormons and Jews. He did not seek to work with them in the crusades themselves—the theological chasms were too wide to bridge—but he never targeted them, either. And he quietly found reasons, both cultural and theological, to keep those ties in good repair.

SCENE 50

1. When a reporter asked an elderly Ruth, with Billy sitting next to her, how the marriage had gone, she twinkled, "98% good." Not to be outdone, Billy instantly asked, "What was the other two per cent?" Elsewhere Billy described their marriage as "happily incompatible."

SCENE 51

1. The BGEA billed *Where I Am: Heaven, Eternity, and the Life Beyond*, published in September 2015, when Graham was in his late nineties, as his thirty-third book. Aides may have read the pages to him, but internal evidence strongly suggests that Franklin Graham (or writers working under Franklin's supervision) effectively authored the volume.

2. "Jesus saith unto him, I am the way, the truth, and the life: no man cometh unto the Father, but by me."

CONCLUSION

1. Graham's signature print and electronic expressions bore other names—*Decision*, *Hour of Decision*, "My Answer," and World Wide Pictures—but Graham himself was so prominently featured in them, page after page, image after image, that he hardly needed to parade his name.

2. More precisely, Aikman framed the trait as humility. I am framing it as obedience to calling, which I see as part of humility.

EPILOGUE

1. This chapter reproduces several sentences and examples contained in Katherine and Grant Wacker, "America's (Children's) Pastor," *Christianity Today*, January 21, 2018, 84–85, http://www.christianitytoday.com/ct/2018/billy-graham/billy-graham-through-childrens-eyes.html, and in "Postscript A: Children's Letters," in my *America's Pastor: Billy Graham and the Shaping of a Nation* (Cambridge, MA: Belknap Press at Harvard University Press, 2014), 277–80. Though we adjusted initial capitalization to context, we quoted the letters exactly, creative spelling included. We masked children's identities by shuffling their actual names among those that most commonly appeared among the two hundred or so letters we read. The gender balance between writers was surprisingly equal. For data on the provenance of the letters, see the appendix.

APPENDIX OF WORLD PREACHING EVENTS

1. I am indebted to my research assistant, Max Feiler, for the hard work of researching and compiling these charts.

Further Reading

A comprehensive bibliography of literature by and about Billy Graham does not yet exist. Even so, the Billy Graham Center Archives (BGCA) at the Billy Graham Center, Wheaton College, Wheaton, Illinois, houses thousands of primary and secondary documents. See the online catalogue at https://www.wheaton.edu/about-wheaton/museum-and -collections/billy-graham-center-archives/welcome/, especially the tab for "Resources on Billy Graham." The links to individual collections contain extremely valuable introductions to specific parts of Graham's career.[1]

The BGCA holds several collections of particular interest to readers interested in the story of Graham's life. These include most of his personal papers (some not yet open); thousands of letters posted to Graham from followers between the late 1940s and the late 1980s; thousands of magazine and newspaper clippings and articles, mostly in English-speaking sources; transcripts of hundreds of news conferences, which offer priceless data because they reveal Graham's words before they were edited by the Billy Graham Evangelistic Association (BGEA) and others; 1,600 audio recordings of Graham's sermons and originals of Graham's sermon notes (many available online as well). The sermon notes contain little biographical information, but they are useful for tracking the evolution of Graham's thinking on theological topics and contemporary affairs.

Graham's memoir, *Just as I Am: The Autobiography of Billy Graham* (San Francisco: HarperSanFrancisco; Grand Rapids: Zondervan, 1997), revised and updated (Charlotte: Billy Graham Evangelistic Association, 2007), is detailed and surprisingly self-critical, yet says little about Graham's inner life. Four early autobiographical essays are in some ways more revealing:

1. At the time of this writing (April 2019), Graham's papers in the BGCA are being moved to the Billy Graham Library in Charlotte, North Carolina.

"I Was Born Again," *American Weekly*, January 16, 1955; and a three-part series, "Billy Graham's Own Story: 'God Is My Witness,'" *McCall's*, April–June 1964. I provide an overview of the reviews of *Just as I Am* in *America's Pastor: Billy Graham and the Shaping of a Nation* (Cambridge, MA: Belknap Press of Harvard University Press, 2014), 162–64.

The thirty-three books published under Graham's name between 1947 and 2016 are mostly theological, sermonic, and devotional, but autobiographical details pop up here and there. For a complete list, see the BGEA website, http://billygraham.org/about/biographies/billy-graham. *Nearing Home: Life, Faith, and Finishing Well* (Nashville: Nelson, 2011) is the most autobiographical of Graham's theological works.

Statistics for Graham's career are confusing at best. Different sites in the BGCA link above may be the best place to start, followed by poking around in billygraham.org., "About," "Biographies," "Billy Graham." Several sites maintained by Graham's media outlet, https://demoss.com/newsrooms/billygraham#multimedia, are helpful, too.

Two photo albums offer a rich material record of Graham's career. Russ Busby, *Billy Graham, God's Ambassador: A Lifelong Mission of Giving Hope to the World* (Alexandria, VA: Time-Life Books, 1999), provides an authorized recounting, including scores of priceless photographs. Ken Garfield, *Billy Graham: A Life in Pictures* (Chicago: Triumph Books, 2013), updates Busby's work with different photographs and a very helpful narrative of Graham's life from the perspective of a sympathetic outsider.

Graham biographies abound. Their approaches range from sudsy whitewashes in which it seems Graham could do no wrong to grubby mud washes in which it seems he could do no right. For examples of the far ends of the genre, see George Burnham and Lee Fisher, *Billy Graham: Man of God*, 3rd ed. (Westchester, IL: Good News, n.d.), and C. Bothwell, *The Prince of War: Billy Graham's Crusade for a Wholly Christian Empire* (Asheville, NC: Brave Ulysses Books, 2007).

The gold standard of Graham biographies is William Martin, *A Prophet with Honor: The Billy Graham Story* (New York: Morrow, 1991). Zondervan released an enlarged and updated edition in 2018, weeks before Graham's death. Martin also published a children's version: *Prophet with Honor* (Grand Rapids: Zonderkidz, 2013). Though dated, one of the best article-length overviews of Graham's life remains William Martin, "Fifty Years with Billy," *Christianity Today*, November 13, 1995. Likewise, the best chapter-length summary of Graham's international work is Martin's chapter in *Billy Graham: American Pilgrim* (noted below): "God's Ambassador to the World." All biographers of Graham, most emphatically including me, owe a great debt to Martin's sedulous research, insight, and, not least, wit. I crafted an appreciative review of the first edition of *Prophet with Honor* as "'Charles Atlas with a Halo': America's Billy Graham," *Christian Century*, April 1, 1992, 336–41.

Other biographies started to appear shortly after Graham's breakout crusade in Los Angeles in 1949. Stanley High, *Billy Graham: The Personal Story of the Man, His Message, and His Mission* (New York: McGraw-Hill, 1956), is consistently admiring yet astutely captures key ingredients of Graham's narrative. William McLoughlin, *Billy Graham, Revivalist in a Secular Age* (New York: Ronald, 1960), was the first scholarly biography. Though relentlessly unfavorable, the volume contains a wealth of basic biographical data as well as detailed analysis of the BGEA. Marshall Frady, *Billy Graham, a Parable of American Righteousness* (Boston: Little, Brown, 1979), is florid and tendentious yet projects perceptive insights into Graham's relation to American culture.

The new century saw fresh entries into the Graham biography market. Two relatively short yet comprehensive ones designed for general readers include Roger A. Bruns, *Billy Graham: A Biography* (Westport, CT: Greenwood, 2004), and David Aikman, *Billy Graham: His Life and Influence* (Nashville: Nelson, 2007). Both incorporate the larger cultural setting. The former volume is more critical of Graham, the latter more sympathetic. Lon Alison, *Billy Graham: An Ordinary Man and His Extraordinary God* (Brewster, MA: Paraclete, 2018), does not pretend to be objective but offers unique biographical details drawn from long personal acquaintance.

My *America's Pastor* does not aspire to serve as a biography in the conventional meaning of the term but focuses on a dozen themes running across Graham's entire career. I pay particular attention to the power of context: How did Graham shape the age and how did the age shape him? As noted, *One Soul* is not an abbreviated version of *America's Pastor* but rather an entirely different volume. It concentrates not on the setting but on the man himself.

Over the years John Pollock, a prodigiously productive "amateur" historian and Anglican cleric, wrote a series of authorized biographies of Graham (and many other Christian leaders). They include *Billy Graham: The Authorized Biography* (New York: McGraw-Hill, 1966); *Billy Graham: Evangelist to the World; An Authorized Biography of the Decisive Years* (Minneapolis: World Wide Publications, 1979); and *The Billy Graham Story: The Authorized Biography* (Grand Rapids: Zondervan, 2003). Pollock consistently views Graham through very sympathetic eyes, yet he is not entirely blind to his faults. He offers a great deal of data, based on long personal association with the Graham family and organization, not available elsewhere. Pollock's attention to Graham's international work is especially useful.

A number of biographies concentrate on specific aspects of Graham's career. Four especially masterful ones include, in chronological order, Nancy Gibbs and Michael Duffy, *The Preacher and the Presidents: Billy Graham in the White House* (New York: Center Street, 2007); Garth Rosell, *The Surprising Work of God: Harold John Ockenga, Billy Graham, and the Rebirth of Evangelicalism* (Grand Rapids: Baker Academic, 2008); Andrew S. Finstuen, *Original Sin and Everyday Protestants: The Theology of Reinhold Niebuhr, Billy Graham, and Paul Tillich in an Age of Anxiety* (Chapel Hill: University of North Carolina Press, 2009); and Steven P. Miller, *Billy Graham and the Rise of the Republican South* (Philadelphia: University of Pennsylvania Press, 2009). Harold Myra and Marshall Shelley, *The Leadership Secrets of Billy Graham* (Grand Rapids: Zondervan, 2005), is more theological than biographical yet provides a keen analysis of Graham's administrative style, an important yet rarely addressed subject.

Two additional biography-related items merit notice. Kevin M. Kruse, *One Nation under God: How Corporate America Invented Christian America* (New York: Basic Books, 2015), is not a biography of Graham, but he appears so often that the book almost serves as a biography of an important aspect of the first half of his career. Journalist/historian Mike Hertenstein offers new data on the first and second conversations between Graham and Nixon regarding Jews in "Billy Graham & the Synagogue of Satan," *Medium*, July 28, 2018, https://medium.com/@mikeh_50175/billy-graham-the-synagogue-of-satan-681360ae5b99.

Journal articles and book and dissertation chapters about Graham are too numerous to list, but six merit special notice. They are Uta Balbier, "Selling Soap and Salvation: Billy Graham's Consumer Styled Revival Meetings and the Reshaping of German Evangelicalism in the 1950s," *Amerikastudien/American Studies Quarterly* 59, no. 2 (2015); Larry Eskridge, "'One Way': Billy Graham, the Jesus Generation, and the Idea of an Evangelical Youth Culture," *Church History* 67, no. 1 (1998): 83–106, doi:10.2307/3170772; Helen Jin Kim, "Gospel of the 'Orient': Koreans, Race and the Transpacific Rise of American Evangelicalism in the Cold War Era, 1950–1980" (PhD diss., Harvard University, 2017), chap. 4; Mark A. Noll, *American Evangelical Christianity: An Introduction* (Malden, MA: Blackwell, 2001), chap. 3, "The Significance of Billy Graham"; David Aikman, *Great Souls: Six Who Changed the Century* (Lanham, MD: Lexington Books, 2003), chap. 1, "Billy Graham—Salvation"; and Peter J. Boyer, "The Big Tent: Billy Graham, Franklin Graham, and the Transformation of American Evangelicalism," *New Yorker*, August 22, 2005, https:// www .newyorker.com/magazine/2005/08/22/the-big-tent.

Anthologies are useful for specific purposes. For personal reminiscences about Graham that encompass a wide range of personalities, religious views, and social locations, see Amy Newmark, Steve Posner, and A. Larry Ross, *Chicken Soup for the Soul: Billy Graham & Me; 101 Inspiring Personal Stories from Presidents, Pastors, Performers, and Other People Who Know Him Well* (Cos Cob, CT: Chicken Soup for the Soul, 2013). Collections of Graham's own observations about a variety of topics are useful too. One of the best for the scope of the subjects addressed is Billy Graham and Bill Adler, *The Wit and Wisdom of Billy Graham* (New York: Random House, 1967), updated as *Compiled by Bill Adler: Ask Billy Graham* (Nashville: Nelson, 2007, 2010).

Graham's story cannot be told without attention to his wife, Ruth Bell Graham, and, to a lesser extent, his children. The only sustained biography of the former is Patricia Cornwell, *Ruth: A Portrait; The Story of Ruth Bell Graham* (Garden City, NY: Doubleday, 1997). Though Cornwell is a renowned mystery writer, not a historian by training, this fine volume offers a wealth of data. For Ruth's own voice, with commentary by daughter Gigi Graham Tchividjian, see *Footprints of a Pilgrim: The Life and Loves of Ruth Bell Graham* (Nashville: Word, 2001). For the texture of Billy and Ruth's life together, see Hanspeter Nüesch, *Ruth and Billy Graham: The Legacy of a Couple* (Grand Rapids: Baker Books, 2013). Daughter Ruth and son Franklin offer autobiographical reflections about themselves and the Graham family—dramatically different in tone as well as in content—in *In Every Pew Sits a Broken Heart: Hope for the Hurting* (Grand Rapids: Zondervan, 2004) and in *Through My Father's Eyes* (Nashville: Nelson, 2018).

Researchers might find four of my other publications about Graham helpful. I road tested some of the ideas in *America's Pastor* and in *One Soul* in "Billy Graham's America," *Church History: Studies in Christianity and Culture* 78, no. 3 (2009): 489–511, condensed in *ChristianHistory.Net*, November 4, 2009, http://www.christianitytoday.com/ch/bytopic/preachers evangelists/billygrahamsamerica.html. "The Billy Pulpit: Billy Graham's Career in the Mainline," *Christian Century*, November 15, 2003, 2, 26, explores an underexamined topic: Graham's influence outside the evangelical tradition. In "Billy Graham, Christian Manliness, and the Marketing of the Evangelical Subculture," in *Religion and the Marketplace in the United States*, ed. Jan Stievermann, Philip Goff, and Detlef Junker (New York: Oxford University Press, 2015), I look especially at the role of gender in how Graham marketed, and others appropriated, his image and message. And in "Rising in the West: Billy Graham's 1949 Los Angeles Revival," in *"A Straight but Thorny Road": Turning Points in the History of American Evangelicalism; Essays in Honor of Mark Noll*, ed. Heath W. Carter and Laura Romiger Porter (Grand Rapids: Eerdmans, 2017), I examine the origins and influence of Graham's breakout crusade.

Pathbreaking essays on unexplored or underexplored parts of Graham's career appear in Andrew S. Finstuen, Anne Blue Wills, and Grant Wacker, eds., *Billy Graham: American Pilgrim* (New York: Oxford University Press, 2017). The thirteen Graham scholars that contribute to the volume—Margaret Bendroth, Edith L. Blumhofer, Elesha Coffman, Darren Dochuk, Seth Dowland, Curtis J. Evans, Andrew Finstuen, Ken Garfield, Michael Hamilton, David P. King, William Martin, Steven P. Miller, and Anne Blue Wills—move beyond easy stereotypes and treat him with the analytic precision he merits. Nearly every page of *One Soul* bears the imprint of their careful research and fresh imagination.

Graham's death in 2018 released a flood of obituary ruminations on his life and legacy. Four of the most balanced and perceptive are Kenneth L. Woodward, "America's Preacher: Remembering Billy Graham," *Commonweal*, February 23, 2018, www.commonwealmagazine.org/america's -preacher; Ken Garfield, "I Saw Graham Preach to Hundreds of Thousands— but I'll Remember Him for a Very Different Reason," *Charlotte Observer*, February 21, 2018, www.charlotteobserver.com/news/special-reports/billy -graham-life/article201410924.html; Tim Funk, "'America's Pastor': Evangelist Billy Graham Dead at 99," *Charlotte Observer*, February 21, 2018, https://www.charlotteobserver.com/news/special-reports/billy-graham -life/article201269154.html; and Laurie Goodstein, "Billy Graham, 99, Dies; Pastor Filled Stadiums and Counseled Presidents," *New York Times*, February 21, 2018, www.nytimes.com/2018/02/21/obituaries/billy-graham-dead.html.

Two additional works will constitute major contributions to Billy Graham studies: Edith Blumhofer's forthcoming book on the music of the crusades and Anne Blue Wills's biography of Ruth Bell Graham. Both will be published by Eerdmans, the latter in the Library of Religious Biography series. Both have strongly influenced my thinking in *One Soul at a Time*.

The memorial edition of *Christianity Today* contains twenty-six essays devoted to Graham's life and legacy. Not surprisingly, few are critical in either the academic or commonsense meaning of the word. Even so, the issue contains numerous insights, raw data, and unique facts useful to serious students of Graham. *Christianity Today*, April 2018, https://www.christianitytoday.com/ct/2018/billy-graham/. Michael S. Hamilton, "How a Humble Evangelist Changed Christianity as We Know It," in that issue, is the best article-length overview of Graham's life available anywhere.

Studies of the broad landscape of evangelicalism after World War II are legion. For the American setting, two that offer a clear view of the whole, with considerable attention to Graham, include Frances Fitzgerald, *The Evangelicals: The Struggle to Shape America* (New York: Simon & Schuster, 2017), and Steven P. Miller, *The Age of Evangelicalism: America's Born-Again Years* (New York: Oxford University Press, 2014). For the global story, see Melani McAlister, *The Kingdom of God Has No Borders: A Global History of American Evangelicals* (New York: Oxford University Press, 2018), and Mark Noll, *The New Shape of World Christianity: How American Experience Reflects Global Faith* (Downers Grove, IL: InterVarsity Press, 2009).

Finally, some of my publications about Graham, not already noted, may be useful for students of Graham's life and legacy. They are listed in chronological order.

"Presidential Preacher." Review of *The Preacher and the Presidents: Billy Graham in the White House*, by Nancy Gibbs and Michael Duffy. *Chicago Tribune*, August 18, 2007, Books section, 3.

"Billy Graham Was a Model for What Americans Wanted to Be." *Faith and Leadership: A Learning Resource for Christian Leaders*, December 14, 2014. https://www.faithandleadership.com/grant-wacker-billy-graham-was-model-what-americans-wanted-be.

"'Unbroken' and Billy Graham." *Wall Street Journal*, January 1, 2015, A13. http://www.wsj.com/articles/grant-wacker-unbroken-and-billy-graham-1420156042.

"Response" to essays about my work on Graham by Randall J. Stephens, Mark Noll, Joel Carpenter, Heather D. Curtis, Amanda Porterfield, Catherine Brekus, Nathan O. Hatch, Kate Bowler, and Laurie Maffly-Kipp. In "Special Section: The Scholarship and Career of Grant Wacker," *Fides et Historia*, Summer/Fall 2015, 112–19.

"Response to Randall Balmer," "Response to Vincente Bacote," "Response to Kathryn Lofton," and "Response to Nathan Walton." Book Symposium on *America's Pastor*. *Syndicate Theology*, May 2016. https://syndicatetheology.com/symposium/americas-pastor/.

"The Remarkable Mr. Graham." *Christianity Today*, November 7, 2016. http://www.christianitytoday.com/ct/2016/november-web-only /remarkable-billy-graham.html.

"Billy Graham and American Culture: Legacies." In *Great Awakenings: Historical Perspectives for Today*, edited by David Horn, 86–79. Peabody, MA: Hendrickson, 2017.

"Introduction: 'He Brought the Storm Down.'" In *American Pilgrim: Billy Graham, Religion, Politics, and Culture*, edited by Andrew Finstuen, Anne Blue Wills, and Grant Wacker, 1–22. New York: Oxford University Press, 2017.

"Billy Graham and Christian Humility." *Faith and Leadership: A Learning Resource for Christian Leaders*, April 4, 2017. https://www .faithandleadership.com/category/topics/news-ideas.

"Sixty Years Ago: Billy Graham's Madison Square Garden Crusade—an Interview with Grant Wacker." *TGC: The Gospel Coalition*, May 15, 2017. https://blogs.thegospelcoalition.org/evangelical-history/2017 /05/15/billy-grahams-madison-square-garden-campaign-60-years -later/.

With Katherine Wacker. "America's (Children's) Pastor." *Christianity Today*, February 21, 2018, 84–85. http://www.christianitytoday.com /ct/2018/billy-graham/billy-graham-through-childrens-eyes.html.

"Billy Graham's Legacy for Christians, Evangelical and Otherwise." *Christian Century*, February 21, 2018. https://www.christiancentury.org /article/critical-essay/billy-graham-s-legacy-christians-evangelical -and-otherwise.

"How an Aging Billy Graham Approached His Own Death." *Washington Post*, February 21, 2018. https://www.washingtonpost.com/news/acts- of-faith/wp/2018/02/21/how-an-aging-billy-graham-approached- his-own-death/?utm_term=.c039d62b5e07.

"The Legacy of Billy Graham." *(Durham, NC) Herald Sun*, February 21, 2018. https://www.heraldsun.com/opinion/article201453109.html.

"Leaving a Legacy." *Alabama Baptist*, March 1, 2018, 1 and 3.

Permissions

Harvard University Press for permission to quote eight brief paragraphs from Grant Wacker, *America's Pastor: Billy Graham and the Shaping of a Nation* (Cambridge, MA: Belknap Press of Harvard University Press, 2014), 33–34.

Oxford University Press for permission to adapt scattered phrases from my "Billy Graham, Christian Manliness, and the Marketing of the Evangelical Subculture," in *Religion and the Marketplace in the United States* ed. Jan Stievermann, Philip Goff, and Detlef Junker (New York: Oxford University Press, 2015).

Oxford University Press for permission to adapt scattered phrases from my "Introduction: 'He Brought the Storm Down,' " in *American Pilgrim: Billy Graham, Religion, Politics, and Culture*, ed. Andrew Finstuen, Anne Blue Wills, and Grant Wacker (New York: Oxford University Press, 2017).

Hendrickson Publishers and *Christianity Today* for permission to adapt scattered lines and phrases from "Billy Graham and American Culture: Legacies," in *Great Awakenings: Historical Perspectives for Today*, ed. David Horn (Peabody, MA: Hendrickson Publishers 2017), 86–99, and from "The Remarkable Mr. Graham," *Christianity Today*, November 7, 2016, http://www.christianitytoday.com/ct/2016/november-web-only/remarkable-billy-graham.html.

The first three paragraphs of the Appendix on Letters are adapted with permissiom from my "Introduction: 'He Brought the Storm Down,' " in *American Pilgrim: Billy Graham, Religion, Politics, and Culture*, ed. Andrew Finstuen, Anne Blue Wills, and Grant Wacker (New York: Oxford University Press, 2017), 1–2.

Chapter [Scene] 49 is adapted with permission from "Billy Graham and American Culture: Legacies," in *Great Awakenings: Historical Perspectives for Today*, ed. David Horn (Peabody, MA: Hendrickson, 2017), 86–99, and from "The Remarkable Mr. Graham," *Christianity Today*, November 7, 2016, http://www.christianitytoday.com/ct/2016/november-web-only/remarkable-billy-graham.html.

Index

Note: In this index BG stands for Billy Graham.

Index

Titles published in the

LIBRARY OF RELIGIOUS BIOGRAPHY SERIES

Aimee Semple McPherson: Everybody's Sister
by Edith L. Blumhofer

Damning Words: The Life and Religious Times of **H. L. Mencken**
by D. G. Hart

Thomas Merton *and the Monastic Vision*
by Lawrence S. Cunningham

God's Strange Work: **William Miller** *and the End of the World*
by David L. Rowe

Blaise Pascal: *Reasons of the Heart*
by Marvin R. O'Connell

Occupy Until I Come: **A. T. Pierson** *and the Evangelization of the World*
by Dana L. Robert

The Kingdom Is Always but Coming: A Life of **Walter Rauschenbusch**
by Christopher H. Evans

A Christian and a Democrat: A Religious Life of **Franklin D. Roosevelt**
by John F. Woolverton with James D. Bratt

Francis Schaeffer *and the Shaping of Evangelical America*
by Barry Hankins

Harriet Beecher Stowe: *A Spiritual Life*
by Nancy Koester

Billy Sunday *and the Redemption of Urban America*
by Lyle W. Dorsett

Assist Me to Proclaim: The Life and Hymns of **Charles Wesley**
by John R. Tyson

Prophetess of Health: A Study of **Ellen G. White**
by Ronald L. Numbers

George Whitefield: *Evangelist for God and Empire*
by Peter Y. Choi

The Divine Dramatist: **George Whitefield**
and the Rise of Modern Evangelicalism
by Harry S. Stout

Liberty of Conscience: **Roger Williams** *in America*
by Edwin S. Gaustad